PUEBLOS, VILLAGES, FORTS, AND TRAILS

A GUIDE TO
NEW MEXICO'S PAST

Pueblos, Villages, Forts & Trails

DAVID GRANT NOBLE

University of New Mexico Press
Albuquerque

Library of Congress
Cataloging-in-Publication Data

Noble, David Grant
    Pueblos, villages, forts, and trails: a guide
to New Mexico's past / David Grant Noble.
        p.   cm.
    Includes bibliographical references (p.)
and index.
    ISBN 0-8263-1514-3 (cl).—
    ISBN 0-8263-1485-6 (pbk.)
    1. Historic sites—New Mexico—
Guidebooks. 2. New Mexico—Guidebooks.
3. Automobile travel—New Mexico—
Guidebooks. 4. New Mexico—History,
Local. I. Title.
F797.N63 1994
917.8904'53—dc20   93-42192
CIP

Design by Stephanie Jurs

CONTENTS

PREFACE

I am an explorer by nature, always ready to take off in the car, watch the landscape roll by and the afternoon clouds boil up over the plains, stop at small-town cafes, and photograph in the late afternoon light. In the evenings, I sometimes pull off the road and stretch out by a juniper tree to observe Venus as she drops below the horizon.

The process of writing this book brought many rewards. As I explored, I sought out places with history—old fort ruins, ancient villages, remnants of trails—traveling in the present to discover the past. A parallel journey occurred in libraries where, in books, I tried to make contact with the people who recorded what happened in New Mexico years ago—priests and conquerors, travelers and journalists, scholars and popular writers. Sometimes the immediacy of their thoughts and feelings evaporated the intervening centuries.

Perhaps the most meaningful reward for me was internal, arriving at some personal understanding of why history happened as it did. This can be a disturbing process. Not infrequently, I found myself wishing for a time machine to take me back a century or two to redirect the actors, as if history were a play. But while history is constantly being reinterpreted, the past is done and gone. Still, with our diverse backgrounds, each of us sees it differently, and even if the facts often seem apparent, their significance can be elusive. Like a southwestern sunset, meaning changes color and shape as you watch; and yet the sun moves.

Once I led a study group up a canyon in Arizona to view an Anasazi cliff house tucked under a ledge. The little dwelling appeared to have belonged originally to the ancient Anasazi, but was reoccupied centuries later by Navajos hiding from U.S. troops in Canyon de Chelly some miles upstream. I told my group a little about the last Navajo war: Kit Carson's campaign, the Long Walk, the tragedy at the Bosque Redondo. One of my listeners began to shake his head. Finally, with much emotion, he let it be known that after two hundred years of killing New Mexicans, the Navajos had had it coming. What was more, Carson's soldiers were Hispanos, "not blue-eyed!" His comments touched on the main difficulties of understanding New Mexico history; indeed, in the 1860s, Indians, Hispanos, and Anglo-Americans were all caught up in a terrible resolution of prior social and historical developments. Collective memories are long-lasting.

The greatest single frustration I experienced in studying New Mexico's past was the void of written material from the Native American perspective. Writings by the common people of Hispanic heritage also are rare. As we all know, every word in our vocabulary carries some emotional weight, and even to write in English about Pueblos, Athapascans, and Hispanos, for example, inevitably involves a measure of ethnic bias.

Most of our biases date to our earliest years and lie in a place deeper than conscious thought. My grandmother, for example, used to tell me stories about her father, who left his home in Maine and went to Michigan where he became a teacher and judge. Absorbing Grandma's stories as a child, I'm sure I viewed my ancestor as someone who had helped bring the torch of enlightenment and the banner of justice to the American West. Fifty years later, as I wrote about events in the nineteenth century, it seemed only too natural to speak of "the opening of the West." Such notions, of course, are laughable to Native Americans, or would be if they did not evoke a painful era in their history.

Easier questions arose as I did my research. One was what sites to include and what to leave out. History begins yesterday, doesn't it? But then, a historian told me, no, it ended in 1900. So the choice was mine. The places that most interested me were the older ones; indeed, my first book, *Ancient Ruins of the Southwest,* only dealt with prehistoric sites. So I decided to emphasize the earlier sites and end with the coming of the railroad, after which a truly new era begins.

I also have selected places we can still visit. Fort Fillmore, which I excluded, has virtually disappeared, but Pecos Pueblo has become the centerpiece of a national park. In addition, I wanted the places in this book to reflect New Mexico's four main historic cultures. Thus, you will find chapters dealing with the history of the Pueblos, Apaches and Navajos, Hispanos, and Anglo-Americans.

It is the guidebook writer's temptation to be encyclopedic—there's always one more site just over the horizon with a story to be told. Of course, they are not all here. You may wonder at the exclusion of ghost towns and mining camps. Assuredly, these abandoned settlements, whose heydays flashed like the gold and silver that made them boom, are part of New Mexico's history. The problem is that there are so many of them, and so many books already published on the subject! Historic houses were another temptation, but they are even more prolific than ghost towns. However, the following pages include leads to publications about historic buildings, and as you travel, you will find many useful walking-tour guides.

As Ralph Waldo Emerson aptly wrote, "Foolish consistency is the hobgoblin of little minds." Accordingly, this "pre-railroad" guide includes a chapter on the Cumbres & Toltec Scenic Railroad, a functioning museum, as well as one on the Trinity Site, where, in a blinding burst of light in 1945, we entered the Atomic Age.

Having mentioned the elusiveness of the truth about history, let me now say that the past can have a substantive, tangible quality as well. You can drive or hike somewhere and there it is. At Hawikuh, for example, you can stand on the very spot where Zuñi warriors and Spanish soldiers did battle more than four centuries ago. And in the old Lincoln Country Courthouse, you will be in the very room in which a shackled Billy the Kid leaned out the window and shot his jailer. Experiences like that bring history alive.

This book is written mainly for those of us who live in or are traveling through New Mexico and wish to know more about where we are. You can use it for trip planning, too, noting the many historic places and sites in the state where you can still discover the fascination of New Mexico's rich cultural heritage. As you visit native pueblos and villages or explore old fort ruins, I hope the following pages help to enrich your experience by bringing a distant and elusive past into the present.

ACKNOWLEDGMENTS

I would like to thank the following people for reviewing parts of my manuscript and generously sharing their knowledge and insights with me: Patti Bell, Charles Carroll, Stanley M. Hordes, Charles H. Lange, Dan Murphy, Mike Mallouf, Douglas P. Peterson, George Rivera, Orlando Romero, Marc Simmons, Robert J. Torres, Linda Tigges, Ann M. Rasor, Gregory Scott Smith, Cordelia Snow, and John P. Wilson.

For assisting me in my research, let me thank Laura Holt, Michael Miller, Arthur L. Olivas, Richard Rudisill, and Betty Sena; and for her proofreading and perceptive editorial comments, Ruth J. Meria.

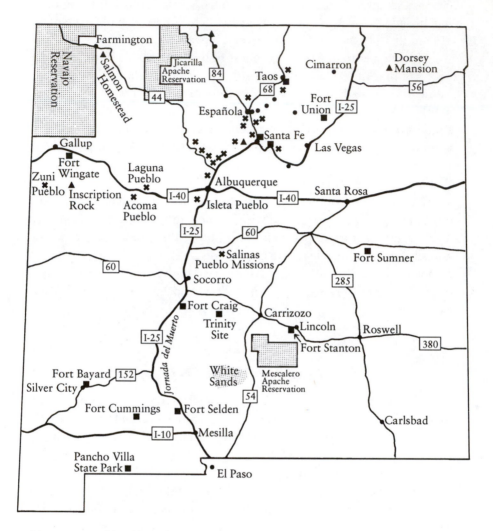

Historic sites in New Mexico.

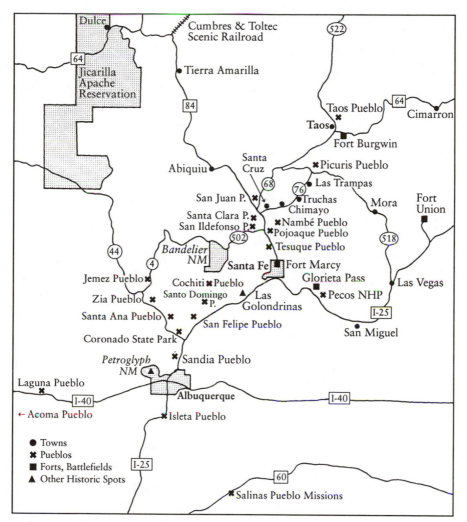

Historic sites in north-central New Mexico.

THE ANASAZI-PUEBLO PAST

The Pueblo Indians live in a series of villages, or *pueblos,* on small reservations in the northern Rio Grande Valley, in western New Mexico, and in northeastern Arizona. Some pueblos, such as Zuñi and Acoma (see pp. 103 and 90), are believed to be more than seven hundred years old, while others date to the 1500s or after the Pueblo-Spanish wars of the late 1600s.

The various Pueblo communities share a common background and value system and have many similar customs. From their agrarian life emerged a common religion and worldview and a similar material culture, which is especially apparent in craft arts and architecture. However, throughout their history, they have operated as independent, autonomous villages and only once, in 1680, acted in concert. The Pueblos speak several distinct native languages and dialects and, according to their linguistic group and village affiliation, have differing specific customs. Each pueblo has its own land base and has had its own singular historical experience.

Native Americans and European Americans tend to approach history somewhat differently. In Pueblo culture, for example, time is cyclical and the linear sequence of past events is not significant. The Pueblos view all of life, including their own past, as being influenced by religious factors, which are woven into the fabric of oral narratives. In contrast, the Western tradition emphasizes the chronology of historical events, the potency of economic and political forces, and the role of individuals in determining historical developments.

Much of the published literature on the prehistory of the Pueblo Indians derives from the work of archaeologists, who have long been investigating ancient sites throughout the Southwest. Scholars trace Pueblo, or *Anasazi,* culture back about two millennia, when it emerged from a hunter-gatherer background. The main initial catalyst for change was the introduction of corn from Mexico and the adoption of agriculture.

The need for moisture and fertility to raise crops stimulated the rise of an elaborate religion based on the magical relationship between the Earth, as mother, and the Sky, as father, and harmony between people and Nature. Over time, the Anasazi developed a social and religious structure, within each pueblo, in which chosen individuals took special

Cliff Palace, Mesa Verde National Park. (Photo by David Grant Noble.)

responsibility for sacred activities. Today, more than a millennium later, these traditions, in modified form, are still strongly adhered to by the Pueblo people, and, in most pueblos, an inherited system of religious and civil governance is still practiced.

For more than a thousand years, Anasazi culture centered on the Colorado Plateau, especially along the San Juan River where it flows through the "Four Corners" region. In this area, with its propitious combination of natural resources, wildlife habitat, rainfall, and long

Taos Pueblo, 1977. (Photo by Peter Dechert.)

growing season, the people thrived and multiplied. By around A.D. 1100, burgeoning regional centers had developed, the most noted of which were in Chaco Canyon, in the Montezuma Valley/Mesa Verde area, and in the canyon country around present-day Kayenta, Arizona. The Anasazi eventually became skilled arid-land farmers, traded with other peoples near and distant, and produced a wide variety of beautiful crafts. Many lived in compact multistoried apartment dwellings somewhat resembling those in the pueblos of Taos (p. 89) and Acoma.

Toward the end of the 1200s, the Anasazi left their Four Corners homeland and seem also to have experienced a population collapse. These events coincided with a twenty-four-year drought. During these challenging years, Anasazi population centers shifted to the northern Rio Grande Valley, the Hopi mesas, the Zuñi area, and the Little Colorado River, where other Puebloan peoples already lived.

One fateful day in 1540, the Zuñis, in central-western New Mexico, watched from the rooftops of Hawikuh as an army of three hundred Spanish soldiers and eight hundred Mexican Indians, accompanied by Catholic priests, approached their village; their world was about to change. Hawikuh was stormed and conquered by the foreigners, who spent nearly two years exploring the Southwest from the Gulf of California to the plains of Kansas. In 1541, the Tiwas (p. 59), who lived along the Rio Grande, defended themselves against Spanish attacks but lost many warriors in battle, and two of their pueblos were destroyed. These events marked a watershed in Pueblo history, where links to an Anasazi past would begin to break and influences from Europe would bring about profound transformations.

After the departure of Francisco Vásquez de Coronado and his troops in 1542, the Pueblos saw few Spaniards until 1598, when Juan de Oñate brought a colony of soldier-settlers, priests, and Mexican Indians to New Mexico. They initially settled at the Tewa pueblos of Ok'he and Yunqe at the confluence of the Rio Chama and the Rio Grande, but after a dozen years here, they relocated to a site at the foothills of the Sangre de Cristo Mountains, which they named Santa Fe (p. 89).

Under this new regime, the Pueblos were required to pay tribute to the Spaniards in the form of goods and services, and they were forbidden to freely practice their own religion. In addition, they were repeatedly stricken by contagious diseases of European origin against which they had almost no natural immunity. To worsen matters, an extended drought beginning in the mid-1600s brought famine, and nomadic tribes from the southern plains raided New Mexico pueblos, often at harvest time. By the late 1660s, the Pueblos were in a desperate condition. For example, at the Pueblo of Las Humanas, later renamed Gran Quivira (p. 55), hundreds died from warfare, famine, and disease. The few survivors took refuge among the Tiwas and Piros along the Rio Grande. In 1675, forty-seven Indian religious leaders were imprisoned by the Spanish authorities on charges of sorcery. Three were hanged, others flogged in Santa Fe's plaza, and one committed suicide. The hatred generated by this incident finally exploded five years later when the Indians rose up in concert, killed most of the Franciscans and hundreds of settlers, burned churches, and drove the Spanish survivors into exile in El Paso del Norte.

While the revolt itself was brilliantly planned and executed, Pueblo unity proved to be short-lived. Its principal leader, Popé, had died by 1692, when Spanish soldiers under Diego de Vargas marched back into the territory and demanded pledges of allegiance from each pueblo. The complete reestablishment of Spanish rule took four years, facilitated by the collaboration of several pueblos and the disintegration of the former Pueblo confederation.

The crown awarded the Pueblo Indians grants of land, the sizes of which reflected residential and farming needs but ignored the more extensive areas the Indians used for hunting, gathering, and religious activities. The *encomienda,* or tribute system, was discontinued, and the Pueblos were allowed more religious freedom. The natives and colonists, most of whom were subsistence farmers, often lived as close neighbors, traded with each other, sometimes intermarried, and often joined forces in defense against attacks by Navajos, Apaches, and Comanches.

The seventeenth and eighteenth centuries witnessed repeated epidemics of smallpox, influenza, measles, and other diseases; in 1780–81 alone, one-quarter of the Pueblo population (approximately five thousand people) and many colonists succumbed to smallpox. In general, lands owned by the Indians included the most desirable agricultural areas, and when their population shrank, unused fields were hard to protect from encroachment by non-Indian settlers, whose numbers were swelling because of immigration.

When Mexico gained its independence from Spain in 1821, conditions among New Mexico Indians changed little; even after the United States' occupation of the territory twenty-one years later, life in most pueblos carried on about the same. It was not until the arrival of the railroad in the early 1880s that Anglo-American culture began to strongly affect the Indians' way of life. The railroad introduced a new cast of characters—entrepreneurs, miners, ranchers, missionaries, teachers, Indian agents, doctors, anthropologists, and even a new subspecies, which one observer described as "American tourists who in shoals and swarms are now invading the Rio Grande valley."

With the twentieth century came many developments affecting all Americans, including New Mexico's native-born people: urban centers; mechanized farming methods; highways and cars; educational and health services; the growth of a cash economy; two world wars; and radio and television. Indian women now used tin pots in their kitchens and sold their traditional ceramic vessels as decorative items to non-Indians. At the same time, many Pueblo men gave up farming in favor of wage work in nearby towns, and Indian children were sent away to schools that promoted assimilation and forbade them to speak their native tongues.

There were other developments that helped to change Pueblo life. Many men, for example, served in the military, received specialized training, and saw the outside world. The Pueblo Lands Act (1924) initiated a lengthy legal process to reaffirm Pueblo ownership of Spanish land grants and adjudicate claims by Hispanic settlers within these grants. The Indian Reorganization Act (1934) concerned itself with

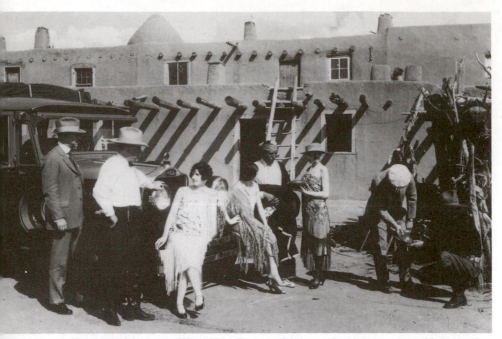

Tourists at Tesuque Pueblo, 1926. (Photo by T. Harmon Parkhurst, courtesy Museum of New Mexico, neg. 132440.)

tribal autonomy and democratic self-government and put into effect a number of beneficial economic and educational programs. In the same year, other legislation was enacted to allow Indian children to attend public schools, rather than Bureau of Indian Affairs or religious schools. And in 1948, Native Americans in New Mexico were granted full voting rights.

Today, the pueblos of Sandia (p. 59) and Isleta (p. 25) lie on the fringes of Albuquerque, and many residents of the Tewa villages to the north work in the "Atomic City" of Los Alamos, returning home each evening to a world still infused with traditions from an Anasazi heritage. Inevitably, many Pueblo people live permanently off their reservations and have become integrated into the mainstream of the dominant society. But even these "expatriates" usually come home for holidays and special occasions. At these special times they find renewal and strength in their native roots.

Since 1540, the Pueblo Indians have absorbed or embraced a mixed bag of cultural attributes while still maintaining their own identity. Even their villages reflect cultural diversity: the kivas reflect an Anasazi heritage; the churches derive from Spain; the *hornos* (adobe bread ovens) are Middle Eastern in origin; and the TV antennas and carports are contributions from Anglo-America.

When you visit a pueblo, please bear in mind that you are a guest on Indian land and should respect local rules, customs, and sensitivities. You can find out about each pueblo's regulations and obtain other information at the governor's office, which is usually well marked. Feast days, when outsiders are always welcome, are a good time to visit; you will be able to watch public dances, meet people, buy crafts and food, and enjoy the generally festive atmosphere.

SUGGESTED READING:

Pueblo Nations, by Joe S. Sando (Santa Fe: Clear Light Publishers, 1992).

Handbook of North American Indians, vol. 9, edited by Alfonso Ortiz (Washington: Smithsonian Institution, 1979).

ACOMA PUEBLO

Acoma Pueblo is located sixty miles west of Albuquerque, off Interstate 40. To reach the pueblo from Albuquerque, drive forty-five miles west on I-40, then twelve miles south on New Mexico 23.

Acoma's general appearance today, when viewed from the surrounding lowlands, is little changed from that of centuries past. The historic feeling of the pueblo, which is situated atop a steep mesa, has made it a popular site to visit.

Archaeologists believe Acoma Pueblo was founded in the late 1200s, when migrants from the north moved here to join other Puebloan people who had been living in the vicinity for several centuries. The earlier residents lived in small scattered communities on the plains below, where they could conveniently tend their fields and obtain water. The defensive posture of the mesa pueblo is a clue to a possible external threat perceived by its builders.

Acoma's defensibility was an asset when Spanish soldiers came to the pueblo in the sixteenth century. In 1541, Hernando de Alvarado, one of Francisco Vásquez de Coronado's officers, stopped here to reconnoiter and obtain supplies. A member of the expedition reported that "The natives . . . came down to meet us peacefully, although they might have spared themselves the trouble and remained on their rock, for we

The trail to Acoma Pueblo, c. 1883. (Photo by Ben Wittick, courtesy School of American Research collections in the Museum of New Mexico, neg. 16173.)

would not have been able to disturb them in the least." Three decades later, Antonio de Espejo, whose explorations were generally marked by good relations with the Southwest's natives, stayed here, too. He noted that the Acomas had "*mantas* (woven shawls), deerskins, and strips of buffalo-hide, tanned as they tan them in Flanders, and many provisions, consisting of maize and turkeys." He also witnessed their Snake Dance, a ceremony that has since disappeared here, but still is practiced by the Hopis.

Very likely, as at Zuñi, some native leaders favored a policy of co-operation with the Spaniards while others argued for active resistance. In 1598, Juan de Oñate's colonists experienced both policies at different times. When Oñate visited the pueblo in October, the pacifist faction led by Chumpo made diplomatic overtures and allowed Oñate to carry out the Spanish oath-of-allegiance ritual.

If the diplomats prevailed during Oñate's visit, the militants, led by one Zutacapan, took control of the pueblo's foreign policy later in the year, when a party of some thirty soldiers led by Oñate's young nephew, Captain Juan de Zaldívar, camped at the foot of their stronghold. Only the Spaniards chronicled the ensuing events, and their records predict-ably tell a tale of Indian treachery. What appears certain is that a battle took place in the pueblo and the Acomas prevailed. Many Spanish sol-diers, including Zaldívar himself, died either in the fighting or in falls from the cliffs as they tried to retreat.

Oñate was angered when he learned of the defeat and, in January, sent a seventy-man punitive expedition under Zaldívar's brother Vi-cente. Vicente's soldiers climbed to the summit under cover of darkness and won a decisive battle, in which hundreds of Indians were killed, some five hundred occupants captured, and the pueblo destroyed.

In February, the fate of the captives, who had been removed to Santo Domingo Pueblo, was determined in a trial presided over by Oñate himself. Since the Acomas had sworn allegiance to Spain, the charges against them included treason, of which they were found guilty. A shocking punishment was handed down to serve as a deterrent to other potential native dissidents. Men over twenty-five years of age suf-fered the amputation of one foot and twenty years of personal servitude; women of the same age group and young men aged twelve to twenty-five received twenty years of servitude; children under the age of twelve were placed under the authority of priests, to be distributed to monas-teries and other places "to attain the knowledge of God and the salva-tion of their souls." All persons sentenced to servitude were assigned to Oñate's soldiers, to be held as slaves for twenty years.

In 1629, Acoma Pueblo received its first missionary, Fray Juan Ramírez. Under his direction, the Indians built San Estevan mission, a monumental adobe structure. They also completed the rebuilding of the pueblo; many of the lower-story rooms in use today date to this time.

The distance to Acoma Pueblo from Santa Fe protected its members from some of the impact of Spanish colonization. In 1680, they participated in the Pueblo revolt only to the extent of killing their priest. When Vargas reconquered New Mexico, the Acomas only allowed him to enter the pueblo for a brief inspection tour. Acoma's old independent spirit reemerged in the following four years, when the pueblo took in many Keresan refugees and malcontents from the Rio Grande and sent warriors to assist the Pueblo of Jemez in its fight against Spanish rule.

The scant historical records extant from the eighteenth century emphasize Acoma's hard times and the stagnation of the Christian missionary program at the pueblo. For a time, the Spaniards recruited some Acomas to assist them in converting and pacifying nearby Navajo bands, but this effort bore little fruit. A dispute with neighboring Laguna Pueblo (p. 35) over water rights began in the mid-1700s and was not legally resolved for many generations. Laguna had been founded around 1699 by refugees from the Rio Grande. Acoma's population, already diminished, dropped still further as a result of epidemics and raids by nomadic tribes. The people subsisted by farming in the canyons and drainages near their mesa and by raising some livestock, which they brought up on the mesa at night for protection from marauders. The blankets they wove were also highly acclaimed, though the craft of weaving subsequently disappeared here. In the late eighteenth century, the Acomas and Lagunas joined the Spaniards in many expeditions against the Navajos, who posed an increasing threat to settlers and pueblo dwellers alike. This military support continued through the Mexican period (1821–1846) and sometimes resulted in obtaining considerable bounty in the recovery of sheep that the Navajos had stolen from the Indians and settlers.

After New Mexico was seized by the Americans in 1846, Lieutenant James William Abert visited Acoma and left a vivid description of the pueblo:

> Each family occupies those rooms that are situated vertically over each other; the lowest stories used as a store-room, in which they put their corn, pumpkins, melons, and other eatables. The fronts of the houses are covered with festoons of bright red peppers, and strings of pumpkins and musk melons that have been cut into ropes and twisted into branches to dry for winter use.

Horses corralled in Acoma Pueblo, c. 1883. (Photo by Ben Wittick, courtesy School of American Research collections in the Museum of New Mexico, neg. 16169.)

The late 1800s were marked by continuous land and boundary disputes with Laguna Pueblo as well as encroachments by Mexicans and problems over fraudulent real estate schemes. Poverty was made more acute by drought, and repeated epidemics of smallpox and diptheria took a frightful toll. Acoma's population at the time of the census of 1900 was less than five hundred, a tragic drop from the sixteenth century, when this tribe is thought to have numbered several thousand.

Western-style medical care and education were slow to arrive at Acoma due to a combination of American bureaucratic apathy, geographical isolation, and the Indians' natural cultural conservatism. When health conditions did improve, they soon were reflected in rising population. Acoma and nearby villages remained economically depressed for many years; even in the 1960s, annual per-capita income was under 750 dollars. In 1970, the Acomas negotiated a compensation of 6,107,157 dollars with the Indian Claims Committee for lands lost that they had used and occupied from time immemorial. After centuries of suffering a diminishing and depleted land base, this compensation

Acoma from the air. (Photo by Peter Dechert.)

represented an important accomplishment. Since then, other economic
developments have occurred on the Acoma reservation, including the
building of a visitor center and tribal museum.

In some respects, the old mesatop Pueblo of Acoma was never a
practical village site. It was too far from agricultural fields, grazing
lands, and water, and, after many Acomas took wage jobs in Albuquerque, too far from public-transportation routes. Consequently, the
pueblo has become primarily a ceremonial place, lived in year round by
only a few families. Even so, the homes and church are well maintained
and regarded with deep ties by the people. The pueblo is open to visitors
on a daily basis. You should register and purchase a camera permit at

the visitors' center and await a guided tour; tour frequency varies according to seasonal demand. Attached to the visitors' center are a museum and cafeteria. A tour guide will lead you through the village's winding lanes and to the historic and beautifully restored San Estevan Church. Along the way there are numerous opportunities to buy crafts and curios. One of the best times to see Acoma dances is on September 2, the Feast Day of Saint Stephen.

TIPS FOR THE TRAVELER:
You many be interested in seeing Laguna Pueblo while you are in the area. Also, the newly formed El Malpais National Monument in Grants offers a dramatic volcanic terrain which is crossed by an ancient trail linking Acoma to Zuñi. El Morro National Monument (p. 321) and the Pueblo of Zuñi (p. 103) lie due east, while farther to the north and west is Chaco Canyon, whose prehistoric pueblo ruins were probably ancestral to the Acoma people.

SUGGESTED READING:
Acoma: Pueblo in the Sky by Ward A. Minge (revised edition; Albuquerque: University of New Mexico Press, 1991).

COCHITI PUEBLO

Cochiti Pueblo sits on the west side of the Rio Grande, thirty miles from Santa Fe. From Santa Fe, drive south on Interstate 25 to the Cochiti exit (New Mexico 16) and follow signs for 12.5 miles to the pueblo. From Albuquerque, take the Santo Domingo exit and follow New Mexico 22 to the pueblo.

The Cochiti Indians live on the west bank of the Rio Grande, just below the imposing Cochiti Dam and Reservoir, which was completed in the early 1970s. Their reservation extends north of the pueblo, nearly to the southern edge of Bandelier National Monument on the Pajarito Plateau.

The Cochitis are Keresan-speaking Pueblos whose oral narratives tell of a mythological dwelling place in the long-distant past, referred to as "White House." It was here the people lived following their emergence into the present world. From White House (no connection to the well-known cliff dwelling in Canyon de Chelly, Arizona), the Keres migrated south and east, some eventually settling on the Pajarito Plateau near other Puebloan farmers.

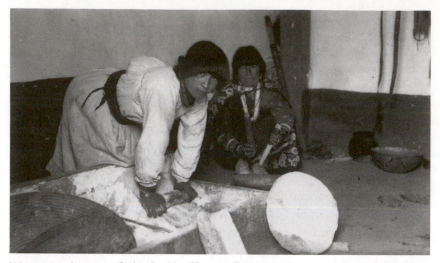

Women grinding corn, Cochiti Pueblo. (Photo by T. Harmon Parkhurst, courtesy Museum of New Mexico, neg. 30227.)

Archaeological research has revealed that the southern Pajarito Plateau, lying on the east flank of the Jemez Mountains, had a major influx of Anasazi homesteaders around A.D. 1175. These migrants, who came from the west, established numerous small pueblos, which they usually occupied for only a few years before moving on to new homesites near other tillable land. Their mobility may have reflected inexperience in subsisting in the unfamiliar environment of the high-elevation, volcanic plateau, cut through by narrow and steep-sided canyons. But more probably, local soils became depleted, requiring frequent moves.

By around A.D. 1300, the population of the southern Pajarito began to swell as a new influx of migrants from the recently abandoned Four Corners region poured into the Rio Grande Valley and surrounding environs. Despite the area's agricultural limitations, the Pajarito settlers thrived; soon, their settlements grew from hamlets of fifteen or twenty rooms to villages of a hundred, and, in the fifteenth century, to towns eight or ten times this size. They also developed a distinctive glazeware style of ceramics, which was a technologically innovative departure from the earlier black-on-white pots decorated with carbon paints. To better control the uncertainties of dryland farming, the Cochiti ancestors constructed terraces, checkdams, and small-scale irrigation systems. Interestingly, there is some evidence that a territorial boundary existed along Frijoles Canyon, separating the people of the southern Pajarito, probably Keresan speakers, from those of the northern plateau, who spoke the Tewa language. Today, these groups are represented, respectively, by the pueblos of Cochiti, Santo Domingo, and San Felipe to the south and San Ildefonso and Santa Clara to the north. The Cochitis still visit sacred places in their ancestral areas, including the Stone Lions hunting shrine within the boundaries of Bandelier National Monument.

Archaeologists also have conducted examinations of limited excavations in Cochiti Pueblo itself, and uncovered ceramics indicating that part of the village may have originated as early as 1225. If this is true, Cochiti is one of the longest continuously occupied villages in North America.

Cochiti was an active community in 1581, when members of the Rodríguez-Chamuscado expedition paid a visit, and at this time the pueblo consisted of 230 houses, two and three stories high. The Spaniards initially called the village Medina de la Torre. The following year, the explorer Antonio de Espejo and a small party stopped at Cochiti and traded bells and small iron articles for buffalo skins and food. In both these instances, the Spaniards and Indians enjoyed cordial relations.

Because of its location on the west bank of the river, Cochiti Pueblo was bypassed by travelers along the Camino Real (see p. 293), the historic trail linking Santa Fe with Mexico City. The Indians may well have viewed being off the beaten track as a blessing, for they had less interference from foreigners and less contact with germs that caused epidemics in other native communities.

In the seventeenth century, the Cochitis sometimes had their own Spanish priest in residence, but at other times the pueblo was a *visita,* or adjunct mission, of nearby Santo Domingo Pueblo. After the 1630s, Cochiti's leaders conspired in more than one rebellious plot against their Spanish rulers, foreshadowing the 1680 revolt, in which they wholeheartedly supported their Pueblo neighbors to the north. To his good fortune, when the revolt did break out, Cochiti's priest was one of the few in the entire territory to save his own life.

After the rebellion, the Cochitis withdrew from their riverside village to a stronghold on the Potrero Viejo, a steep-sided mesa several miles to the northwest. Here, they successfully repulsed a Spanish attack in 1681 led by the exiled governor Antonio de Otermin. Vargas found them still here in 1692 and, the following year, laid siege to the refuge in order to force the Cochitis back to their home village. While the Spaniards were in exile, the Cochitis and their Keres neighbors overthrew Popé, the Tewa leader who had led the 1680 revolt, and appointed their own individual headmen. The Cochitis chose Lucas Naranjo, who led them in a second rebellion against the Spaniards in June of 1696. At this time, Vargas brought his army down from Santa Cruz (p. 184) and defeated the rebels. His soldiers killed and decapitated Naranjo and presented his head as a trophy of victory to their Indian allies at Pecos Pueblo (p. 42).

Following the turmoil of the 1680s and 1690s, a group of Cochitis joined other Keres to found the Pueblo of Laguna (p. 35) far to the southwest. Those who remained rebuilt the destroyed San Buenaventura Church on its original site. It has since been restored and holds a prominent place in the pueblo. On San Buenaventura Day, July 14, the Indians dance in front of the church before going to the main plaza.

For many years, Cochiti has had a few Spanish-American residents. Around the time of the Mexican Revolution, the Cochitis transferred some property within the confines of the village to Mexicans, an unusual occurrence among the pueblos. This was done in exchange for assistance against the raiding Navajo Indians. Some non-Indian residents, however, already had moved into the pueblo for security from attackers.

In historic times, the Cochitis hunted game in the Jemez Mountains, organized rabbit hunts in the vicinity of the pueblo, and participated in fall buffalo hunts in the eastern plains. Today, the tribe has a relatively small land base—less than thirty thousand acres—and much of their reservation is unsuitable for cultivation and only marginally useful for grazing livestock. But strips of irrigable land along the Rio Grande have long been used for floodwater and small-scale agriculture. Ironically, the enormous reservoir just north of the village caused an elevation of the water table to a point of waterlogging fields. In 1993, the tribe negotiated a settlement with the federal government to compensate for damages incurred.

Following construction of the dam, the tribe negotiated a ninety-nine-year lease of seventy-five hundred acres of reservation land north of their village to a land development company. Today, this area encompasses a modern subdivision including a small shopping center, golf course, and other facilities for retired people. This business enterprise, which was highly controversial among members of the pueblo, has helped to accelerate cultural change on the reservation. In addition, the U.S. Corps of Engineers has developed boat ramps and camping sites to accommodate boaters and fishermen. Cochiti's former isolation is no more.

Cochiti remains a small pueblo whose old section around the plaza retains a strong historical character. As many pueblo members live off

San Buenaventura Mission Church at Cochiti Pueblo, c. 1900. (Courtesy Museum of New Mexico, neg. 12286.)

the reservation, a good time to observe traditional life here and to join in the excitement of ceremonial activity is the Feast of San Buenaventura, July 14. Cochiti craftspeople are noted for their fine drums, carved from cottonwood trunks, and their pottery, especially the popular ceramic storyteller figurines, which depict an elder talking to children. One of the originators of this art form is Helen Cordero, whose early figurines command high prices if they can be found.

TIPS FOR THE TRAVELER:

A trip to Bandelier National Monument, near Los Alamos, will introduce you to prehistoric Pueblo sites (Tyuonyi, Ceremonial Cave, Yapashi, San Miguel) that may have been inhabited by Cochiti ancestors. Two other Keresan pueblos, Santo Domingo and San Felipe, are located a few miles south of Cochiti. Other Pueblo ruins can be seen at Coronado State Monument, near Bernalillo. Tent Rocks, five miles west of the pueblo, provides a short hike in a Bureau of Land Management designated area amidst an unusual geological formation. Santa Fe is the best place to find travel and tourist services, but camping areas are available at Cochiti Lake and several miles up the Bland Canyon Road, north of the lake.

SUGGESTED READING:

Cochiti: A New Mexico Pueblo, Past and Present, by Charles H. Lange (reprinted; Albuquerque: University of New Mexico Press, 1990).

CORONADO STATE MONUMENT

Coronado State Monument is located along New Mexico 44, one mile west of Bernalillo.

Coronado State Monument commemorates in name Spain's first explorer/conqueror in New Mexico, Francisco Vásquez de Coronado; however, the site consists of the excavated and partially restored ruins of an ancient Tiwa Indian pueblo called *Kuaua*.

Coronado traveled to New Mexico in the summer of 1540, initially occupying the Zuñi Pueblo of Hawikuh (see p. 103). He sent detachments in all directions to reconnoiter the land and its peoples, look for gold, and find a suitable place for his army to spend the oncoming winter. One subordinate, Captain Hernando de Alvarado, led a party east to the valley of the Rio Grande, where he found a dozen Tiwa villages strung along the river between Kuaua, to the north, and Isleta (p. 25), to the south. The Tiwas, who were farming the alluvial plains along the Rio Grande, appeared better off than the Zuñis and received the Spaniards cordially. Alvarado urged his commander to quarter the army in this area, which he called the Province of Tiguex. Coronado agreed, and the Spaniards arrived in Tiguex in the fall, short of food and supplies and with winter storms nipping at their heels. They selected a Tiwa pueblo they called *Alcanfor*, and moved in.

Where are the remains of Alcanfor today? The question has intrigued archaeologists and historians for many years. Coronado's followers included more than three hundred Spaniards (most of them cavalrymen), nearly a thousand Mexican-Indian allies, and more than a thousand livestock. His men had spears, bows and crossbows, shields, coats of mail, helmets, and other paraphernalia that one would expect to find traces of in the archaeological record. But the 1934–39 archaeological excavations at Kuaua did not reveal such items. Kuaua was not "Alcanfor." Someday, perhaps, a road cut will be widened or a house footing dug, exposing a Spanish spearpoint or helmet. Then excavations will begin anew in search of Coronado's elusive winter camp.

Kuaua's excavators did, however, learn a lot about an Indian pueblo. The village is believed to have been founded in the early fourteenth century, a time of intensive Pueblo-settlement expansion in the Rio Grande Valley. In those times, the river flowed some distance to the east of its present location, which is within a stone's throw of the ruins. The inhabitants of Kuaua and other nearby Tiwa pueblos—Puaray, Alameda, Sandia (p. 59)—tilled fertile fields along the river to produce

The ruins of Kuaua along the Rio Grande. (Photo by David Grant Noble.)

corn, beans, squash, tobacco, and cotton, and they gathered wild plant foods in the lush riparian environment. They also hunted, both along the river and in the sacred Sandia Mountains in whose shadow they lived. Most of what they needed in the way of tools, utensils, and cloth, they either made at home or acquired through trading with their neighbors. They stored enough food in the ground-floor back rooms of their pueblo to see them through a poor harvest or two, but extended droughts meant famine.

Kuaua Pueblo was constructed of adobe, which its builders puddled in courses to form walls. Its rooms were small (cramped and claustrophobic by modern standards), but practical for heat conservation. They were built as solid multistoried apartment blocks surrounding courtyards, where people worked, raised turkeys, played, and held ceremonies. Entrance to the apartments was by hatchways in the roofs, which were attained by retractable ladders. An absence of exterior doors in the roomblocks forced one to enter the plaza through a narrow passageway. Kuaua was no fortress, but potential attackers would have had to overcome serious obstacles before getting at its food stores.

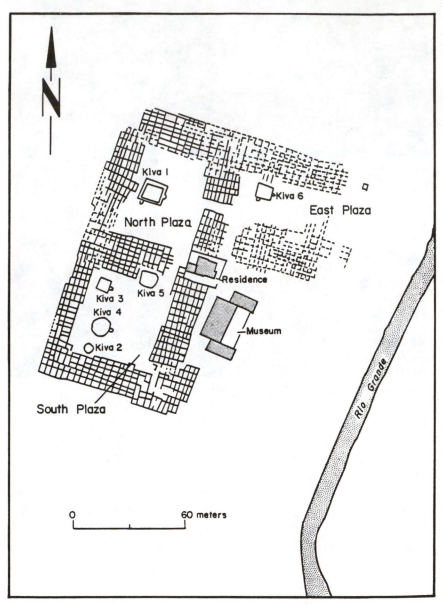

Plan of Kuaua Pueblo. (Courtesy Laboratory of Anthropology, Santa Fe.)

When Coronado appropriated Alcanfor, its inhabitants dispersed, probably to join friends and relatives in nearby villages. To feed and clothe his troops, he sent soldiers among the Tiwa villages to requisition food and clothing. As the weeks passed, the Indians increasingly begrudged giving their food and clothing to the Spanish soldiers. The situation ultimately led to war. By spring, two Tiwa pueblos had been destroyed and many Indians buried.

Kuaua, no doubt, was one of the communities upon which the Spaniards depended for supplies; one can only imagine the experiences of its inhabitants through the winter of 1540–41. Archaeologists believe the village survived to the early 1600s. If so, the Kuauans certainly met other Spanish explorers—Fray Agustín Rodríguez and Captain Francisco Sánchez Chamuscado in 1581, for example, and Juan de Oñate in 1598. Perhaps one of Oñate's clerics came here to proselytize and, following colonial policy, urged the pueblo's inhabitants to leave their village and consolidate with nearby Puaray or Alameda.

Kuaua ruins, while they may not be the site of Coronado's camp, can still be a memorial to everything that happened in the winter of 1540–41. Those fateful events, indeed, set the stage for the Pueblo revolt, which occurred 140 years later. Today, an interpretive trail leads through the ruins, whose waist-high adobe brick walls (resurrected by archaeologists) reflect the pueblo's original structure and layout. Bear in mind that the wall stubs you see supported a multiroom structure reaching a height of two to three stories. Families lived in suites of upper-level rooms connected by doorways and stored their grain in the cooler, less accessible rooms below. They ground their corn on *metates,* sundried meat and fruits on their rooftops, and raised turkeys in pens around the plazas. There are numerous kivas (subterranean chambers) where religious societies met and young men were initiated into the pueblo's cultural mysteries. You can enter one reconstructed kiva and see an extraordinary set of painted mural reproductions depicting religious motifs. These frescoes caused great excitement when they were discovered in the 1930s. Archaeologists carefully removed them to a laboratory at the University of New Mexico, where conservators painstakingly peeled away seventeen layers of painted plaster to reveal a trove of prehistoric Pueblo religious art. The monument also has a small cultural museum, which includes examples of the original kiva paintings. Adjoining the monument is a small park with picnic tables and camping facilities.

Kiva painting at Coronado State Park. (Photo by David Grant Noble.)

TIPS FOR THE TRAVELER:
Sandia Pueblo is located only a few miles to the south. It is one of two extant Southern Tiwa villages, the other being Isleta, south of Albuquerque. Along New Mexico 44 to the west is the Keres pueblo of Zia (p. 99), which is also worth a visit. The newly formed Petroglyph National Monument in Albuquerque contains thousands of examples of rock art of the Tiwa Indians. To the east are the Sandia Mountains, which are sacred to all the Rio Grande Pueblo Indians and provide a beautiful area for hiking, picnicking, camping, and, in winter, skiing.

SUGGESTED READING:
Coronado: Knight of Pueblo and Plains, by Herbert E. Bolton (reprinted; Albuquerque: University of New Mexico Press, 1991).

ISLETA PUEBLO

Isleta Pueblo is located fourteen miles south of Albuquerque. From Albuquerque, take Interstate 25 south to the Isleta Pueblo exit and follow signs to the pueblo.

Isleta Pueblo is on the fringe of the greater Albuquerque metropolitan area and thus has joined, to a large extent, the mainstream of American life. Situated on a 200,000-acre reservation with irrigable bottomland on the west bank of the Rio Grande, Isletans have long enjoyed a measure of prosperity not available to other Indian communities. In addition to farming, they also obtain revenue from a substantial cattle operation and have many nearby opportunities for employment, including a bingo gambling establishment on pueblo land.

Opinions differ as to just when Isleta was founded. When Spaniards first entered New Mexico, the Southern Tiwa Indians lived in a dozen or so villages strung along the Rio Grande between Isleta and Bernalillo. Of these, only Isleta and Sandia remain. Although an older settlement may have existed where Isleta now stands, the pueblo probably was formed in the sixteenth century as an aggregation of local Tiwa villages.

The Tiwa name for Isleta is *Shiewhibak* (knife laid on the ground to play *whib*). The "knife," in this case, probably refers to the nearby sharply shaped lava ridge, and *whib* is a native foot race. The original Spanish name, *San Antonio de la Isleta* (Saint Anthony of the Little Island), reminds us that the flooding Rio Grande sometimes developed a western channel, placing the pueblo on an island. During the Pueblo revolt, some converted Isletan refugees brought their patron, Saint Anthony of Padua, to El Paso del Norte, where they established a new settlement. Some years later, when Isleta Pueblo was refounded, its inhabitants adopted San Augustín as their new patron saint.

According to Tiwa oral tradition, some of the pueblo's ancestors originated in the northwest, while others came here from the south. While the concept of a prehistoric migration from the north is shared by all of the Pueblo Indians, the legendary southern origin points to an even earlier influx of Mogollon people into the Rio Grande region. The Mogollon culture emerged over two thousand years ago and survived until the 1300s. It was thriving in southwestern New Mexico while the Anasazi culture was developing in the northern San Juan region. Archaeologists have found evidence of an ancient Mogollon migration to the Salinas Basin southeast of Isleta, and in the mid-1600s, many Salinas Indians (see p. 55) abandoned their pueblos and came as refugees to Isleta and to other Tiwa and Piro villages.

In 1581, two Spanish explorers, Agustín Rodríguez and Francisco Sánchez Chamuscado, led a small group of explorers up the Rio Grande Valley and through the pueblos of the Piro and the southern Tiwa Indians. At the first major Tiwa pueblo they encountered—possibly Isleta itself—they were graciously welcomed and offered food. Reportedly, the Indians also made "the sign of the cross with their hands as a sign of peace, as the people before [the Piros] had done." The Spaniards left us an interesting description of their hosts:

The men have their hair cut in the fashion of caps, so that they leave . . . on the crown of their heads, a sort of skull cap formed by their own hair. Others wear their hair long, to the shoulders, as the Indians of New Spain formerly did. Some adorn themselves with painted cotton pieces of cloth three spans long and two thirds wide, with which they cover their privy parts. Over this they wear, fastened at the shoulders, a blanket of the same material, painted with many figures and colors. It reaches to their knees like the clothes of the Mexicans. Some, in fact most of them, wear cotton shirts, hand painted and embroidered, that are very charming. They wear shoes. Below the waist the women wear cotton skirts, colored and embroidered, and above, a blanket of the same material, painted and worked like those used by the men. They wear it after the fashion of the Jewish women. They gird themselves over it with cotton sashes adorned with tassels. They comb their hair, which is long.

For reasons not entirely clear to historians, Isleta was the sole pueblo that did not join the Pueblo revolt in 1680. A likely reason for their inaction, however, is that when the revolt ignited, the Spanish lieutenant governor was in the pueblo with forty soldiers, and soon after, about fifteen hundred settlers from around Bernalillo sought safety here. The refugees and three hundred Tiwa, Piro, and Tompiro Indians withdrew to El Paso, believing that the northern colonists had been wiped out in the insurrection. In fact, the colonists escaped from Santa Fe and also went south.

In the turmoil of the rebellion, many Isletans scattered in fear of both the fleeing Spaniards and the insurgent Pueblos who were caught up in the fervor of victory. But some remained at Isleta and others returned later to be joined by some Piros from Pilabo Pueblo (see p. 203), which had been attacked by Apaches. In December 1681, Governor Antonio de Otermín led Spanish troops up the Rio Grande to assess damages and test Pueblo forces. He was dismayed to find Isleta's mission burned and the church being used by the natives as a stock corral.

Interior of the Isleta mission, 1881. (Photo by Ben Wittick, courtesy School of American Research collections in the Museum of New Mexico, neg. 15590.)

Otermín learned that, even after a year, the spirit of rebellion still glowed. He recaptured and burned Isleta, took 519 captives, and attacked Zia Pueblo (p. 99) before being stopped at Cochiti (p. 15). The Isletan refugees in El Paso established a new settlement there, Isleta del Sur. However, some deserted to return home and others took up residence in other Rio Grande pueblos or lived among the Apaches. Some even journeyed to Hopi country, where they established the village of Payupki on Second Mesa. Here they lived for several generations before being persuaded by the Spanish to come back.

In 1692, when Governor Diego de Vargas led another effort to recover New Mexico, he found the lower parts of the nave walls of Isleta's church in good condition; very likely, these stubs were retained when the church was rebuilt. If so, these portions of the present church date to the original construction in 1613.

Simon Zuni, an Isleta leader, 1900. (Courtesy Museum of New Mexico, neg. 52866.)

In 1776, when it was visited by Fray Francisco Atanasio Domín-guez, Isleta was a thriving village consisting of three apartment blocks that formed a large plaza in front of the church. Its mission also served several other nearby Spanish communities. The Indians reaped copious harvests from fields along a belt for three miles up and down the river. In addition, they tended fruit orchards and a vineyard from which wine was produced. Isleta's proximity to a series of Spanish settlements en-couraged acculturation, but after Mexican independence in 1821, they experienced less colonial interference. The influence of the church also diminished; indeed, New Mexico's contingent of priests was reduced to a mere handful.

In the nineteenth century, Isletans still grew corn as their main crop, but they also tilled fields of wheat and continued to be successful with their orchards and vegetable gardens. They also raised horses, cattle, goats, sheep, and poultry. Rabbits were a common source of meat around the pueblo, and hunters went to the nearby Manzano Mountains for deer or traveled to the more distant plains for buffalo.

In the early 1880s, Laguna Pueblo (p. 35), to the west, was rife with religious factionalism that pitted religious traditionalists against a group of Protestant reformists. After two kivas were burned, the conservatives moved to Isleta, bringing with them their potent kachina masks and religious paraphernalia.

The Pueblos believe that the kachina gods are instrumental in bringing rain. The kachina cult had disappeared at Isleta, and village elders recognized the potential benefit to the pueblo of having the Laguna migrants settle here. Accordingly, they made the Laguna kachina chief, Francisco Correo, an offer: a new home and land in return for a pledge always to keep the masks at Isleta. The migrants were accepted into various Isleta religious societies and given a parcel of land around Oraibi Hill for their small colony. However, the integration of the Lagunas and their kachina rituals became problematical, and before long many of the Lagunas returned home. But, as promised, the masks and their keepers remained and the rituals continued.

Isleta has not been immune to political factionalism, which began in the late 1870s and is still present. As in other pueblos, internal dissensions have often been traceable to conflicts between those who wish to keep old ways and those who want change. In one 1940s dispute over leadership succession, the traditional canes of office were actually snatched during a ceremony from the hands of one faction's leader by a member of a rival party. The breakdown of the traditional political system ultimately led to Isleta's adoption of a constitution and a democratic form of government.

Another dispute at Isleta in recent times generated wide press coverage and caused much embarrassment in the pueblo. In 1965, the governor, with the support of his council, served the resident Roman Catholic priest a tribal court order of eviction. They felt the cleric had expressed disrespect and intolerance for their religious traditions. When the priest refused to obey the order, he was forcibly removed from the reservation by tribal authorities. For a pueblo that had ostensibly espoused Roman Catholicism for more than three centuries, this act, which thwarted the wishes of the archbishop, caused much disturbance. In a mild way, history was repeating itself.

Nearby Albuquerque has numerous sites of historical and anthropological interest, including Old Town and the Maxwell Museum of Anthropology. Petroglyph National Monument, located along Albuquerque's West Mesa, is a preserve of thousands of petroglyphs pecked onto basalt boulders by the ancestors of the Tiwa Indians. For information to visit these sites, call (505) 766-8375. Albuquerque's South Valley was settled by Spanish colonists in the early 1700s, and if you drive along New Mexico 47 between Pajarito and Tomé, you will pass through a series of communities that had their beginnings in this era.

SUGGESTED READING:
"Isleta: The Pueblo That Roared," by John Phillip Olguin and Mary T. Olguin, *The Indian Historian,* (Fall 1976).

JEMEZ PUEBLO AND JEMEZ STATE MONUMENT

Jemez Pueblo is located on New Mexico 4, forty-five miles northwest of Albuquerque. From Interstate 25 at Bernalillo, follow New Mexico 44 west to San Ysidro; then turn north on New Mexico 4 and continue six miles to the pueblo. Jemez State Monument is in Jemez Springs, twelve miles farther north on New Mexico 4.

On November 12 of each year, the people of Jemez Pueblo celebrate the feast day of their patron, San Diego. Dancers fill the pueblo's long plaza, and along the narrow streets merchants sell refreshments, jewelry, pottery, weaving, and local produce. Locals and outsiders of many backgrounds mingle as they watch the dances, meet friends, shop, and enjoy the festive atmosphere. The aromas of burning piñon and food cooking drift in the crisp fall air against the sounds of talk, laughter, drumming, and chanting. Feast days and trade fairs are old traditions in New Mexico, and at them one feels the remarkable continuity of Pueblo cultural traditions.

The Pueblo of Jemez, known by its Towa inhabitants as *Walatowa,* probably goes back to the early 1600s, when it was one of a series of villages inhabited by the Jemez Indians. Its first mission, founded soon after 1621, was a *visita* of San José de Jemez Church at Giusewa Pueblo, several miles upriver, near the hot springs. Today, these sites are the main features of Jemez State Monument.

Jemez Pueblo, c. 1885. (Courtesy Museum of New Mexico, neg. 31251.)

In 1541, Spanish explorers counted seven pueblos in the mountainous Jemez country, some perched safely atop steep mesas. Their defensive posture suggests some foe threatened their inhabitants before the coming of the Spaniards. Walatowa's first occupants were pressured to move here by Franciscans, who, to facilitate proselytizing and civil control, followed a policy to consolidate scattered, small native communities around their missions. A 1651 decree stated that "Indians should be brought together in settlements and should not continue living separated and apart in the mountains and forests, deprived of every spiritual and temporal benefit." In time, the Jemez were consolidated, first in the villages of Giusewa, Patoqua, and Astialakwa, then, after attacks by Navajos, in the single pueblo of Walatowa.

The history of the Jemez Indians extends much further back in time than 1541, when their presence was first recorded by European chroniclers. Historian Joe S. Sando describes an earlier homeland of his people as "a vast wilderness of sparsely peopled, piñon covered rolling hills, flat-topped mesas, and deep desert canyons. From their homes they could see the snow-covered San Juan mountain range about forty miles to the north, in present-day Colorado." Jemez oral accounts of their past are largely reinforced by the findings of archaeologists, who believe Jemez ancestors lived in the upper San Juan River country, east of the Animas River in Colorado. Sometime prior to A.D. 950, they migrated south to the area of Stone Lake, which lies south of Dulce, New Mexico, now on the Jicarilla Apache reservation. The people made their lives here for some three centuries before moving to the region they now occupy.

While their villages and farmlands were concentrated on the mesas and in the river valleys, the Jemez used a much wider territory for hunting and gathering and religious functions. This distinction between *settlement* and *use* areas would become, in the twentieth century, a key issue in tribal land claims, not just here but at other pueblos, too.

In their relations with Spaniards, the Jemez were among the more independent and resistant Indian pueblos. In a minor revolt of the late 1640s, they killed a Spaniard, an offense for which twenty-nine pueblo members were hanged. They joined in the 1680 rebellion, when they murdered their priest, Fray Juan de Jesús María, and set fire to the church.

The Jemez strongly resisted reconquest. In his drive to retake New Mexico, Diego de Vargas enlisted the aid of the subdued Zia, Santa Ana, and San Felipe pueblos (see pp. 99, 77, and 64, respectively), which supported his efforts. At the same time, the Jemez secured the assistance of warriors from Acoma and Zuñi, and were joined by refugees from Santo Domingo. During these years, most Jemez found refuge in their ancestral mesatop villages, while others went west to join the Navajos and Hopis. In 1694, those who stayed suffered a disastrous defeat to Vargas's forces on San Diego Mesa. Most of the refugees eventually returned to their homeland, although some stayed in the west and assimilated with the Navajos.

In the 1830s, Pecos Pueblo (p. 42), which had long been in decline as a result of warfare and epidemics, finally found it impossible to maintain a viable community. The Jemez invited its few surviving residents to join them. The Pecos Bull Ceremony, which occurs on August 2 at Jemez, is one tradition that survives from another time and place.

Jemez enjoys a tradition of long-distance running, which takes the form of both a ceremonial activity and a sport. Stories are told of past runners of great prowess, and as the pueblo's youth continue to compete in local races and national runs, new stories are born to pass on to future generations.

The traditional Jemez economy, based on agriculture, hunting, and gathering, was broadened by contact with Europeans, who introduced new seeds such as wheat; domestic animals, including horses, cattle, and sheep; and metal implements. Although the Jemez still do some farming, more and more people have wage-earning jobs and come into close contact with the outside world.

After the Pueblo revolt, the Spanish king had issued the Jemez a 17,331-acre land grant. With this limited base, the tribe began a long struggle to regain ownership over a portion of their wider territory.

Woman and child, Jemez Pueblo, 1912. (Photo by Jesse L. Nusbaum, courtesy Museum of New Mexico, neg. 61712.)

Their efforts to increase the size of their reservation have met some success: Congress added nearly 16,000 acres in the early 1900s, and 9,648 more acres were received in 1942 through the Pueblo Lands Act. In addition, the Jemez lease over 40,000 acres of federal land.

Jemez State Monument, which has a visitor center and a small museum, is open daily. An interpretive trail goes by the mounds of Giusewa

Laguna Pueblo, c. 1935. (Photo by T. Harmon Parkhurst, courtesy Museum of New Mexico, neg. 2787.)

Pueblo to the ruins of San José de los Jemez Church. Archaeological excavations in 1921–22 revealed that the pueblo was founded in the fourteenth century and attained at least two stories in height. The church and mission, built of sandstone and adobe, bears testimony to the remarkable building abilities of the Indians and Franciscans. Two fascinating discoveries in the church remains were a series of colorful murals depicting floral patterns and Indian motifs and windows of selenite, a transparent form of gypsum.

TIPS FOR THE TRAVELER:
Other nearby historic sites you may find interesting to visit include nearby Zia Pueblo; Coronado State Monument (p. 20), in Bernalillo; and Bandelier National Monument, along New Mexico 4 near Los Alamos. The closest tourist facilities are along New Mexico 44 in San Ysidro and to the east in Bernalillo.

SUGGESTED READING:
Nee Hemish: The History of Jemez Pueblo, by Joe S. Sando (Albuquerque: University of New Mexico Press, 1982).

LAGUNA PUEBLO

Laguna Pueblo is located forty-two miles west of Albuquerque, along U.S. 66 and just off Interstate 40.

Drivers between Albuquerque and Grants often are struck by the contrast between the modern interstate they are traveling and the appearance of a historic native village clinging to a hill just opposite the highway. Many pull into the rest stop to gaze across a narrow wash, and seemingly vaster gulf of time, at Laguna Pueblo.

Laguna is often cited as New Mexico's newest pueblo, having been officially founded in 1699. Governor Cubero did indeed dedicate the village on July 4 of that year and gave its residents a likeness of their patron, San José. Laguna Pueblo's founding, however, does not mark the beginning of settlement by Puebloan people in this area. Researchers have found nearby the remains of Indian habitations that predate the arrival of Spaniards in New Mexico by many centuries. Some archaeological sites, indeed, go back to the even earlier Archaic Period, when bands of hunter-gatherers made their camps in the vicinity.

The Lagunas, who speak Keresan, are closely related to their neighbors at Acoma Pueblo, only fourteen miles away. The two groups share many customs and traditions. The Lagunas, like other Keres, have a strong oral tradition whose narratives speak of long-ago migrations here from a land to the north. En route, the migrants stopped for periods of time, but always moved on, helped by their guiding Spirit, Iatiko. Some stories are about two leaders, White Hands of the Lizard Clan and Broken Prayer Stick of the Water Clan. Broken Prayer Stick is said to have used his powers to rid the mesa of Acoma of its many troublesome snakes; later, he led followers northeast to Laguna, where he recognized the place where Iatiko, their Mother, wished them to settle. Here, along San José Creek, where beavers had created a lake, the people established new roots and later built a pueblo, Kawaika. The archaeological remains have not been identified, but they may lie under Old Laguna.

The Laguna narratives transmit certain truths down through the generations. One of these was the necessity of leaving the north country. Another was the role of a vital religion in surviving in harmony with nature in a challenging environment. Still others included the importance of mutual assistance among Pueblo groups and the joy of ultimately finding a nurturing new home. Some elements of Laguna oral tradition are reinforced by archaeologists' findings. The country to the north, for example, probably represents the San Juan region, which the Anasazi certainly did vacate in the late 1200s.

Between the time of the Pueblo revolt in 1680 and the final regaining of control by the Spaniards in 1696, many of New Mexico's Indian pueblos were in a state of turmoil. Villages were abandoned and reoccupied, new pueblos were built, and various groups moved from place to place in search of safety, freedom, and a return to traditionalism. Many refugees found their way to Laguna, some coming from Keresan villages such as Santo Domingo and Cochiti in the northern Rio Grande Valley, and others arriving via Acoma, which also harbored refugees. The newcomers strengthened Laguna and helped area residents in defending themselves against Apache and Navajo raids.

The threat from nomadic tribes continued well into the 1800s, making life hazardous for the pastoral Lagunas and their neighbors at Acoma. The pueblo continued to accept new residents, both Pueblo and Navajo, and as the Laguna population grew, the people established new farms, grazing camps, and hamlets in outlying areas and acquired some additional parcels of land, owned outright by the tribe.

Laguna was situated along a well-traveled route, and in the nineteenth century, Hispanic and Anglo-American farmers and ranchers moved west from the Rio Grande Valley into the vicinity of the pueblo. As elsewhere, the newcomers brought their own culture to bear upon the Indians, and some encroached upon traditional Acoma and Laguna lands, causing conflicts and property disputes.

As outside influences intensified, progressive and conservative factions developed at Laguna. In 1851, the Reverend Samuel Gorman, a white Protestant missionary, took up residence in the pueblo. He was followed by other Anglo-Americans—teachers, surveyors, merchants, missionaries—some of whom married Laguna women. The newcomers encouraged change and promoted their own religion, Presbyterianism. Two non-Indians, Walter and Robert Marmon, were even elected to terms as governor, an unthinkable occurrence in most other pueblos. Political and religious factionalism eventually tore Laguna asunder. In the 1870s, two kivas were destroyed, motivating some traditionalists to move to Mesita, the nearest outlying village, and then to Isleta (p. 25), a Southern Tiwa pueblo south of Albuquerque. The disputes over modernization and religion caused a serious intrapueblo rift, the repercussions of which are still not forgotten.

Other external forces also brought change and directed Laguna's future. In the early 1880s, the railroad came to Albuquerque, then cut west past Laguna, placing these native people directly in the path of

Laguna people, c. 1935. (Photo by T. Harmon Parkhurst, courtesy Museum of New Mexico, neg. 2885.)

Anglo-American progress. Of course, many men found employment laying track and were introduced to a wage-earning type of economy. More recent generations of Lagunas have worked in uranium mines and other business enterprises on the reservation as well as for federal agencies.

Even as the modern world encroached more and more on Laguna's way of life, traditional activities such as farming and herding continued to be practiced. A drought in 1935 stimulated the pueblo to institute range-conservation measures and adopt scientific animal-husbandry techniques to save the land and ameliorate economic conditions. Livestock associations also were formed to help improve sheep and cattle raising on the reservation. In addition, federally funded programs have introduced modern housing and medical services as well as college scholarships for promising high school graduates. One widely recognized Laguna writer is Leslie Marmon Silko, author of the novel *Ceremony* and other books. With relatively high employment, a population of over six thousand, and about 420,000 acres of land, Laguna is one of New Mexico's more affluent pueblos.

If you visit Laguna, be sure to walk through the old pueblo. The massive stone church, San José de Laguna, originally built in 1699, remains in good condition as a result of restorations in the 1930s. Laguna Feast Days are held on March 19 and September 19, both good times to come here. To see more of the area, you might also drive through Laguna's outlying hamlets of Mesita, Paguate, Paraje, Encinal, and Seama, and continue west on Route 66 through Cubero and San Fidel. At San Fidel the old highway rejoins I-40.

TIPS FOR THE TRAVELER:
Acoma Pueblo, sometimes called "Sky City," is located nearby and is well worth seeing. If you are headed west, you will enjoy visiting El Morro National Monument and the Pueblo of Zuñi. North of Interstate 40 at Thoreau, you may visit Chaco Culture National Historical Park, whose ancient pueblos represent a highlight of the Anasazi culture. You will find motel accommodations, restaurants, and other travel services in Grants and Albuquerque along Interstate 40.

SUGGESTED READING:
"An Outline of Laguna Pueblo History and Social Organization," by Florence (Hawley) Ellis, *Southwestern Journal of Anthropology* (V. 15, No. 4, 1959).

NAMBE PUEBLO

Nambe Pueblo is located between Santa Fe and Española. From U.S. 285/84, drive two miles east on New Mexico 503, then take a right turn to the pueblo.

Five hundred years ago, the western foothills of the Sangre de Cristo Mountains were dotted with a series of Indian villages, ancestral to Nambe Pueblo. Behind them, the terrain rose to the wooded game-rich slopes of the mountains, while below flowed fresh streams, whose waters could be diverted to fields and gardens. Most of these pueblos were situated along easily defended ridges and mesas, suggesting the presence of some external threat to their inhabitants. Tewa oral narratives mention invaders "from the east"; however, such stories may refer to the Comanches, whose aggression toward the communities in the Rio Grande Valley came later in time. Although little archaeological research has been done on these foothill sites, they appear to have been abandoned in the early 1500s, when some of their inhabitants joined friends or relatives at Nambe.

The unauthorized Spanish colonizer, Castaño de Sosa, visited Nambe Pueblo in 1691 and was given food by the villagers. As he was looking for a place to settle his colony, the occupants of the pueblo were probably concerned that he and his followers would appropriate their village, as Coronado had done earlier at Alcanfor in the Province of Tiguex. But Castaño and his followers traveled on, eventually to Santo Domingo Pueblo, where they were arrested by Spanish officials. One wonders how the Pueblo Indians appeared four centuries ago, and fortunately, Castaño included an account in his journals. The following description is from his journal entry at Pecos Pueblo, which he had occupied in January.

> The dress of the men . . . [consisted of] a blanket (*manta*) of cotton and a buffalo hide over it. Some of them cover their private parts with very gay and highly decorated cloths. The women [dress] with a blanket drawn in a knot at the shoulder and a sash the width of a palm at the waist. At one side, the blanket is completely open. Over it are placed some other very gaily worked blanket or some turkey feather robes and many other curious things, which is remarkable for savages.

At Pecos, Castaño was impressed by the large quantities of corn he saw, for "every house had two or three rooms full. . . . The corn was of many colors, and the same [is true of] the beans. Apparently there was

Potshuno, a Nambe warrior, 1879. (Photo by John K. Hillers, courtesy Museum of New Mexico, neg. 55217.)

corn from the two previous years." In his journal, he also mentioned the farm produce at Nambe. What is especially interesting from an historical perspective are the agricultural surpluses that Castaño and other early Spanish explorers observed at the pueblos. The experience of many centuries had taught the Pueblos that farming was an unpredictable business, at best, and it was wise to lay up food stores to cover possible future crop failures. No doubt, Castaño, like Coronado before him and Oñate after, realized that the Pueblos' surpluses could be appropriated by others as well.

Castaño did not stay, but only a few years later, a "legitimate" Spanish colony came up the Rio Grande and settled at nearby Yunge, across the river from San Juan Pueblo (see p. 72). Missionaries spread out among the pueblos from Yunge, and by 1617 Nambe had a missionary and church. The people of Nambe joined the revolt of 1680 and enjoyed the dozen years of independence that followed until the Spaniards returned in 1692.

In 1696, after nearly a century of missionary teachings, the Nambes and their fellow Tewas continued to reject Catholicism and were on the verge of a second rebellion. The frustration that this caused Nambe's missionary, Fray Antonio Carbonel, is vividly revealed in a letter he wrote to his superior on March 31 of that year. The friar bitterly complained that the Indians "mock the ministers and even Christ transubstantiated in the host." Describing his relationship with the Indians, he refers to himself as "an ant . . . against a thousand bloodthirsty wolves." He accused the Tewas of idolatry, wicked acts, theft, banditry, and rebelliousness, and urged strong punishments. He also bemoaned the failure of the missionary program, suggesting that he had been deceived in coming here "to die among infidels." Paraphrasing texts from the Old Testament, the distraught cleric recommended: *Ubi no fuerint accepti fugiam in alia terra cum benedictione Dei* ("Where you have not been accepted flee into another land with the blessing of God").

Not long after writing these words, Carbonel and several other Spaniards from Nambe were murdered and the pueblo's mission looted of its sacred vessels. In retaliation, Governor Vargas arrested Nambe's *cacique* (religious leader), Diego Xenome, and had him executed. The 1696 revolt of the Pueblos, however, did not have the planning, organization, or cohesiveness of that of 1680. Five pueblos were Spanish allies, and some factions within even the rebellious villages did not support the movement. It was the Pueblos' last effort to oppose foreign rule and it failed.

In the seventeenth and eighteenth centuries, the pueblo was repeatedly struck by epidemics, reducing its population at times to only a few dozen families. However, unlike their neighbors at Pojoaque, they never left, and in the present century they have increased to several hundred people. In the late 1700s, an observer commented on Nambe's river and its "swift current full of crystalline water." It flowed, he said, from a canyon in the hills to the southeast, where "there is trout fishing." This stream was responsible for Nambe's well-irrigated fields and gardens and good crops of vegetables and fruit. And like the fresh stream that runs through Taos Pueblo from Blue Lake, it must have given the pueblo's inhabitants spiritual reinforcement as well. Nambe Falls, above the pueblo, remain a sacred site to the Indians and a popular place for outsiders to visit.

The pueblo's small size and its proximity to Hispanic and Anglo-American communities have resulted in many marriages with outsiders. By the mid-1900s, the pueblo had lost much of its traditional culture, ceremonial functions had nearly disappeared, and few people spoke the

Tewa language. In 1961, however, soon after Santa Clara Pueblo began holding an annual ceremonial at Puye Cliffs, the Nambes initiated their own ceremonial, held at Nambe Falls. The event, which tourists are welcome to attend, was conceived to raise funds to restore the church, but it has provided revenue for other purposes, too. The villagers enthusiastically support the event because it introduces their children to their old traditions.

TIPS FOR THE TRAVELER:
Nambe Pueblo is just off the "high road" to Taos (p. 208). From here you can continue to Chimayo (p. 147), the mountain villages of Truchas (p. 218) and Las Trampas (p. 157), to Picuris Pueblo (p. 48), and on to Taos. Tourist facilities can be found in Española and Santa Fe. Other Tewa villages such as San Ildefonso (p. 68) and San Juan may also make interesting side trips.

SUGGESTED READING:
The Pueblo Indians of North America, by Edward P. Dozier (reprinted; Prospect Heights: Waveland Press, 1983).

PECOS NATIONAL HISTORICAL PARK

Pecos National Historical Park is located off Interstate 25, twenty-eight miles east of Santa Fe. From Santa Fe, take the Glorieta-Pecos exit and proceed eight miles through Pecos village to the park. Southbound travelers on the interstate should take the Rowe-Pecos exit and continue four miles to the park.

Pecos Pueblo, whose ruins are the focus of a historical park near Santa Fe, was a major population and trading center between around A.D. 1450 and 1700. After 1700, this fortified town also functioned as a buffer between the Pueblo and Spanish farming communities to the west and the nomadic, often warlike tribes of the southern plains.

The Pecos site, on a hill just west of the Pecos River at the edge of the Sangre de Cristo Mountains, was first settled by Puebloan people as early as A.D. 1300. After 1400, however, an influx of newcomers arrived, probably from several less-defensible settlements down the valley, including one whose remains are known today as Forked Lightning Pueblo. Pecos commands a full view over the valley, allowing its inhabitants to spot anyone approaching.

Remains of the Pecos mission. (Photo by David Grant Noble.)

Pecos was a highly defensible town. Consider the obstacles that an attacker would have faced. First, there was a perimeter wall, parts of which are still visible. Then, within the wall was the multistoried pueblo itself, with no exterior doors or windows and only two narrow entranceways. If an enemy gained entrance to the quadrangle, he would have found access to the pueblo's interior even more challenging: a scramble to rooftops; a leap down a dark hatchway, perhaps to meet a lance point; a search through labyrinthine corridors and rooms for defenders.

Pecos had more advantages than good defense. Out of the nearby mountains, which still abound in game and other resources, flowed reliable streams, which the Indians used to irrigate their crops in the valley. Equally important to the pueblo's two thousand inhabitants was their strategic position between the fertile and populous northern Rio Grande Valley to the west and the vast buffalo plains to the east. The Pecos carried on a vigorous trade, exchanging farm products from the pueblos for hides, robes, and jerked meat brought in by Plains tribes.

When news reached Pecos in 1540 that foreigners had attacked Hawikuh Pueblo (see p. 103), the Pecos sent a diplomatic mission to the land of the Zuñis to make contact with the invaders. They chose a person of stature, nicknamed "Bigotes" by the Spaniards because he had a mustache. Bigotes made peaceful overtures to Coronado and his officers, and agreed to guide an exploratory party, led by Captain Hernando de Alvarado, to the Rio Grande and Pecos. Another guide took them eastward across the plains to the mythic land of "Quivira," rumored to be rich in gold. It is reasonable to assume the Pecos leaders had a strategy behind their guiding service: to lead the invaders far into the waterless wilderness of the Great Plains, hopefully never to return. To some extent, it worked, for by the time the Spaniards did find their way back, they were so weakened and demoralized that they decided to return to Mexico City. Pecos Pueblo was left alone for another fifty years.

In 1590, in the dead of winter, a score of armed Spanish soldiers and their following of Mexican Indian servants appeared at the gates of Pecos Pueblo. They called out and waved their arms, but the Indians ignored them. To express her scorn, one woman even flung a pot of ashes in the face of the Spanish leader, Gaspar Castaño de Sosa, an outcast petty official and slaver from Nuevo León. Still, the soldiers persisted, for they were the vanguard of a group of prospective colonists. With cannon, arquebus, and spear, they stormed the pueblo and overwhelmed its five hundred armed warriors, who were reinforced by twice

Reconstruction of Nuestra Senora de Los Angeles de Porciuncula Mission. (Courtesy National Park Service.)

as many residents. One wonders at the seeming ease of their victory, or the inability of Pecos's defenders to drive off a much smaller force. Castaño stayed at Pecos less than a week. The Indians, meanwhile, vanished, probably to take refuge in nearby villages.

Eight years later, another colonizer, Juan de Oñate, arrived in New Mexico and sent a missionary to Pecos. This aging friar began building a small church which was never finished. His successors, however, renewed the task and in 1625, *Nuestra Señora de los Angeles,* was completed at Pecos, built by the Indians under the direction of Friar Andrés Juárez. This edifice, which measured 145 feet from doorway to altar and contained over 300,000 adobe bricks in its massive, forty-foot high, white-washed walls, must have deeply impressed all who saw it.

Pecos Pueblo's experience in the seventeenth century reflects that of most New Mexican Indian villages. Some aspects of daily life continued normally but the impact of foreign rule—loss of religious freedom, heavy tribute, epidemics— was formidable. The Pecos joined the Pueblo revolt of 1680, then enjoyed twelve years of independence. When the Spanish returned, the Pecos, under Juan de Ye, accepted reconquest and even helped their former enemy bring resistant pueblos into submission. Despite this policy, Pecos was split between competing pro- and anti-Spanish factions. Perhaps a similar factionalism had lain behind their lack of resolve in 1690.

Diorama of life in Pecos Pueblo in the museum at Pecos National Historical Park. (Photo by David Grant Noble.)

By the early 1700s, Pecos's power and prestige was in decline. Epidemics struck about every decade, and beginning in the 1740s, a new enemy, the Comanches, repeatedly raided the pueblo in forces of up to three hundred mounted warriors. The Indians and Spanish joined in mutual defense against these fearsome invaders. By 1750, Pecos's population had been reduced to 500, and in the late 1700s, only 150 Indians lived at the pueblo. By this time, a Spanish-Comanche truce had been concluded, and Spanish farmers were settling the broad valley of the Pecos River, often encroaching on Pecos lands. Pecos's priests ignored the Pecos mission in favor of growing congregations at San Miguel del Vado (p. 179), Tecolote, and other villages. Land disputes arose, too, with some simmering for years in the courts. After 1821, when the Santa Fe Trail opened, caravans often stopped overnight at Pecos. The Americans were impressed by the large pueblo, despite its deteriorated condition, and enjoyed campfire talks with its dwindling inhabitants. How could they have guessed the pueblo's former strength?

In 1838, Pecos's final occupants, led by Juan Antonio Toya, decided the time had come to leave. The Jemez Indians (p. 30), who also spoke the Towa language, invited Pecos's twenty survivors to move into their pueblo in the foothills west of the Jemez Mountains. In so doing, the Pecos forfeited title to their Spanish land grant. Over the generations, they have merged with the population of their hosts.

Your visit to Pecos Pueblo will be much enhanced by the park's fine historical and cultural museum, which was developed with the financial assistance of E. E. Fogelson and Greer Garson. Stop here first, then proceed to the ruins to see a reconstructed kiva, the immense mound of the North Pueblo, and a series of excavated dwellings thought to have belonged to a Christianized segment of the community. As you stand on the mound and look over the beautiful Pecos Valley, try to visualize Castaño's winter camp or a Comanche war party storming the pueblo walls. The trail continues to the monumental church ruins and the remains of the mission complex, which include the residential quarters of the friars and the cloisters, workshops, stables, and other structures.

Pecos National Historical Park has acquired a large portion of the adjacent Forked Lightning Ranch, whose additional Pueblo sites and historic ranch house have been incorporated into the park's interpretive program. In addition, the park administers two nearby sites relating to the Civil War battlefield at Glorieta Pass (p. 271). Further information on these new areas is available at the visitor center.

TIPS FOR THE TRAVELER:
The nearby village of Pecos, which was settled in the mid-1800s, has restaurants, service stations, and grocery stores. The best overnight accommodations, however, are to be found in Santa Fe. Pecos Canyon, north of the village, is a popular spot for fishermen, hikers, and campers. Other nearby historical sites you may wish to visit are the Glorieta Battlefield, San Miguel del Vado, Las Vegas (p. 161), and the ruins of Fort Union (p. 264) along the Santa Fe Trail (p. 309).

SUGGESTED READING:
Kiva, Cross, and Crown: The Pecos Indians and New Mexico, 1540– 1840, by John L. Kessell (reprinted; Albuquerque: University of New Mexico Press, 1987).

PICURIS PUEBLO

Picuris Pueblo is located along New Mexico 75, twenty-three miles south of Taos and fifty-five miles north of Santa Fe.

In early historic times, Picuris Pueblo, up in the mountains, was the least known of New Mexico's Indian pueblos. Members of Coronado's expedition missed it when they explored the region in 1540–41, as did two subsequent Spanish parties. It was not until a cold January day in 1591, when the snow lay so deep horses could hardly walk, that Castaño de Sosa trudged up to the pueblo with a few soldiers. For him, the visit was disappointing; the Indians seemed to shun him, would not let him enter their pueblo, and made him fear attack.

The Picuris Indians are Northern Tiwa, closely related in language and culture to their neighbors at Taos Pueblo (p. 89) and of the same stock as the Sandians (p. 59) and Isletans (p. 25). Some of their ancestors appear to have come here in the twelfth century, when they built a pit-house village and later constructed a number of small adobe dwellings above ground. Others may have arrived around A.D. 1350, when the inhabitants of Pot Creek Pueblo, lying between Picuris and Taos, abandoned their village.

By the late 1300s, Picuris's population had grown, stimulating the construction of several massive apartmentlike buildings of coursed adobe, which were added to in the 1500s. In his journal, Castaño described Picuris as being seven or eight stories high; in all probability, much of the structure he saw was two hundred years old. If he did not exaggerate his account, Picuris was certainly the tallest pueblo in New Mexico.

Picuris Pueblo's size and remoteness gave its inhabitants a measure of power and independence and initially helped shield them from the many problems introduced by Spaniards. Their mountain location also gave them access to special natural resources, which they traded at San Juan Pueblo (p. 72) and other villages along the Rio Grande and with the nomadic tribes of the eastern plains. Castaño noted the presence of some huts near Picuris in which "foreigners" were living; historians speculate that these may have been Jicarilla Apaches (p. 115), for this tribe frequented regular campsites in the surrounding mountains.

Although a Catholic mission was established here in the early 1620s and a church and *convento* built by 1650, Picuris still remained off the well-traveled routes of the expanding European colony. The Spanish observed that Picuris's inhabitants, like those of Pecos Pueblo (p. 42) to the

Tower kiva at the ruins of Old Picuris. (Photo by David Grant Noble.)

south, enjoyed a profitable middleman role in the Plains–Rio Grande trade. The Apaches, who spent much of the year on the buffalo plains, came here with robes, hides, pelts, and jerky to trade for produce of the Pueblos, including corn, pottery, turquoise, and textiles. Picuris thrived, and its population climbed to an estimated three thousand people.

By the mid-1600s, however, Picuris was feeling the impact of Spanish rule. In 1639, their neighbors at Taos rebelled against the religious program imposed on them by the Europeans. The Picuris made payments to their *encomendero*, but stubbornly resisted the Franciscans' attempts to convert them to Christianity. In 1680, led by a man the Spanish called "Don Lorenzo," they joined the Pueblo revolt, killed their priest and four Spanish settlers, and sent a force south to assist in the siege of Santa Fe (p. 189).

Another Picuris leader during the revolt and post-revolt period was Don Lorenzo's brother, Don Luis Tupatú. In 1681, he led a small armed force south from Picuris to Cañada de Cochiti to reinforce Keres warriors who opposed a Spanish drive to retake New Mexico. They succeeded, and Tupatú replaced Popé as leader of the still-unified Pueblos.

When Diego de Vargas marched up the Rio Grande from El Paso del Norte in 1692, he found that the former Pueblo union had disintegrated. The Picuris initially expressed a desire for peace and cooperated with the *reconquistador*. But as they watched Spanish rule reassert itself, they changed their minds, rebelling in 1694 and again in 1696. The priest assigned to Picuris complained that he feared for his life and pleaded with Santa Fe authorities to send help.

, When Vargas came up, the Indians had left. Together with some Tanos and Tewas, they had fled to the plains to join their Apache friends. Vargas set out in pursuit and captured eighty-four women and children whom he turned over to his soldiers to be servants. The rest of the Indians fled east to Cuartelejo, in what is now western Kansas, where they lived for ten years with the Apaches. Over time, some, probably relatives of Vargas's captives, filtered back home. In 1696, word came to Santa Fe that the Apaches were treating the Picuris refugees as slaves, and Captain Juan de Ulibarrí went to the plains to bring them back. After 1706, the Picuris resigned themselves to Spanish rule and Picuris warriors joined their former foe in campaigns against the Comanches and Utes.

Picuris Pueblo's population fell precipitously during the century following the Pueblo revolt. Their numbers, once around three thousand, had fallen to scarcely over two hundred by 1776, and many perished in a virulent smallpox epidemic four years later. Over the same years, Spanish farmers were encroaching on tribal land that the Indians had ceased to cultivate. In addition, the government issued land grants to nearby settlers so that, by 1796, the pueblo was surrounded by European settlers. The Indians' challenge now was to stop further encroachment and loss of their land. They sought assistance from Spanish, then Mexican, and finally United States authorities, but by this time, their strength had so diminished that complaints drew little serious consideration. In 1890, there were fewer than a hundred Picuris Indians.

After the Civil War and especially toward the end of the nineteenth century, Anglo-American culture began to have an impact on Picuris. The buffalo hunts on the plains had ended; wage jobs drew men away from the pueblo; logging operations conflicted with traditional irrigation farming; children went to school and learned English; and traditional religious practices were discouraged. In 1881, the pueblo was reportedly in a ruinous state.

In the twentieth century, all these trends continued and were even accelerated when men returned home from overseas wars. In recent years, however, the pueblo's economic and cultural life has taken an

Threshing wheat with goats at Picuris Pueblo, c. 1905. (Photo by Ed Andrews, courtesy Museum of New Mexico, neg. 15123.)

upward turn. As in many pueblos, interest has revived in native religious ceremonies. In addition, efforts to rebuild the collapsed San Lorenzo Church, originally built in the 1770s, has helped to draw the community together. As one member commented, "Preserving this church is a way for us to once again establish a connection with our tribal elders, to preserve the traditions of our pueblo." It was rededicated in 1993.

Perhaps the most recent surprising development, however, happened in the late 1980s, when the tribe went into partnership with a private developer to build and operate an eleven-million-dollar hotel in Santa Fe. This enterprise promises to bring the tribe continuing revenues as well as employment for its members.

When you visit Picuris Pueblo, go first to the museum-restaurant complex to obtain a visitor permit and tour information. You may walk or drive from here to the church, then continue to the hilltop site of the old pueblo. Here you can view archaeological excavations, a standing block of rooms, and an unusual round tower kiva. The pueblo's cemetery lies just beyond. Picuris Pueblo celebrates its Feast Day on August 10, the day the Pueblo revolt began in 1680. Many nonresidents return at this time, and visitors are invited to come watch the dances and running races and buy native crafts.

TIPS FOR THE TRAVELER:
To see Picuris Pueblo in context, plan to visit nearby Spanish-American villages such as Las Trampas (see p. 157), Penasco, and Taos, as well as Taos Pueblo. The latter's five-story house blocks offer a hint of how Picuris Pueblo may have looked in centuries past. You will find travel services available in Española, Taos, and Santa Fe.

SUGGESTED READING:
A Brief History of Picuris Pueblo, by Albert H. Schroeder (Adams State College, 1974).

POJOAQUE PUEBLO

Pojoaque Pueblo is located fifteen miles north of Santa Fe, off U.S. 84/285. The pueblo runs the Poeh Center, a crafts store and museum along 84/285, just south of the New Mexico 502 turnoff.

The early history of the Pojoaque Indians coincides with that of other Tewa pueblos in the region. Pojoaque ancestors were a blend of indigenous northern Rio Grande Puebloan people and migrants from the Four Corners region, who arrived here in the thirteenth and fourteenth centuries.

Pojoaque Pueblo is a study in survival. When Spaniards first explored the Rio Grande Valley north of El Paso del Norte in the sixteenth century, they counted as many as eighty Indian villages, including Pojoaque. Due to the upheaval caused by Spanish colonization, by the end of the following century most of these villages were no longer extant. Pojoaque is the smallest of six Tewa pueblos today, but once it was among the larger communities in the valley. Remarkably, its people have managed to survive foreign invasion, epidemics, rebellion and warfare, social disruption, economic hardship, and loss of land. Today, the pueblo is experiencing a renaissance.

Pojoaque was abandoned after the Spanish-Pueblo wars (1680–96), but it was resettled in 1706. In 1712 its population numbered only seventy-nine people, and this small group had shrunk to a mere thirty-two in the late 1800s. In addition, much of the pueblo's ceremonial life also disappeared and other tribal activities diminished. In this condition, the pueblo was even more vulnerable than its neighbors to encroachments by Spanish, Mexican, and American farmers and ranchers.

Pojoaque Pueblo, 1899. (Photo by Adam C. Vroman, courtesy Smithsonian National Anthropological Archives.)

Like Pecos Pueblo (see p. 42), Pojoaque reached a critical survival point in its history. But unlike the last survivors of Pecos, who left their land grant as a group and moved to Jemez (p. 30), Pojoaque's residents just slowly drifted away from their homes. Some joined relatives in neighboring Tewa villages, while others went to Santa Fe or other cities, or left New Mexico altogether. Still, wherever they were, they remembered their roots.

Pojoaque's church, dedicated to Our Lady of Guadalupe, had been completed in 1773, and was soon described by a visiting Spanish priest in rather disparaging terms. He said its windows were "ugly," its pulpit "very ugly," and its confessional "fully as ugly" as the pulpit. Captain John G. Bourke, who visited Pojoaque in 1881, was impressed by the paintings of saints hanging in the church, especially one of Our Lady of Guadalupe hanging over the altar. Fray Domínguez had also noted this painting, which had been a gift from the king of Spain. As it must have been cherished and cared for by the parishioners, one wonders what happened to it. Bourke was astonished by another feature within the church, a human skull over the confessional to remind sinners of "Life's destiny."

In the first decade of this century, anthropologists F. W. Hodge and J. P. Harrington reported that Pojoaque was abandoned. Harrington did, however, locate two Pojoaque families living in Santa Fe who had property at the pueblo. Very likely, more Pojoaque members were using their old homes occasionally, and others were perhaps visiting the pueblo from time to time to check on the condition of their property. Even so, the village was in a ruinous and seemingly deserted condition. Fortunately, their Spanish land grant had been patented by the United States government in 1864, an act that gave legal status to the tribe and helps account for its survival to the present day.

The previous year, Pojoaque's governor, with other Pueblo leaders, had received a ceremonial cane with "A. Lincoln" inscribed on its ebony head in recognition of the pueblo's neutrality in the Civil War. The Pueblos have received a series of such canes as symbols of the authority of their governors. The king of Spain gave the first canes in 1620, and the Mexican government gave the Pueblos silver-headed canes after that country gained its independence from Spain. In 1980, to mark the tricentennial of the Pueblo revolt, another set of commemorative canes were created and given to the Pueblo governors.

In the early 1930s, a Pojoaque man named José Antonio Tapia, who had been living in Colorado since 1912, returned to New Mexico and, with the assistance of several family members, reclaimed and resettled the Pojoaque land grant. Within a few years, they had fenced the reservation and evicted non-Indians, who had moved onto the grant or were using it for grazing stock. Tapia's efforts were not in vain, for within fifty years Pojoaque's population, formerly listed as zero, had surpassed a hundred.

As a result of their close association with Hispanic residents of the Pojoaque valley, the Pojoaque Indians have a mixed cultural and ethnic background. Since 1900, they had been without a *cacique* and other traditional officials, and thus they were unable to carry on a ceremonial life at the pueblo. Even so, some members continued to hold a strong interest in their Pueblo heritage and, in recent years, invited elders of surrounding Tewa villages to share their culture with them. In 1990, Pojoaque installed a war chief and two war captains.

Pojoaque Pueblo has an elected governor and tribal council. This group manages the pueblo's affairs, which include operating the Poeh Center and a number of tribally owned corporations and retail businesses at a mall along U.S. 84/285. If you are driving along this route, you will enjoy stopping at the center.

TIPS FOR THE TRAVELER:
Pojoaque Pueblo is in the heart of Tewa country and close to Bandelier National Monument and Puye Cliffs, where you can explore ancestral Pueblo sites and cave dwellings. In addition, you may find Chimayo, and its famous *santuario* worth a visit. Santa Fe, within half an hour's drive from Pojoaque, has many historical sites and is a tourist and travel center.

SUGGESTED READING:
Then and Now: A Historical Photo Sourcebook of Pojoaque Pueblo, introduced by Alfonso Ortiz (Santa Fe: Sunstone Press, 1991).

SALINAS PUEBLO MISSIONS NATIONAL MONUMENT

The main visitor center of Salinas Pueblo Missions National Monument is at the corner of Broadway and Ripley streets in Mountainair, along U.S. 60 south of Albuquerque. The monument's historic attractions, however, are the ruins at Abo, Quarai, and Gran Quivira. Abo is located a mile north of U.S. 60, nine miles west of Mountainair. Quarai is eight miles north of Mountainair, in Punta de Agua. Gran Quivira is twenty-six miles south of Mountainair, along New Mexico 55.

The Spanish province of *Las Salinas,* lying east of the Middle Rio Grande Valley, once contained a group of thriving Indian villages which, like Pecos Pueblo (see p. 42), actively traded with the nomadic tribes of the southern plains. These pueblos survive today only as gentle mounds; however, three sites, which had Catholic missions, form Salinas Pueblo Missions National Monument. At Gran Quivira, Abo, and Quarai, you can enjoy a glimpse into the area's Pueblo and Spanish colonial past.

A time traveler might have encountered Native Americans in the Salinas region as long ago as ten or twelve thousand years. They would have been Paleolithic hunters, stalking big game along the margins of shallow lakes. The Paleoindians and Archaic hunter-gatherers who followed them disappeared millennia ago, to be followed by agriculturalists. First living in pithouse settlements, they later developed the technique of laying up stone and adobe walls to construct above-ground

Remains of San Gregorio de Abo Mission. (Photo by David Grant Noble.)

pueblos. By A.D. 1300, there were numerous densely populated, multi-storied apartment complexes dotting the basin.

The Salinas Indians spoke dialects of the Piro language, as did other pueblos along the Rio Grande around present-day Socorro (p. 203). They tilled fields of corn, beans, and squash along streambeds and hunted game in the Manzano Mountains. In addition, they excavated chunks of salt from the nearby dried-up saline lakes to trade with other tribes, some of whom traveled long distances to acquire this valued mineral.

When Spaniards first came into the Southwest, with gold rather than salt on their minds, they bypassed the pueblos of Las Salinas. It was not until 1598 that mounted soldiers of Juan de Oñate rode into their villages. Franciscan friars followed them, establishing missions and planning construction of the majestic churches whose ruins are still impressive. In 1601, the Indians of Abo killed two Spanish soldiers, bringing Oñate's wrath down upon them. The governor dispatched his nephew, Vicente de Zaldívar, with seventy troops on a punitive campaign. Vicente was the brother of Juan de Zaldívar, who had been killed at Acoma Pueblo (p. 9) two years before. Warriors from Abo and Acolocu (later named Quarai) were defeated by the Spaniards, who set fire to Acolocu and claimed to have killed nine hundred Indians.

The power of the military allowed privileged soldier-citizens, known as *encomenderos,* to exact tribute from the Salinas pueblos; officially, this took the form of corn, meat, or cloth although labor, too, was sometimes demanded. Pueblo labor was also exploited to extract quantities of salt for export to Parral, Mexico, to process silver ore. In the 1620s, Spanish missionaries ardently tried to convert the Indians of Salinas to Catholicism. The mission of *Nuestra Señora de la Purísima Concepción* was built by 1628 at Quarai, and another at Abo, with their massive sandstone walls and voluminous interior spaces, no doubt, greatly impressing the Indians, whose compact pueblos had such small rooms. Like other missions, it was designed by the friars—architecture and building were a part of their training—who then directed Indian workers in the construction. Quarai soon had a congregation of 658 Indians as well as a choir, which sang to the accompaniment of an organ.

The Salinas pueblos experienced more than their share of suffering in the seventeenth century. A drought, which struck New Mexico in the mid-1600s, affected every human being in the region and brought famine to many communities. European diseases decimated the Indian population, and still others died in battle, not just with Spaniards but also with nomadic tribes from the Plains, who raided for food. They sometimes seized captives as well, though usually in retaliation for losses of their own people to Spanish slavers. In 1668, when over four hundred inhabitants of Gran Quivira died of starvation, the survivors packed up their few belongings and headed west to the Rio Grande to find shelter with Piro friends. Within but a generation or two, Gran Quivira, whose population had been two or three thousand, was abandoned, and soon its sister pueblos, also, stood vacant. Today, its ruins, consisting of twenty-one pueblo house mounds and two churches, sit on a windswept hill as stark reminders of a truly bleak era in history.

Archaeologists have conducted excavations at all three of the Salinas pueblos and missions, trying to supplement the scarce historical data found in documents. The oldest sections of the pueblos are thought to date to the late 1200s. Around 1545, an influx of migrants arrived at Gran Quivira, probably from Zuñi, which had been attacked by Coronado's army five years before. Excavations at Abo uncovered Old World watermelon and mission grape seeds and the presence of turkey pens within the mission complex. In addition, researchers found a kiva in the

Prehistoric carving found at Gran Quivira. (Photo by David Grant Noble.)

west patio. One wonders what circumstances led to the construction of this "pagan" structure in the heart of a Catholic mission. The ruins at Quarai remain unexcavated; perhaps future research here will tell us more about the relationship of this pueblo's inhabitants and their Spanish rulers.

Between 1668 and 1670, Quarai was the seat of the Holy Office of the Inquisition in New Mexico. One victim, whom we know a little about, was a German trader, Bernardo Gruber, accused of superstition. Church officials had him shackled and jailed at Abo and ordered his property to be confiscated. For two years, this unfortunate awaited trial, then he escaped and fled down the Camino Real (p. 293) and into the desert, where he perished. This desert came to be known as the Jornada del Muerto, "Journey of the Dead Man," and the site where his bleached bones were discovered is still called El Aleman, the German.

Abo, Quarai, and Gran Quivira are all open to the public on a daily basis. At each site you can follow interpretive trails through the pueblo and mission ruins and view exhibits, which provide further historical and cultural background. The monument's headquarters in Mountainair also has a small museum.

TIPS FOR THE TRAVELER:
Mountainair is a small southwestern ranching town in which you will find several restaurants and a motel and a few other travel services. Manzano State Park, near Quarai, has a large campground. You will find Pecos National Historic Park, east of Santa Fe, and Jemez State Park (p. 30), west of Bernalillo, of related interest. In addition, the historic town of Socorro (p. 203) is only a short drive from here.

SUGGESTED READING:
Salinas: Archaeology, History, Prehistory, edited by David Grant Noble (Santa Fe: Ancient City Press, 1993)

SANDIA PUEBLO

Sandia Pueblo is located along New Mexico 313, between Albuquerque and Bernalillo. The Sandia reservation borders Albuquerque's northern city limits.

When a detachment of Vázquez de Coronado's soldiers journeyed east from Zuñi in August of 1540, they entered a region they called *Tiguex,* located along the Rio Grande. This was the land of the Southern Tiwa Indians, who resided in a dozen pueblos strung along a corridor on both sides of the river between Isleta Pueblo (see p. 25) and present-day Bernalillo. One was Sandia.

The Spaniards initially did not stay long in Tiguex. Led by Coronado's captain of artillery, Hernando de Alvarado, they accepted needed supplies from the Tiwas, took note of the Indians' friendliness and food stores, and continued upriver under the guidance of Bigotes, an official of Pecos Pueblo (p. 42). Little did the Sandias and their neighbors realize that Alvarado had urged his commander to leave the Zuñi pueblos and send his entire army here to spend the oncoming winter. The Spaniards—Coronado had 336 armed soldiers equipped with 559 horses, and 800 Mexican Indians under his command—had meager knowledge how to survive in the desert Southwest and thus depended upon its indigenous peoples for support.

In autumn, the Tiwas met more troops under Lieutenant García López de Cardenas, who moved into the Pueblo of Alcanfor on the west bank of the Rio Grande. (Archaeological research has shown that Kuaua Pueblo at Coronado State Monument was not Alcanfor; Santiago Pueblo, however, is a likely candidate.) Later, even more arrived.

The Tiwas had little choice but to cooperate. Spanish troops made the rounds of nearby pueblos—Puaray, Mojo, Alameda, Santiago, Arenal, and others—to appropriate food and clothing. Descriptions contained in Spanish chronicles suggest that Arenal might have been the pueblo later called Sandia.

While Alvarado's needs in August had been light, the supplies being requisitioned to feed the army through the winter months became a heavy burden to the Tiwas. Even before Coronado himself arrived, the Indians felt misgivings about their situation. Incidents, including the alleged rape of one of their women, caused mistrust, then resentment, and finally open hostility.

In late December, a group of daring Indians from Arenal drove off a portion of the soldiers' horse herd. They headed south, but when Spanish pursuers drew near they slaughtered more than a dozen of the animals and disappeared. According to Spanish writings, the Tiwas "shouted their war cries to heaven and waved as banners the tails of the Spanish horses they had killed" as soldiers rode through their villages. With a general uprising seeming to be imminent, Coronado ordered his troops to attack Arenal. After a fierce battle on the first day, the soldiers set the pueblo ablaze and killed many of its inhabitants as they fled. Many captives were lanced or burned at the stake. The fate of Arenal sent a signal to all the Tiwa, who fled for refuge toward Oku Pin, the sacred mountain overshadowing their pueblos.

With Arenal defeated, the Spaniards set their sights on the Pueblo of Moho, which had become a gathering point of refugees. But Moho was stronger than Arenal, and in the initial stage of battle its defenders held their own and wounded more than eighty soldiers. Thwarted, the Spaniards changed tactics, laying a siege to the pueblo that lasted eighty days. By spring, Moho's inhabitants were desperate from thirst, and many women and children gave themselves up to a future of servitude. Finally, the men either escaped to the mountains or were killed or captured. Mojo, too, was burned.

After the Tiwa wars, Coronado continued on his quest for gold, traveling as far as eastern Kansas. When he returned, Arenal and Mojo were vacant. The Tiwas were still in shock from events of the spring. Some villages would never again be occupied. Their population, counted in the thousands, began a decline that would continue for more than three centuries.

Sandia Pueblo saw Spaniards again in 1581 and 1582, though to little consequence to themselves. After the founding of Spain's first New Mexico colony in 1598, Franciscan friars started a mission at the

Sandia Pueblo, 1880. (Photo by John K. Hillers, courtesy Museum of New Mexico, neg. 3371.)

pueblo. As the seventeenth century progressed, the Middle Rio Grande Valley grew popular for colonization and the Tiwa population was consolidated into four pueblos: Sandia, Puaray, Alameda, and Isleta (p. 25). When the Pueblo Indians rebelled in 1680, the Sandias burned their church and vacated the pueblo. After the Indians' siege of Santa Fe (p. 192), Governor Otermín and his surviving northern colonists retreated south to El Paso del Norte. Finding Sandia empty, they set fire to its buildings. The following year, Otermín returned and burned the pueblo once again.

Sandia history between 1680 and the mid-1700s is somewhat hazy. Some Indians apparently went north for a time to live with the Tewas, while another larger contingent, in 1692 or soon after, journeyed west to join the Hopis. With refugees from Isleta, they founded the village of Payupki on Second Mesa. Here they stayed until the 1740s, when Spanish clerics persuaded them to come back to their former home along the Rio Grande. Some Hopis apparently came with them. By this time,

Juan Avila, governor of Sandia Pueblo, 1923. (Photo by DeLancey Gill, courtesy Smithsonian National Anthropological Archives.)

Puaray and Alameda were ghost towns, leaving only Sandia and Isleta as survivors of the once numerous Southern Tiwa pueblos.

By the beginning of the eighteenth century, the Middle Valley had become a highly desirable area for Spanish colonists to establish their *ranchos*, and Sandia Pueblo soon found itself surrounded by settlers. The Indians could not help but feel the influences of Spanish culture at linguistic, religious, social, and economic levels. Some tribal members married outside the pueblo, further intermingling the cultures. At the same time, raiding Navajos and Apaches forced both groups to collaborate in matters of defense. Pueblo warriors became a vital element in campaigns against the nomads.

After the United States occupied New Mexico, Albuquerque burgeoned as a commercial and industrial center and the Sandias became further acculturated. Their close proximity to the city had a dual effect on their culture. On the one hand, they learned English, were introduced to Anglo-American customs, found employment in the city, and increasingly quit farming as a livelihood. On the other hand, being so close to Albuquerque, Sandia workers were able to commute home after work, bringing their wages with them. This reinforced the cohesion and integrity of the pueblo. Over the generations, Sandia Pueblo has sustained a sense of itself as a separate Indian community, upholding native religious traditions and, until the mid-1900s, continuing to speak Tiwa.

Since World War II, the city of Albuquerque has expanded to the very border of the Sandia reservation, and commercial ventures, including bingo gambling, have brought outsiders onto Pueblo land. Despite these trends, the pueblo is still strongly Indian and its members enjoy a sense of emotional, social, and economic security. Its population, while still relatively small, has tripled since the turn of the century, and its members have successfully adapted to a rapidly changing external society.

TIPS FOR THE TRAVELER:
Sandia's Feast of St. Anthony is celebrated on June 13, a good time to visit the pueblo and see its Corn Dance. Other places of historical interest in the area include Coronado State Monument, Albuquerque's Old Town, and Isleta Pueblo. In addition, you may enjoy hiking through Petroglyph National Monument, noted for its collection of rock art, much of which was pecked on boulders by ancestors of the Sandia people. For information on this new preserve, call (505) 766-8375. Finally, if you are interested in Pueblo craft arts, be sure to stop at the Indian Pueblo Cultural Center at 2401 Twelfth Street in Albuquerque.

SUGGESTED READING:
"The Cultural and Social Survival of a Pueblo Indian Community," by Suzanne (Lee) Simons, in *Minorities and Politics*, edited by Henry J. Tobias and Charles E. Woodhouse (Albuquerque: University of New Mexico Press, 1969).

SAN FELIPE PUEBLO

To reach San Felipe Pueblo, drive twenty-five miles north of Albuquerque on Interstate 25, then take the San Felipe Pueblo exit west and continue three miles to the pueblo.

The San Felipe people believe that in a long-ago time they emerged into the present world "from the womb of the earth." Accompanying them was the Spirit (Corn Mother), who acted as their guide as they slowly traveled southward to the Rio Grande Valley. By migrating in groups, rather than all together, they could more easily live off the land and had a greater chance of tribal survival. As they went, the Spirit taught them many lessons about their new world and how to live together in safety.

The San Felipeans tell of arriving in the Rio Grande region and living first at a site on the west side of the river. Archaeologists believe there are habitation sites on the southern Pajarito Plateau, in the vicinity of Bandelier National Monument, that are ancestral to the San Felipeans and other Keres groups. Some may be around Frijoles Canyon; and another candidate is Kuapa Pueblo, just north of Cochiti Pueblo. According to legend, Kuapa was attacked and destroyed by outside invaders, called *Pinimi*.

After Kuapa's destruction, the San Felipe ancestors moved again, eventually going south to found their own village, Katishtya, along the Rio Grande. As San Felipe elders have recounted, the Spirit "warned of the dangers to come as more people inhabit the new continent . . . and reminded her people of their past experiences of building dwelling places in fortress style." The Spirit also instructed them in how to live and work together as a harmonious community, how to cultivate corn, and where to gather wild edible plants for food. Of utmost importance was adherence to the laws of nature and the orders of their chief, the *cacique*. "The Cacique, said the Spirit, will guide you henceforth, and as the head of the tribe he will be concerned with your spiritual lives as well as with your government." To assist him in governance, the Spirit endowed the *cacique* with spiritual and jurisdictional powers. Eventually, as his responsibilities increased, he created the two offices of war captain (*tsiyakiya*), which he gave first to the twin gods of war, Masewi and Oyoyewi. The war captains, who are chosen each year from the pueblo's two kiva groups, carry out the directions of the *cacique*.

After Spaniards settled in the land of the Pueblos in the seventeenth century, they added new offices to the existing theocratic government of

San Felipe Pueblo, c. 1935. (Photo by T. Harmon Parkhurst, courtesy Museum of New Mexico, neg. 3436.)

San Felipe and the other pueblos, which mirrored the offices of their own system of government. At the head was the governor, who was an individual in the pueblo with whom they felt they could carry on their administrative business. This system worked well for the Indians, who selected a trusted citizen for the position and closely supervised his duties as liaison officer to the foreign rulers. While the governor concerned himself with external affairs, the *cacique* and his assistants carried out their religious and political responsibilities. This dual governance has allowed the pueblo to manage its internal affairs in privacy, while maintaining an acceptable and effective system to deal with the Spanish and, later, the Mexican and American authorities. As external authorities became more repressive in their dealings with the Pueblos, prohibiting native religious expressions, for example, the *cacique*'s realm of activity became increasingly secretive. Even to the present day, outsiders know little of the internal workings and sacred life of San Felipe Pueblo.

The village of Katishtya moved a couple of times before finally being located on the west bank of the river in the early 1700s. For a time, there were communities on either shore whose inhabitants crossed back and forth using canoes and rafts, sometimes assisted by a rope. In the 1890s, the Indians built a bridge spanning rock-filled wicker cribs that were stabilized by wooden braces sunk into the river bed.

San Felipe woman at a spinning wheel, c. 1900. (Photo by Mary E. Disette, courtesy Museum of New Mexico, neg. 45441.)

San Felipe Pueblo fully supported the Pueblo revolt in 1680 and the following year, when the exiled governor Antonio de Otermín attempted to reconquer the territory, its inhabitants withdrew north to join other Pueblo refugees in a defensive mesatop redoubt near Cochiti Pueblo. In their absence, Otermín destroyed Katishtya. He also captured two San Felipe Indians, who provided him with a few details on post-revolt events. They blamed the Spaniards' religious repression for causing the Indians to rebel, and they said that after the revolt the Pueblo leader Popé had come to San Felipe with his forces and "ordered the churches burned and the holy images broken up and burned." With his cohort from Santo Domingo, Alonso Catiti, he also encouraged the San Felipeans to rebuild their kivas and revive their traditional religious practices.

It was at the Cochiti refugee site that Vargas found the San Felipe people in 1692. He camped at the foot of the mesa with sixty soldiers, and persuaded the people to come down to hear him. Then his priest reportedly baptized more than a hundred children born since the revolt. Vargas also persuaded the people to return peacefully to their home village. From this time on, the San Felipeans became allies of the Spaniards, sometimes even assisting them in campaigns against recalcitrant pueblos. On more than one occasion, this policy brought them into violent conflict with Jemez Pueblo and its Zuñi, Acoma, and Navajo allies. In 1696, when the Pueblos again rebelled against the Spaniards and the church, it was to San Felipe that the priest from Cochiti fled for protection. At this time, the San Felipeans moved their village from the mesa to where it is today.

There exist only the most meager historical references to San Felipe during the eighteenth and nineteenth centuries, suggesting that its residents had little interaction with the Spanish colony and that Spanish officials interfered little with its political life. In 1694, San Felipe's priest reported the pueblo's population as 240 people. By 1776, this figure had grown to 406; however, it had dropped to under 300 people in the early nineteenth century, reflecting the continuing deadly toll of epidemics.

Historically, San Felipe was a successful farming community with abundant fields under cultivation and usually good harvests. The periodic flooding of the Rio Grande, which once damaged homes and fields, is presently controlled by Cochiti Dam upstream. Today, of course, agriculture plays a much lesser role in the pueblo's economy, as many San Felipeans hold jobs in the greater Albuquerque metropolitan area.

San Felipe's church, built in the early eighteenth century, is a striking example of mission architecture. Religious services continue to be held here, and on the pueblo's Feast Day, May 1, they are followed by a Green Corn Dance that lasts all day in the large sunken square plaza. San Felipe is a conservative pueblo and most of its religious activities are closed to outsiders; however, on Feast Day, outsiders are welcome to attend.

TIPS FOR THE TRAVELER:
In nearby Albuquerque, you will enjoy visits to the Maxwell Museum of Anthropology, on the campus of the University of New Mexico, and to the Indian Pueblo Cultural Center, located at 2401 Twelfth Street N.W. Other Keresan pueblos close to San Felipe are Zia, Santo Domingo, and Cochiti. Just west of Bernalillo, you can tour the ruins of Kuaua Pueblo at Coronado State Park (p. 00), a prehistoric Tiwa site.

SUGGESTED READING:
"The Pueblo of San Felipe," *Memoirs of the American Anthropological Association* 38, by Leslie A. White (Menasha, Wisc., 1932).

Corn Dance, San Ildefonso Pueblo, c. 1920. (Courtesy Museum of New Mexico, neg. 74749.)

SAN ILDEFONSO PUEBLO

San Ildefonso Pueblo is located along New Mexico 502, six miles west of this road's intersection with U.S. 84/285. From Santa Fe, drive nineteen miles north on U.S. 84/285, bear west on New Mexico 502 at Pojoaque, and continue to the pueblo's entrance.

The late world-renowned potter, María Martínez (1887–1980), drew much attention to San Ildefonso Pueblo, one of a string of Tewa villages along the northern Rio Grande. Although María had begun making pottery as a young girl, her real passion for the art was sparked in 1908, when she saw potsherds being excavated from ancestral Tewa sites on the Pajarito Plateau above the pueblo. Asked to reproduce the decorated prehistoric vessels, she began making fine ceramic wares in her own style, but with inspiration from Tewa antiquity.

The Tewas trace their distant origins to the northwest, even to Mesa Verde and the great prehistoric towns of the Montezuma Valley near Cortez, Colorado. San Ildefonsans regard certain sites such as Otowi and Tsankawi, on the Pajarito Plateau across the Rio Grande, as more recently ancestral. Archaeologists believe Tsankawi reached its peak in the 1400s and was abandoned around the time of the first Spanish *entrada.*

San Ildefonso Pueblo (*Pohwoge* in Tewa) probably goes back to around A.D. 1300, when the village was located just south of where it is today. Some archaeologists believe its residents drew water out of the Pojoaque River, a Rio Grande tributary, irrigating their fields by means of a network of ditches. In the 1200s, Pohwoge was only one of several small pueblos in the area, but the others merged with it in the 1300s. Still another settlement known as *Perage,* which was occupied between around A.D. 1250 and 1350, was located just across the river. Its villagers probably waded across the river each day to join the Pohwoge inhabitants in the task of farming. Archaeologists speculate that ultimately some Perage occupants relocated permanently to Pohwoge, while others moved to the Galisteo Basin, southeast of Santa Fe.

At the time of first contact with Europeans, San Ildefonso was the largest of nine Tewa villages, and its occupants may have numbered in the thousands. Its population, however, dropped drastically over subsequent generations. From 1760 to 1860, for example, it fell from 484 to 154 people, and after World War I, it reached a low of about 90 people following a devastating Spanish flu epidemic. Since then, the pueblo's numbers have steadily grown.

Historically, San Ildefonso had two main economic problems: loss of land and loss of water. Although reduction of their land base was caused partly by Indians selling parcels of tribal land to local non-Indians, more significant acreage was lost when Spanish or Mexican settlers simply squatted on land that was not being used. This frequently happened following an epidemic. In the eighteenth century, Spanish-American population was rapidly increasing while Indian population was falling. Between 1913 and 1940, the Pueblo Lands Board adjudicated thousands of private claims made by non-Indians living on northern Pueblo grants. The San Ildefonsans were awarded approximately one-third of the claims, most of these being upland (less valuable) acreage, and compensated for other lands.

Although San Ildefonso is situated close to the Rio Grande, most of its irrigation ditches ran off the smaller, more manageable Pojoaque River. Several other Indian and Hispanic communities were located upstream leaving the San Ildefonsans with last water use, a plight that hindered their ability to farm effectively. To compound the problem of water availability, numerous fields were covered by river gravel in the

Maria Martinez and her sister, Santana, firing pottery at San Ildefonso, 1933. (Photo by Louise Everhardy, courtesy Museum of New Mexico, neg. 21661.)

late 1800s, when the Pojoaque flooded, and other agricultural acreage was lost as a consequence of the meandering course of the Rio Grande.

San Ildefonsans played an active role in the Pueblo revolt of 1680. One of its leaders, an individual whom the Spanish knew as Francisco, was a close cohort of Popé, the rebellion's chief instigator. The pueblo rebelled again in 1694 and still again in 1696. During these times, the San Ildefonsans would take refuge on Black Mesa, a dramatic landform standing just north of the village. The pueblo's mission church was repeatedly destroyed and rebuilt, and the present church, which is located just west of the plaza, is of recent construction.

Conflict at San Ildefonso was not limited to revolts against Spanish rule. In the early decades of the present century, the pueblo was afflicted by internal dissension that disrupted its political and religious traditions. This intramural factionalism had complex causes, but it began in the late 1800s out of a dispute over where to locate the plaza as the village expanded northward. Sometime between 1910 and 1923, a South Plaza was built around the old circular kiva, which is still extant; many people, however, remained in the North Plaza. This split residential situation eventually disrupted the traditional dual organization, or moiety system (Summer and Winter people), with the result that family relationships, religious-society memberships, and village governance became undermined. This old problem continues to cause controversy today in San Ildefonso politics.

As agriculture diminished, San Ildefonsans developed other economic pursuits. Some found wage jobs in Española and Santa Fe, and after World War II many became employed at Los Alamos. Other members of the pueblo, especially women, revived ancient native crafts, with pottery becoming a local specialty. María Martínez was especially prominent in this development, reviving the ancient black-on-black style for which the pueblo is now noted. Her husband, Julian, painted the designs on her pots. Today, San Ildefonso has numerous pottery-making families who sell their wares at the pueblo, at native craft fairs, and in stores in Santa Fe. By special arrangement, some of these artists will demonstrate their craft to visitors or invite potential buyers into their homes to see samples of their work. There are several craft shops around the plaza and a small tribal museum in the tribal administrative office building. Each summer, a huge Indian craft fair held in the plaza is attended by hundreds of exhibitors and thousands of visitors. If you are interested in attending, contact the tribal offices (505-455-3549) for further information. San Ildefonso's Feast Day, on January 23, is an occasion when visitors can expect to see the Comanche dance and a buffalo dance.

TIPS FOR THE TRAVELER:
For a more historical experience in driving to San Ildefonso, take the first left after the Route 502 turnoff and follow this old road through Jacona and El Rancho to the pueblo. After seeing San Ildefonso, you will certainly enjoy Bandelier National Monument, located along New Mexico 4, just beyond White Rock. Here, trails lead to numerous prehistoric pueblo and cave-dwelling sites. Tsankawi Ruins forms an adjunct to the monument and may be reached by a hiking trail from the Tsankawi parking area, between the junction of routes 4 and 502 and White Rock. More ancient Pueblo sites are found at nearby Puye Cliffs, administered by Santa Clara Pueblo, and Taos (p. 89) is an hour's drive to the north. You will find an abundance of tourist and travel facilities in Española and Santa Fe.

SUGGESTED READING:
María by Richard Spivey, (Flagstaff: Northland Press, 1979).

Corn harvest at San Juan Pueblo, c. 1935. (Photo by T. Harmon Parkhurst, courtesy Museum of New Mexico, neg. 3984.)

SAN JUAN PUEBLO

San Juan Pueblo is located along the Rio Grande just north of Española. From Española, take New Mexico 68 north approximately three miles, then turn west on New Mexico 74 and continue one mile to the pueblo.

Like other Tewas, the people of San Juan believe that long ago their ancestors migrated to the Rio Grande Valley from the north. San Juan narratives tell how the people lived in a series of villages as they migrated here, and mention specific pueblos where they resided toward the end of the journey. Some of these sites, like Poshuouinge and Posiouinge, lie on terraces of the Rio Chama. Others are defensively situated at the top of steep mesas. Most of these pueblos were inhabited throughout the fifteenth century, but were abandoned by the time of the first Spanish *entrada* (1540–41). Tewa narratives concerning this history are reinforced by the findings of archaeologists, who have found innumerable Pueblo sites in the Four Corners region, which were abandoned in the 1200s, and identified many ancestral Tewa pueblos along the Rio Chama.

In the sixteenth century, the San Juan people lived in two companion pueblos, *Ok'he* and *Yunge,* which lay across the Rio Grande from each other. Coronado's soldiers came here in 1541 and looted the villages, extending into Tewa country the fearsome reputation they had already earned in the land of the Tiwa (see p. 59). Then, in 1598, the residents of *Ok'he* and *Yunge* became the first indigenous New Mexicans to feel the impact of Spanish colonization. In that year, Juan de Oñate led four hundred colonists up the Rio Grande to these pueblos and decided to establish a permanent Spanish settlement here. His following included soldiers, Franciscan missionaries, prospective settlers, and Mexican Indian servants, not to mention a lumbering herd of cattle and a convoy of supply carts. The colony, which was nearly out of food and unprepared for the approaching winter, first moved into *Ok'he,* which Oñate renamed *San Juan de los Caballeros* (San Juan Pueblo). Later, he appropriated *Yunge,* renamed San Gabriel, making it his headquarters for ten years.

The people of San Juan provided the Spaniards with food, fuel, shelter, and clothing, and some of these supplies probably were donated by nearby Tewa villages. They were experienced farmers and skilled hunters, and it was their custom to maintain surplus food stores as a buffer against the possibility of poor harvests. Still, once the colonists had gone through these reserves, their continued demands must have been a significant economic burden on the Tewas.

As an administrator, Oñate proved inept, preferring to explore the Southwest for gold rather than attend to the urgent needs of his followers. In his absence, the San Gabriel colony foundered; some members even deserted. Still, with the Indians' assistance, the settlement survived, eventually stabilized, and, in 1610, relocated to the site of present-day Santa Fe.

After the departure of the San Gabriel colonists, conditions at San Juan Pueblo should have improved. However, under the Spanish *encomienda* (the tribute system), the Indians still had to provide corn, venison, cloth, or labor to their overlord. In addition, an alien religious faith was imposed on them, and their own ceremonies were forbidden. Dissension was not tolerated. One dissenter was a religious leader named Popé. In 1676, Spanish authorities accused him and other Pueblo leaders of sorcery, a potentially capital crime under the laws of the Inquisition. Popé and his colleagues were imprisoned in Santa Fe, then flogged in the plaza. Several were hanged. The incident generated outrage and resentment throughout the Pueblo world and motivated Popé to formulate a plan to free his people. He was joined by other Pueblo leaders, who gathered in the kivas of Taos Pueblo to organize what some have called the "first American revolution." They succeeded, with their crowning accomplishment being the overthrow of Spanish rule in New Mexico and, for twelve years at least, independence. Underlying this victory, however, was another significant achievement: Pueblo unification. If this had lasted, freedom would certainly have endured much longer.

The Spaniards' experience of defeat and exile led to their adoption of a looser, less repressive policy toward the Pueblos. Still, true tolerance was not achieved. In 1694, San Juan's resident missionary, Fray Gerónimo, repeatedly tore down a village religious shrine. To his frustration, members of his flock rebuilt it just as often. Finally, village elders explained the shrine's significance and admonished the priest about his behavior. As Fray Gerónimo wrote to his own superior, the Indians told him "that the kingdom had revolted [in 1680] because this [religious custom] had been taken away from them, and that if it were to be taken away from them they would again rise in rebellion." He replied "that it was a deception of the devil, that the stones could give them nothing, that only God was the all powerful to whom they should appeal for help . . ."

Native religious beliefs and practices have survived many onslaughts; even at an acculturated pueblo like San Juan, they remain an active and cohesive force in the community, manifested in an invigorating annual cycle of ceremonial dances. One ceremony, which is attended by many outsiders, occurs on June 24, the Feast of St. John, when as many as a hundred dancers fill the plaza. A journal notation by the anthropologist Adolph F. Bandelier offers a glimpse of this ceremony as it was held more than a century ago. Today, at San Juan's Feast Day, one would recognize much in Bandelier's description. What Bandelier calls "tambourines" were actually Plains-style flat drums.

> After Mass, the dance began, about 120 persons taking part in it. The singers, as usual, with one big drum and 8–10 tambourines. . . . The men wear long crests of eagle-feathers, or fur caps with eagle-feathers and plumes. They wore gaudy, fancy costumes, buckskin leggings, mostly embroidered with beads, but no manta. Their paint was very diversified and as gaudy and horrible as that of the Qöshare at Cochiti, all colors of the rainbow being represented. They carried pistols, lances, muskets, bows and arrows, also sabres, and wands of various sizes and shapes, all profusely adorned with plumes, and evident "fancy arrangements." The flags were of calico with feathers pending. The girls gaudily

Deer Dance, San Juan Pueblo, 1973. (Photo by David Grant Noble.)

dressed with calico skirts, wool, even some with silk, and a few old mantas. Some had white down on their heads. Necklaces, etc., of silver, turquoise, coral, etc. were abundant. Everything looked new and as if just made for the occasion. The dancers remained at the east side of the plaza, and advanced in an irregular double file, then wheeled about, dancing as usual, in a double row, treble, and quadruple row . . .

In the twentieth century, and especially since World War II, San Juan Pueblo, like the rest of northern New Mexico, has experienced many changes. Subsistence farming and bartering nearly disappeared in favor of wage work and a cash economy, and some youths have pursued higher education leading to professional jobs.

In this century's early decades, Pueblo land rights, especially as regards the status of historic Spanish grants and encroachments by non-Indians, became a focus of public controversy and federal legislation. When the infamous Bursum Bill of 1922 threatened to deprive the Pueblos of much prime land, the All Pueblo Council was revived and Sotero Ortiz of San Juan Pueblo was elected its chairman. The Bursum Bill was defeated, to be replaced in 1924 by the Pueblo Lands Act, and Ortiz served as an all-Pueblo spokesman for twenty-five more years. He died in 1962 at the age of eighty-six.

Today, the federal government has a strong presence at San Juan through what the anthropologist Alfonso Ortiz has described as "an almost bewildering plethora of federally funded programs . . . [which are] so extensive in their reach throughout San Juan life as to almost conceal, except on ritual occasions, the traditional soul of the Pueblo." In its own way, Washington's impact in the present day is as potent as Spain's was three centuries ago.

TIPS FOR THE TRAVELER:
The ancestral Tewa pueblo, Poshuouinge, is located along U.S. 84, 2.5 miles south of Abiquiu, and is open to visitors. An interpretive trail leads around the site. If you are headed north, be sure to reserve time to see Taos (p. 89) and Taos Pueblo (p. 89). To the south, also along the Rio Grande, are the pueblos of San Ildefonso (p. 68) and Santa Clara (p. 81) and the ancient dwellings at Puye Cliffs.

SUGGESTED READING:
The Tewa World, by Alfonso Ortiz (Chicago: University of Chicago Press, 1969).

SANTA ANA PUEBLO

The old pueblo of Santa Ana is located on the north side of New Mexico 44, ten miles west of its intersection with Interstate 25 at Bernalillo. This historic village is only open to the public on the Feast Day of Santa Ana, July 26.

When the ancestors of the Santa Ana Indians arrived in the Rio Grande region, they probably passed through the Galisteo Basin (southeast of Santa Fe) and split into groups. Archaeological findings point to one group having founded the Paako Pueblo on the eastern slope of the Sandia Mountains around A.D. 1300; another may have settled near present-day Corrales, and still another along the Jemez River, near their Keresan relations at Zia Pueblo (see p. 99). The eastern faction left Paako around 1425 to rejoin their friends on the west bank of the Rio Grande. Around the same time, other villages sprang up around the mouth of the Jemez River (near Ranchitos), where farmlands were so good the settlers named one hill "Grain Box."

No doubt, some Santa Anans met Spaniards in 1540–41, for Coronado spent his first winter nearby and Captain Barrionuevo conducted an exploration into the Jemez country. In 1598, leaders of Santa Ana and other Keres pueblos assembled at Santo Domingo Pueblo (p. 85), where they took the oath of obedience to the Spanish king. One wonders how the Indians interpreted this foreign ritual.

There is an interesting footnote in the historical record of the mid-1600s. It concerns a claim by Santa Ana Pueblo to the Spanish governor, Bernardo López de Mendizábel, of payment for washing eighty hides. The task, they said, had taken 160 workdays. Other Indian pueblos joined in the claim, requesting that they be paid for a variety of services, including preparing and tanning hides; collecting piñon nuts; manufacturing stockings, shoes, and doublets; and building wagons. We do not know if the claimants won, but the complaint itself exposes the type of exploitation that the Pueblo Indians experienced under colonization. Mendizábel, incidently, was a notoriously corrupt governor, who exploited Spanish colonists as well as Indians.

During the Pueblo revolt, the Santa Anans deserted Tamaya, or old Santa Ana Pueblo, on the north bank of the Jemez River, eight miles northwest of its junction with the Rio Grande. In 1687, an army of Spanish exiles from El Paso del Norte attacked and defeated them and burned their village. The following year, another Spanish force destroyed nearby Zia Pueblo after a fierce battle in which some Santa Anans lost their lives. After these defeats, the Santa Ana and Zia people

Aerial view of Santa Ana Pueblo along the Jemez River, 1977. (Photo by Peter Dechert.)

moved to a new site near Jemez Pueblo (p. 30). It was here that the Spanish *reconquistador* Diego de Vargas found them in 1692. After the devastating experiences of 1687 and 1688, the Santa Anans and Zians toed the line with Governor Vargas and his soldiers. Their collaboration with the former enemy brought contempt upon them from their Jemez neighbors and other independent-spirited pueblos.

According to legend, in 1692 Spanish soldiers lured Santa Ana warriors away from their pueblo under the pretense of joining a large hunt;

while they were absent, other Spaniards seized many Santa Ana women and children, whom they held as hostages. Using this leverage, they coerced the Indians to accept Roman Catholicism and to agree to having their children removed to Mexico for education.

The Zia leader, Bartolomé de Ojeda, went to Mexico several times to check on the well-being of the children, who were never returned to their pueblo homes. Ojeda, a *mestizo,* was wounded and captured in the battle at Zia, lived with his captors for four years in El Paso, and returned with them in 1692 as a Spanish collaborator. On several occasions, warriors from Santa Ana, Zia, and San Felipe (p. 64) joined Vargas's troops when they made war on the Jemez. On July 24, 1694, they reinforced fifty Spanish soldiers in a successful attack on the Jemez village of Astialakwa, then helped their Spanish allies transport bushels of captured Jemez corn to Santa Fe.

The Corrales-Bernalillo area, where Santa Anans settled as early as the fourteenth and fifteenth centuries, had been settled by Spanish farmers in the 1600s. By the early 1700s, however, the Santa Anans needed to relocate from Tamaya, which was in a bleak, arid, and windy area unsuitable for productive farming. They therefore began pooling their resources in order to purchase land in the Ranchitos area along the Rio Grande, between its junction with the Jemez River and Bernalillo. They made eight purchases between 1709 and 1753 and a ninth in 1812. Many families continued to maintain a Tamaya Pueblo residence as well as a Ranchitos farm, but the old pueblo began to serve more and more a ceremonial function.

Toward the end of the nineteenth century, an American observer, Captain John G. Bourke, noted in his journal that he had seen Santa Ana Indians driving twenty ox-drawn wagons and carts, laden with corn, back to Tamaya, which he described as a large, mostly two-story adobe pueblo with glass or selenite windows and water jar chimneys. Its inhabitants owned dogs, cats, chickens, cows, oxen, burros, and several captive eagles. When he was there, they were drying meat, chile, and corn in front of their houses.

In the summer of 1890, an American Indian agent who visited Tamaya wrote that "a complete removal is made in March. Furniture, cooking utensils, mural ornaments, as well as the eagles, dogs, and live stock necessary to farming, are taken to summer quarters 8 miles below. The cats alone remain, prowling like gaunt specters over the roofs and through the deserted street." He also recorded that the tribe owned 600 horses, 2,000 cattle, 30 yoke of oxen, and 150 burros, and that most Santa Anans spoke Spanish and Keres, but not English. Its population

Santa Ana people riding burros, 1901. (Photo by Mary E. Disette, courtesy Museum of New Mexico, neg. 4091.)

was 253 in 1890, a figure that has more than doubled in the succeeding century. Clearly, by the beginning of the twentieth century the Santa Anans had successfully overcome challenges and were prospering.

Today, most Santa Anans live year-round in Ranchitos. Many work in Albuquerque, and their children attend the Bernalillo Consolidated Schools. Farming now plays a minimal role in their life and economy. Tamaya is well maintained but, like Acoma Pueblo (p. 9), is used primarily as a ceremonial site. This accounts for it being closed to outsiders most of the year.

TIPS FOR THE TRAVELER:
While in the Santa Ana area, you should visit Coronado State Monument (p. 20) and Jemez Pueblo and Jemez State Monument. Trips to Petroglyph National Monument and Bandelier National Monument will also be of interest. Many travel services are available in Bernalillo and Albuquerque.

SUGGESTED READING:
Santa Ana: The People, the Pueblo, and the History of Tamaya, by Laura Bayer and Floyd Montoya (Albuquerque: University of New Mexico Press, 1994).

SANTA CLARA PUEBLO

Santa Clara Pueblo is located along New Mexico 30, two miles south of Española and twenty-five miles north of Santa Fe.

On a mesa west of Santa Clara Pueblo lie the remains of Puye Pueblo, one of the largest prehistoric villages in New Mexico. It is also one of the first prehistoric sites in the state to have been studied by professional archaeologists, who, in 1907, excavated a portion of its many rooms. They found that Puye and several other towns on the Pajarito Plateau were built sometime after A.D. 1300 and reached a peak in the 1400s, when their two- and three-story apartment blocks included as many as a thousand rooms.

Puye, which includes a series of cave dwellings along the mesa's cliff, is an ancestral village of the Santa Clara Indians, and it is managed as a public monument by the pueblo. Puye's inhabitants moved down along the Rio Grande to found Santa Clara Pueblo, where they still live. After being abandoned in the 1500s, Puye's walls, constructed of blocks of tufa, fell in and its rooms were filled with windblown dirt. Today, for the sake of tourists, limited restoration had been done, making the extent of the site readily apparent.

Puye's descendants at Santa Clara are Tewa Indians, who share the language and customs of their neighbors at the pueblos of San Ildefonso, San Juan, Tesuque, Nambe, and Pojoaque. Spanish explorers visited Santa Clara in the sixteenth century, and after 1598, when Juan de Oñate settled his colonists at the pueblo of Yunge, near San Juan, Franciscan missionaries came here to proselytize. A mission church was built after 1622, when Fray Alonzo de Benavides took over missionary work here and at San Ildefonso. The priest remained until 1629, when he returned to Spain, wrote his famous *Memorial,* and became a untiring lobbyist to the court of King Philip IV. His efforts to win support for the church's activities in New Mexico bore fruit; in 1631, he negotiated a formal contract with royal officials, which spelled out in minute detail how the crown would subsidize the New Mexico missions.

Royal subsidies or not, the missionary work that took place at Santa Clara and at other pueblos was not well received by their inhabitants, who joined the 1680 Pueblo revolt against the Spanish colony. One of the key rebellion leaders was a Santa Claran named Domingo Naranjo, a mixed blood of black and Indian heritage who understood the Spanish

Cave dwelling, Puye Cliffs, near Santa Clara Pueblo. (Photo by David Grant Noble.)

mentality. At the time of the second revolt, in 1696, Santa Clara's populace virtually abandoned the pueblo, with many taking temporary refuge in the western lands of the Hopis and Navajos (see p. 125). At the same time, the neighboring pueblos of Jacona and Cuyamungue completely disintegrated, never to be revived.

Santa Clara's church was destroyed in 1680 and rebuilt in 1706. After it collapsed, a third was begun in 1758 with a fine bell that, as one visitor wrote, "speaks with its own tongue, unlike others that are rung with stones." This church, too, is gone and the present one dates to 1918.

An interesting insight into Santa Clara, from a missionary's perspective, is provided in a letter of Fray José García Marin, who volunteered for duty at the pueblo in 1694. Marin, who hailed from the province of Burgos in Spain, had learned of the need for missionaries in New Spain where, he was led to believe, "there was an infinity of souls desiring to receive holy baptism." So moved had he apparently been by the New World missionary cause that, as he later wrote, "I decided to leave my holy province, country, parents, brothers, relatives, and friends to sail the expansive and dangerous seas that lie between Spain and New Spain." The support given to this priest by Santa Clara's impoverished inhabitants made him feel accepted; however, he was frustrated by being unable to speak Tewa and not having an interpreter. Under these circumstances, one wonders how he carried on his Christian teachings, or if he was simply a quiet guest in the pueblo. He frankly ascribed the poverty of the Indians to the "continuous wars" that the Spaniards waged against them and the Spaniards' theft of their corn. His apologetic attitude regarding the behavior of his fellow countrymen contrasts with the frequent arrogance and condescension expressed by some of his peers. Interestingly, what appears to have bothered him most in New Mexico were "the rigors of winter [which] are very great. . . . Not even the coldest weather of Flanders can be compared with the severity of the cold in this country." The Rio Grande froze over with some regularity in the sixteenth and seventeenth centuries.

Throughout the eighteenth and early nineteenth centuries, Santa Clara warriors joined campaigns against their traditional enemies, the Navajos, and other aggressive nomadic tribes. The pueblo's war society (which lapsed many years ago, when traditional warfare became obsolete) had lent prestige to warriors who had to demonstrate prowess in battle to gain admittance. But over the centuries, warfare certainly did not account for as many casualties as diseases such as smallpox and

Santiago Naranjo, Santa Clara governor, at home, 1910. (Courtesy Museum of New Mexico, neg. 10325.)

measles, and even the post–World War I epidemic of Spanish flu took a heavy toll in lives at the pueblo.

Intramural factionalism was common among the Pueblos, and was particularly prevalent at Santa Clara between 1894 and 1935. A long-lasting dispute pitted conservatives against progressives, focusing on such issues as the separation of religious and secular activities, whether or not participation in ceremonies should be obligatory or voluntary, and who should be responsible for the maintenance of irrigation ditches. By the 1930s, four separate factions had arisen within the village, with little prospect of resolving disagreements. In 1934, arbitration by the Indian Service in Santa Fe resulted in Santa Clara forming a constitution and adopting an elective form of government. When the constitution was ratified the following year, Santa Clara became the first pueblo to incorporate under the Indian Reorganization Act. This accomplishment represented a major step in resolving internal disputes and in establishing a more modern and harmonious political system.

Today, though it is not one of the larger pueblos, Santa Clara is relatively affluent. Pueblo members find employment in the nearby cities of Española and Los Alamos, and the tribe has developed revenues from tourism, recreation, pumice quarrying on the reservation, and federal grants for development projects. In addition, it is known for its fine potters, some of whom successfully market their wares at craft fairs and in shops in Santa Fe, Taos, Albuquerque, and farther afield. This economic picture represents a major change from a past when farming and hunting were the primary means of livelihood.

Visitors to Santa Clara will find a warm reception and will especially enjoy seeing the pueblo on its Feast Day, which is August 12. Public dances, on this and other days, take place in the old section of the pueblo.

TIPS FOR THE TRAVELER:
You should certainly try to work in a sidetrip to the pueblo ruins and cliff dwellings at Puye. Above the ruins, in Santa Clara Canyon, is a campground and recreational area managed by the tribe, where one can swim, fish, camp, and hike in a beautiful landscape setting. Also nearby is Bandelier National Monument, where trails in Frijoles Canyon lead to more prehistoric Pueblo sites. Tourist accommodations can be found in abundance in Los Alamos, Española, and Santa Fe.

SUGGESTED READING:
Santa Clara Pottery Today, by Betty LeFree (Albuquerque: University of
  New Mexico Press, 1975).

SANTO DOMINGO PUEBLO

Santo Domingo Pueblo lies west of Interstate 25, midway between Albuquerque and Santa Fe. Follow I-25 north from Albuquerque or south from Santa Fe for thirty miles, then take Exit 259 west on New Mexico 22 and continue six miles to the pueblo.

With a population of over twenty-five hundred people, Santo Domingo is the largest of the Rio Grande pueblos and, by reputation, the most conservative in political and religious affairs. The Keres Indians living here have retained their native language, adhered to many traditions, and maintained a strong value system.

The Santo Domingos' first brief contact with Europeans was in 1541, when members of the Coronado expedition stopped here. Knowing of the Spaniards' attack on the Zuñi pueblo of Hawikuh (p. 103), they must have regarded the approaching foreigners with misgivings. However, the visit was peaceable. A half-century later, Castaño de Sosa came here with notions of establishing a permanent Spanish colony

Harvest time at Santo Domingo. (Photo by T. Harmon Parkhurst, courtesy Museum of New Mexico, neg. 4732.)

nearby. But before he could do so, he was arrested by officials from Mexico City for lacking authorization to colonize the territory. To the Santo Domingos, Castaño's fate must have seemed a blessing.

On July 7, 1598, the leaders of Santo Domingo and surrounding pueblos were summoned to the pueblo by Governor Juan de Oñate to swear an oath of allegiance to the king of Spain. The next year, Oñate held an extraordinary war trial here, at which some five hundred captives from Acoma Pueblo (p. 9) were found guilty of treason and were atrociously punished. The trial sent a message throughout the Pueblo world concerning the submissive behavior required by Spanish authorities.

A generation later, the Catholic church chose Santo Domingo for its headquarters in New Mexico. Some Franciscan missionaries even sought refuge here in the 1640s, when conflicts raged between Spanish religious and civil authorities. While the Spaniards disputed among themselves and intensified their repression of Pueblo religious practices, the attitude of the Santo Domingos and their neighbors darkened, and plots of rebellion began to take form.

Alonzo Catiti led the Santo Domingos and all the Keres in the 1680 Pueblo revolt, and according to one report, after the Spaniards' defeat, he and Popé, the rebellion's main organizer, held a victory banquet at Santa Ana Pueblo (p. 77) during which, in mockery of Spanish customs, they raised chalices taken from the churches to toast their victory and curse the Catholic priests. The experience of independence, however, was to be brief, for the following year, Governor Antonio de Otermín led troops north from El Paso del Norte and sacked Santo Domingo. When this happened, the inhabitants sought refuge on nearby mesas and joined allies at a mesatop stronghold near Cochiti Pueblo (p. 15). Some withdrew here again in 1692, when Governor Diego de Vargas began his reconquest of New Mexico, and again in 1693, when Vargas stormed the mesa and set fire to the pueblo. By this time, Catiti had died and there was no unified resistance among the Keres to Spanish rule. In 1694, Santo Domingo's resident priest boasted to his superiors of the success of his missionary program at the pueblo; interesting to note, however, is his comment that the pueblo had only twenty residents. The Santo Domingos had left, some for Acoma and others, under Mateo Hueache, to a fortified pueblo on San Juan Mesa in the Jemez Mountains.

In the eighteenth century, history records little about Santo Domingo, but it is known that about 1793 the dwindling residents of Galisteo Pueblo (thirty miles south of Santa Fe) moved here. When the United States Army occupied New Mexico in 1846, Santo Domingo leaders extended an invitation to the Americans to visit their pueblo. As the U.S. cavalry approached, it was greeted by a party of Santo Domingo elders who indicated that despite appearances to the contrary, the warriors they were about to see were friendly. The American commanding officer's notes on the occasion offer an insight into Santo Domingo's strength and vitality and how its leaders conducted foreign relations:

> The first object that caught my eye through the column of dust, was a fierce pair of buffalo horns, overlapped with long shaggy hair. As they approached, the sturdy form of a naked Indian revealed itself beneath the horns, with shield and lance, dashing at full speed, on a white horse, which, like his own body, was painted all the colors of the rainbow; and then, one by one, his followers came on, painted to the eyes, their own heads and their horses covered with all the strange equipments that the brute creation could afford in the way of horns, skulls, tails, feathers, and claws.
>
> As they passed us, one rank on each side, they fired a volley under our horses' bellies from the right and from the left. Our well-trained dragoons sat motionless on their horses, which went along without pricking an ear or showing any sign of excitement.
>
> Arrived in the rear, the Indians circled round, dropped into a walk on our flanks until their horses recovered their breath, when off they went at full speed, passing to our front, and when there, the opposite files met, and each man selected his adversary and kept up a running fight with muskets, lances, and bows and arrows. Sometimes a fellow

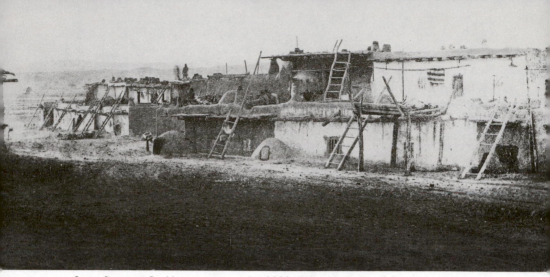

Santo Domingo Pueblo as it appeared in 1880. (Photo by George C. Bennett, courtesy Museum of New Mexico, neg. 4357.)

would stoop almost to the earth to shoot under his horse's belly at full speed, or to shield himself from an impending blow. So they continued to pass and repass us all the way to the steep cliff which overhangs the town. There they filed on each side of the road, which descends through a deep canyon, and halted on the peaks of the cliffs.

The Santo Domingo we know was built in 1886, the previous village having been washed away by a flooding Rio Grande. Despite their traditionalism, the Santo Domingos live in the modern world and have adopted many elements of the surrounding Anglo-American culture. Many work outside the pueblo and have business dealings in Santa Fe, Albuquerque, and other cities. They have an active cottage industry in craft art and are especially noted for their jewelry making.

As you enter Santo Domingo from the east, you will first come upon its Roman Catholic church. This handsome whitewashed and decoratively painted building stands out strikingly against the muted surrounding earth tones and blue sky. You may park near the church and cross a footbridge over a gently flowing and shaded *acequia* to enter the central part of the pueblo. A series of unpaved streets run east to west on either side of the long plaza. Be sure to follow posted regulations regarding photography, sketching, and other prohibited activities, and respect the privacy of the inhabitants.

It is in the plaza that the annual Green Corn Dance takes place on the Feast Day of Saint Dominic. This August 4 ceremonial, with hundreds of dance participants, is famous among Pueblo public ceremonials. In homes, families treat friends and guests to lavish meals, while in the streets, sellers offer a variety of food, refreshments, crafts, souvenirs, and carnival amusements. At a recent Corn Dance here, one visitor was amused to spy two dancers, in full body paint and costume, taking a turn around a ferris wheel between plaza dances. Such is the fascinating counterpoint between Indian traditionalism and modern American culture.

TIPS FOR THE TRAVELER:
You can take a back road from Santo Domingo to San Felipe Pueblo, following the route of the historic Camino Real (p. 293), and take this same road north, crossing the Rio Grande, to Cochiti Pueblo. A visit to Bandelier National Monument, near White Rock, is interesting, for here you can hike to cave dwellings and pueblo sites, some of which housed ancestors of the Santo Domingos. To see fine examples of Pueblo craft arts, plan to visit the Museum of Indian Arts and Culture in Santa Fe (p. 189). Other historic sites, as well as travel services, can be found in the Santa Fe and Albuquerque areas.

SUGGESTED READING:
"The Pueblo of Santo Domingo, New Mexico," by Leslie A. White, *Memoirs of the American Anthropological Association* 43, (Menasha: American Anthropological Association, 1935).

TAOS PUEBLO

Taos Pueblo is three miles north of the village of Taos in northern New Mexico. From downtown Taos, drive north on U.S. 64 to the edge of town, where a well-marked and paved road to the pueblo branches off to the right.

Many people consider Taos Pueblo to be one of the most beautiful architectural structures in North America. Built of adobe and wood more than five hundred years ago, this multistoried monument has become a symbol of the enduring strength of Pueblo culture. Widely known and publicized, it is visited and photographed each year by multitudes from around the world.

The Taos and Picuris Indians speak Tiwa, a Kiowa-Tanoan language; the people of Sandia (p. 59) and Isleta (p. 25) pueblos speak a southern dialect of Tiwa. The linguistic link between the Tiwa and Kiowa Indians is a clue that these two tribes share a long-distant past. In

Taos Pueblo in winter. (Photo by David Grant Noble.)

historic times, they traded with each other, and even in recent generations, Taos and Kiowa families maintained old friendships.

The Taos Valley was first settled nearly a thousand years ago by members of an emerging Puebloan farming culture. Initially living in pithouses, these folk began to build above-ground villages around A.D. 1200 or 1250. At about the same time, immigrants moved here from the north and west, some possibly from Chaco Canyon, which was abandoned in the mid-1100s. Two large villages that were founded in this period were Picuris Pueblo (p. 48) and Pot Creek Pueblo, east of Ranchos de Taos. Archaeologists who have excavated the Pot Creek Site believe that it was abandoned around A.D. 1350. At this time, some of its inhabitants moved to Taos, where they lived for about a hundred years before building the two large apartment dwellings we know as Taos Pueblo. The pueblo was well established when Europeans first explored this region in the sixteenth century.

Life here had many advantages. The Rio Pueblo, which flows from Blue Lake high in the Sangre de Cristo Mountains, provided water for drinking and irrigation. Residents still carry water from it to their homes, albeit now in a metal or plastic bucket rather than in a ceramic pot. The surrounding mountains were rich in game—elk, deer, and turkey—and the broad Taos Valley abounded with antelope and rabbits.

In prehistoric and early historic times, the Taos Indians did much trading: mountain products for cotton textiles produced by their lowland neighbors to the south, for example, or cornmeal for buffalo hides and jerked meat brought in by the Jicarilla Apaches (p. 115).

Taos is the northernmost Rio Grande pueblo and therefore has long enjoyed a degree of isolation. After Spanish colonization of New Mexico, this remoteness served their purposes and helped foster a strong resistance to European influences. Although Christianity held little appeal to the Taos—they had deeply held religious beliefs of their own—they allowed Franciscan friars to establish a mission at the pueblo in the early 1600s; still, like their nearest neighbors at Picuris, they opposed efforts at conversion. In 1639, resentment toward their resident priest led to a rebellion in which they killed him and two other Spaniards and destroyed the church, which was not rebuilt until many years later. This incident foreshadowed the Pueblo revolt of 1680, which was planned in the kivas at Taos by Pueblo religious leaders. Even after the Spanish reconquered New Mexico, the Taos continued to resist foreign domination.

In the eighteenth century, a new enemy appeared on the scene—the powerful Comanches, whose warriors rode over the mountains to raid Indian pueblos and Spanish villages with impunity. All inhabitants of the Taos Valley, regardless of their heritage, cooperated in mutual defense, and the fortresslike pueblo often served as a place of refuge for everyone. In 1776, one visitor reported seeing five defensive towers at strategic points around the pueblo's perimeter walls.

As settlement of the valley increased, the Spaniards founded their own village, Fernando de Taos, three miles away. Relations between the two communities, although generally cordial, were periodically marred by Spanish encroachments on tribal land.

Taos Pueblo held an annual week-long trade fair, during which traditional hostilities between various tribal and ethnic groups were set aside. Buyers and sellers gathered from miles around, regardless of background. Trade goods included agricultural products, craft arts and manufactured items, and captive women and children, who were ransomed or sold as slaves. The fair also functioned as a social occasion, marked by rowdy parties and brawls, and, no doubt, a few unplanned pregnancies. We do not know when the fair originated, probably in prehistoric times, but it thrived throughout the Spanish colonial period. In the latter part of the 1700s, it moved from the pueblo to the village. After the opening of the Santa Fe Trail (p. 309) in 1821, Santa Fe replaced Taos as the region's main marketplace.

In January of 1847, many Taos Indians joined local Hispanic residents in an attempt to overthrow the United States' newly established rule in New Mexico. The insurgents' first act was to assassinate Governor Charles Bent in his Taos home and parade his scalp through town. Afterward, they burned a mill north of Taos and killed several Americans, then headed for Santa Fe. In Santa Cruz de la Cañada (p. 184), they were turned back by U.S. troops. The rebels, whose ranks had swelled to about fifteen hundred, retreated to Taos where they barricaded themselves in the pueblo's thick-walled adobe church. The American soldiers arrived the afternoon of February 3, ineffectively bombarded the church for two and a half hours, then decided to hold further assaults until the next morning.

On the fourth, after the Americans again failed to breach the church walls with cannon fire, Captain John H. Burgwin's company stormed the west side of the building. The troops hacked a small hole in the wall with hand axes and tossed shells inside. Then, one after another, they leaped into the smoke-filled church shooting at the 600 to 700 rebels. Many Indians, escaping death inside, were killed as they ran toward the pueblo. American losses were 7 killed, including Burgwin, and 45 wounded against 150 insurgents dead and an unknown number wounded. The battle was discontinued after nightfall, and the following morning the remaining insurgents, now hidden in the labyrinthine pueblo, recognized the hopelessness of their situation and surrendered.

The Battle of Taos Pueblo graphically demonstrated the defensibility of an adobe building; cannonballs fired at the church walls had either penetrated a few inches and rolled back on the ground or passed through without inflicting serious structural damage. The multistoried pueblo, with rooftop entrances accessible only by ladders, would have proved difficult and costly for the troops to take by force had its occupants continued to fight.

Another more recent battle took place at Taos Pueblo, this one centering in federal courts and legislative offices. In 1906, the U.S. Forest Service appropriated much Taos Pueblo land, including Blue Lake, which is a religious shrine. For more than sixty years, Taos leaders undauntingly opposed the Forest Service's attempts to open the area for recreation and logging and pressed the U.S. government to return control of Blue Lake to the tribe. In 1970, their perseverance was rewarded when President Nixon signed legislation returning the lake and forty-eight thousand acres to the pueblo.

The Taos Indians' natural conservatism, especially with regard to

The remains of the old church at Taos Pueblo. (Photo by David Grant Noble.)

the retention of their traditional values and beliefs, has contributed to the remarkably good preservation of the historic pueblo. The tribal council, which is made up of traditionalists, has long denied modernization of the ancient buildings, including the installation of electricity and plumbing. Even ground-floor doorways and glass windows were disallowed for many years. A fast-growing birthrate, however, has resulted in much of the population moving to modern housing located beyond the confines of the old pueblo. Other people on the tribal rolls have moved away altogether, to return only for reunions and ceremonial occasions.

Today, many sightseers visit Taos Pueblo; on a summer's afternoon, as many as a hundred cars may be parked in the old plaza. At the pueblo's entrance, you must register and obtain a camera permit. This allows you to take general pictures of the pueblo; please ask permission to take portraits. The modest entrance and camera fees are a significant source of tribal income in a region where unemployment is high.

Picuris Pueblo is only a short drive to the south. Historic points of interest around Taos include the Kit Carson home (1825), the Martínez Hacienda (1804), La Morada (1820), the Blumenschein home (1797), San Francisco de Assiz Church, and the Millicent Rogers Museum. The Taos area offers many outdoor activities, such as skiing, river rafting, horseback riding, and hiking. As Taos is a tourist center, motels, restaurants, and other services are readily available.

SUGGESTED READING:
The Taos Indians and the Battle for Blue Lake, by R. C. Gordon-McCutchan (Santa Fe: Red Crane Books, 1991).

TESUQUE PUEBLO

Tesuque Pueblo is located a mile west of 84/285, eight miles north of Santa Fe.

The Tewa Pueblo Indians have resided in the northern Rio Grande region, between Tesuque and San Juan, for many centuries. Of the Tewa pueblos noted by Spaniards in the late sixteenth century, Tesuque, Pojoaque, Nambe, San Ildefonso, Santa Clara, and San Juan still thrive. Yunge Pueblo, at the confluence of the Rio Grande and Rio Chama, was appropriated by Spanish colonists in 1699 (they called it San Gabriel) and abandoned by them eleven years later, and Cuyamungue and Jacona were deserted after the Pueblo revolt. Tesuque, or *Tatsuge* as it is known by its inhabitants, is the southernmost of these villages and the closest to Santa Fe. It is a small community, many of whose members live and work off the reservation. At first glance, outsiders often think it to be empty, which is not the case.

Puebloan ancestors of the Tesuque people are believed to have occupied the Tesuque Valley since around A.D. 850. After A.D. 1000, they lived in many small pueblos and farmsteads that were dominated, it appears, by one larger village whose site archaeologists have imaginatively designated "LA 835." This pueblo, which held about 180 households and had ten kivas and one great kiva, was excavated in the 1950s by archaeologist Stanley Stubbs. LA 835's unified town plan and other features raise the possibility that the village was inhabited by colonists from Chaco Canyon in northwestern New Mexico. Since irrigation

Tesuque Pueblo, 1977. (Photo by Peter Dechert.)

ditches began to appear in the valley at this same time, some researchers speculate that irrigation agriculture was introduced here by the Chacoans, who were well versed in such techniques.

The population of the northern Rio Grande Valley swelled in the late 1200s, causing small farming hamlets to multiply, with some eventually consolidating to form substantial villages. Tesuque Pueblo, which was first situated three miles east of the present village, was one of these. Archaeologists have dated more than a dozen small pueblos and twice as many farm houses in the valley to between A.D. 1200 and 1375; however, between the latter date and the time of the first Spanish *entrada*, these sites diminished in number to four small villages and two large ones, including Tesuque.

In 1541, members of Coronado's expedition estimated the population of Tesuque at 170 people, a number that had risen to about 200 at the time of the Pueblo revolt. In 1591, another Spanish intruder described the Tewa inhabitants of the Tesuque Valley as living in two- and three-storied pueblos, raising crops of corn, beans, and other vegetables, and being friendly and generous with their provisions.

Although the Pueblo revolt of 1680 was secretly planned in the kivas of Taos Pueblo, it first broke out at Tesuque. Rumors of a rebellion reached the ears of the Spanish governor in Santa Fe on August 9, and were soon confirmed when two Tesuque messengers were apprehended. The next morning, Friar Juan Baptista Pío and his personal guard rode into Tesuque from Santa Fe to give Mass. Finding the pueblo deserted, they searched for its inhabitants and eventually found some in a nearby ravine. When Pío approached, they killed him; his guard, however, managed to escape and hurried back to the capital to sound the alarm. Over the following fortnight, Tesuque participated in the siege of Santa Fe and had the satisfaction, on August 20, of watching the defeated Spanish colonists file out of the *casas reales* and begin their retreat to El Paso del Norte.

Being a mere eight miles from the capital, Tesuque was in a difficult position to foment continued rebellion after the Spanish reconquest of New Mexico, which began in 1692. In 1694, they moved to the site of the present pueblo, although it is not clear why. Two years later, some independent elements in the pueblo were more than ready to fight again and tried to recruit residents of San Cristóbal and Pecos pueblos to join them. However, another faction within the pueblo, headed by Governor Domingo Tuhogue, favored appeasement. Tuhogue's influence apparently prevailed, for Tesuque, as a whole, did not join the 1696 revolt.

In the early 1700s, Tesuque's population was swelled by displaced Tanoans from San Cristóbal Pueblo, but these refugees eventually left the Rio Grande Valley altogether to join the Hopis in northeastern Arizona. Their descendants still live on First Mesa on the Hopi reservation.

Some Tesuque Indians lived in a strung-out settlement known as Poshu, along the foothills of the mountains east of the pueblo. Here, they tended irrigated fields on the low benches along several streams. After around 1750, Spanish colonists from Santa Fe pushed northward, thereby competing for the same fields and water being used by the Indians. When the smallpox epidemic of 1780–81 wiped out most of Poshu's population, its few survivors moved to the main pueblo, and much Tesuque Pueblo land was lost. Over the subsequent decades, as water use by non-Indian farmers in Tesuque Village increased, the downstream flow to the pueblo diminished, making agriculture less feasible.

The eighteenth and nineteenth centuries saw a series of epidemics

Ox-drawn carreta, Tesuque Pueblo, 1881. (Photo by George C. Bennett, courtesy Museum of New Mexico, neg. 102139.)

that took a fearful toll on the Pueblo population of New Mexico. Tesuque's population dropped from 187, in 1821, to 119 in 1850, to 94 in 1889, to a low of 77 in 1910. Since then, it has been rising and stands today at around 300 people. In recent years, the tribe has had some success in regaining its access to irrigation waters, which, in turn, has stimulated some revived interest in farming. Still, most employed Tesuque Indians live by wage work in nearby towns. Unlike some other Tewas, notably at Santa Clara and San Ildefonso, the Tesuque Indians have not generated a revival of pottery making and derive little income from craft arts. The pueblo's economy, indeed, has long been depressed.

Among the Tewa pueblos, Tesuque has remained relatively conservative in its customs. This is reflected in the well-preserved architectural layout of the pueblo, where multistoried houseblocks still surround a spacious rectangular plaza. Some of these homes have been restored in recent years. When John Bourke visited the pueblo in 1881, he received directions to the governor's house, but had considerable difficulty in finding the front door. As he wrote in his diary,

> we walked quite around the residence of the gobernador, followed by the whole group of boys and girls laughing and screaming at our ignorance. At last, we found the proper ladder and climbed to the second story. . . . He [the governor] invited us to descend again into the house which, altho' a trifle close, was clean and in good order, warmed by a bright fire of cedar knots blazing on the hearth in one corner. We were first presented to his wife and little daughters; the former making moccasins with soles of rawhide; the latter grinding corn upon metates.

Rooftop entrances to Pueblo homes reflected an architectural style that evolved among the Anasazi many centuries ago, presumably to impede access by potential invaders. The custom continued into historic times and continued to be an asset in the eighteenth century, when Tesuque and other northern Rio Grande villages found themselves under attack by Comanches, Utes, and Navajos. It is interesting that this ancient custom still survived in the late nineteenth century.

Unlike many pueblos, Tesuque's small adobe church faces directly on the village plaza. The original mission collapsed in the 1880s, but was later rebuilt. Should you wish to see the pueblo at its most active time, plan to visit on November 12, when the villagers honor their patron, San Diego, and hold plaza dances all day long.

TIPS FOR THE TRAVELER:
This region is rich in historical sites. In addition to the four other Tewa pueblos mentioned, you will find visits to the Hispanic villages of Santa Cruz (p. 184), Chimayo (p. 147), Truchas (p. 218), and Las Trampas (p. 157) of interest. To learn more about Pueblo prehistory, plan to visit Bandelier National Monument, along New Mexico 4 near White Rock. In addition, Pojoaque Pueblo is developing a museum at its Poeh Center, along U.S. 84/285 north of Tesuque. For accommodations, you will find a campground along U.S. 84/285, near the entrance to Tesuque Pueblo; here, too, is a curious geological feature known as Camel Rock. Many other tourist services can be found in Santa Fe and Española.

SUGGESTED READING:
Dances of the Tewa Pueblo Indians, by Jill D. Sweet (Santa Fe: School of American Research Press, 1985).

Crow Dance, Zia Pueblo, c. 1940. (Photo by Mullarky, courtesy Museum of New Mexico, neg. 74900.)

ZIA PUEBLO

Zia Pueblo is located one mile north of New Mexico 44, nineteen miles northwest of Bernalillo.

Zia Pueblo's location, off heavily traveled tourist routes, has protected it from the streams of visitors with which many Rio Grande pueblos contend, and has given its residents a considerable measure of privacy. The old pueblo perches on a hillside overlooking the Jemez River, its single-story stone and adobe houses clustered around an historic Spanish mission. At the foot of the hill are new single-family housing units that link the old pueblo to modern times.

The Zia people trace their background to the Four Corners region, in particular to a pueblo they call *Kacikatcutiya,* or White House. Their oral traditions delve even further back in time, telling of an original life-giving Being, Tsityostinako, who resided in a series of worlds beneath the present one. This deity had two daughters, Uchtsiti and Naotsiti, who created all living creatures. Eventually, Zian ancestors emerged into the present world, where Uchtsiti taught them how to live by agriculture.

In the 1940s, the archaeologist H. P. Mera identified seven early Zia village sites within six miles of the present pueblo. Potsherd analysis showed that several sites dated to the thirteenth century, and others to the sixteenth and seventeenth centuries. It seems plausible that among them were the five pueblos of the "*Punames*" recorded by the Spanish explorer Antonio de Espejo in 1583. Espejo's chronicler, Pérez de Luxan, described the principal town of the Punames (very likely Zia Pueblo) as

> an important city of more than a thousand houses inhabited by more than four thousand men over fifteen years of age, and women and children in addition. . . . It belonged to the province of the Punamees. . . . There are in this city five plazas and many smaller ones. . . . We raised the flag in the name of his majesty and took possession of the said city and province. A cross was erected and its meaning explained to the natives.

When Espejo came to Zia, he was impressed by the pueblo's size, its many plazas, and its neatly whitewashed and colorfully painted houses. The Indians received him as diplomatically as they had his predecessor, giving the explorers turkeys, corn, vegetables, and more tortillas than the Spaniards could eat. This was a small price for peace and security. Again, according to Luxan,

> The dress of the men consists of some blankets, a small cloth for covering their privy parts, and other cloaks, shawls, and leather shoes in the shape of boots. The women wear a blanket over their shoulders tied with a sash at the waist, their hair cut in front, and the rest plaited so that it forms two braids, and above a blanket of turkey feathers.

The Zians received their first assigned Franciscan missionary, Fray Juan de Alpuente, in 1598. Alpuente was a former philosophy lecturer who often served as Diego de Vargas's military chaplain and was, by his own account, a loner with an irascible temperament who got his flock to obey him through scolding and outbursts of anger. He must have been an unpopular envoy. Still, by around 1612, the Indians built a mission, *Nuestra Señora de la Asunción de Sia,* which still is in use.

In the seventeenth century, Zia's problems were like those of most other Indian communities in New Mexico: food shortages, diseases, and religious persecution. By 1675, the weakened and embittered Indians had reached a point of desperation. At the same time, Spanish administrators and clerics were clashing with each other for control over the province. Five years later, when this tinder box ignited, Zia joined the other rebellious Pueblos in their overthrow of Spanish rule. At this time, they damaged, but did not destroy, their church.

The independence enjoyed by most Pueblo Indians between 1680 and 1692, unfortunately, was interrupted at Zia when a force of Spanish exiles tried to retake the pueblo in 1687. The following year, they returned to storm the village again. This time, after a protracted battle, the Spaniards triumphed; they killed hundreds of Zians, set fire to homes, and captured seventy pueblo members whom they condemned to ten years of servitude in El Paso. After this defeat, the Zia survivors sought refuge in the Jemez Mountains, where they remained until 1692, when Diego de Vargas persuaded them to return home. In a ceremony in the plaza, a Spanish priest baptized 123 members of the pueblo and set a commemorative cross in the ground. The cross, or more likely a replacement, still stands on the west side of the South Plaza.

Although Zia's governor was a man named Cristóbal, a new leader appeared on the scene—Bartolomé de Ojeda. Ojeda, who was of mixed ancestry, had been wounded and captured in the 1688 battle, and had lived for several years among the Spanish exiles in El Paso del Norte. In 1692, serving as Vargas's interpreter and consultant, he urged his people to adopt a policy of accommodation with the Spanish. This they did, joining their Keresan neighbors at Santa Ana and San Felipe as Spanish allies. In 1694, they reinforced an attack by Spanish troops against the Jemez Indians. This act of disloyalty brought them into conflict with their former allies at Santo Domingo, Acoma, and Zuñi; still, they continued the collaboration until Pueblo-Spanish warring ended in 1696.

The Zians suffered one of the most precipitous population declines in the Pueblo world. Between 1541 and 1890, their numbers fell from at least several thousand people to just over a hundred. In 1894, the anthropologist Matilda Coxe Stevenson, who studied Zia customs, wrote,

> All that remains of the once populous pueblo of Sia is a small group of houses and a mere handful of people in the midst of one of the most extensive ruins of the Southwest[,] the living relic of an almost extinct people and a pathetic tale of the ravages of warfare and pestilence.

Population figures at Zia in the twentieth century reflect improving nutrition and health conditions; their numbers have grown from 125 persons, in 1900, to 183 in 1930, to 468 in 1964, to over 600 today. The fact that the Zians did not vanish or merge with nearby Santa Ana

Baking bread at Zia Pueblo. (Photo by T. Harmon Parkhurst, courtesy Museum of New Mexico, neg. 54420.)

Pueblo is a testament to their remarkable hold on life and their love of homeland. Maybe it was fear of extinction that lay behind a long-held tribal law requiring any member to obtain permission from tribal authorities to reside away from the pueblo. The enforcement of such regulations and the adherence to social customs and religious traditions all have helped Zia Pueblo endure. But an underlying life force, perhaps conveyed to them by their creator, Tsityostinako, must also have helped them endure.

Through the twentieth century, Zia people continued to cultivate fields along the Jemez River, but their traditional agricultural base has largely given way to sheep and cattle raising and wage work. Electrification came to the old pueblo in the 1970s, bringing many modern conveniences, but the physical limitations of the hilltop site forced many to build new homes in the valley below. A small federally supported subdivision also has appeared across the river. By the 1970s, half the Pueblo's enrolled members lived away from the reservation, adopting some of the ways of the dominant population.

Zia's most recognizable design symbol is the sun, which appears as a motif on the beautiful pottery for which the Pueblo has achieved artistic fame. The Zia sun symbol was even adopted by New Mexico as the state emblem.

Zia remains a small community, whose members love their home environment and cherish their traditional way of life. The church, although twice damaged by warfare, was never completely destroyed and is well maintained. Zia's Feast Day, celebrated on August 15, begins with an early morning Mass followed by a procession in which the Pueblo's patroness, Our Lady of the Ascension, is carried to the plaza and installed in an arbor. Here, members of the village pay their respects by making an offering. Soon thereafter, the plaza dances begin. This is the best time to see Zia, meet its people, and have a glimpse of the Zia world.

TIPS FOR THE TRAVELER:
While here, you might also visit nearby Jemez Pueblo and Jemez State Monument (p. 30). In addition, Coronado State Monument (p. 20), with its excavated pueblo ruins, is located in Bernalillo. You will find gas along New Mexico 44 at San Ysidro, and restaurants and motels in Cuba and Bernalillo.

SUGGESTED READING:
Recuerdos de los Viejitos/Tales of the Rio Puerco, edited by Nasario García (Albuquerque: University of New Mexico Press, 1987).
The Sia, by Matilda Coxe Stevenson, in *11th Annual Report of the Bureau of American Ethnology for the Years 1889–1890* (Washington, D.C.: 1894).

ZUÑI PUEBLO

Zuñi Pueblo is located along New Mexico 53, thirty-five miles south of Gallup and seventy-one miles west of Grants.

The Zuñis—or *Ashiwi,* as they call themselves—were the first native people of the American Southwest to encounter Europeans. When it happened, in July of 1540, the sight of the mounted foreigners with their armor and guns must have astonished them. The Zuñis were living then in six villages: Hawikuh, Halona (near present Zuñi Pueblo), Kiakima, Matsaki, Kwakina, and Kechipauan. Numbering about three thousand people, they enjoyed a prosperous farming economy and had a highly organized society and strong religion. They also traded widely and ranged over a wide territory to hunt game and gather natural resources.

Dancing the Ka-k'ok-shi, Zuñi Pueblo, 1897. (Photo by Ben Wittick, courtesy Museum of New Mexico, neg. 56120.)

At the time the Spaniards arrived at the Pueblo of Hawikuh, the Zuñis had already been living in their valley for three centuries or longer. Hawikuh was itself at least this old, and other Puebloan sites in the region date even further into antiquity. Between A.D. 1000 and 1150, Zuñi area residents were neighbors of some people with close cultural connections to Chaco Canyon, a major Anasazi ceremonial center to the north. Some years ago, archaeologists excavated a Chacoan site called Village of the Great Kivas, only a few miles from Zuñi Pueblo. One of the more impressive ancestral Zuñi sites is Atsinna, which is perched atop Inscription Rock (see p. 321), some forty miles up the Zuñi River Valley. This fortlike pueblo was inhabited between 1275 and 1325.

Strangely, the first person from Europe to lay eyes on the Zuñis was actually North African—a black Moor named Estebanico, who had been the slave of Spanish explorers shipwrecked off the coast of Texas. Estebanico and his masters wandered for years across the southern Southwest, where they heard stories of a great Pueblo culture to the north. When they reached Mexico City, part of their story reinforced an old legend about gold-laden cities in a land called "Cibola." The account of a populated northern territory (New Mexico) stimulated plans to find the wealth of Cibola.

An expedition was organized in 1539, with Estebanico as its guide and Fray Marcos de Niza as its leader. After an arduous journey, the explorers arrived at the edge of Pueblo country and Estebanico, traveling in advance of the main party with his own native guides, entered the first Pueblo town, Hawikuh. It was a short-lived visit; in some way, the Moor offended the Zuñis and they killed him. Intimidated, Marcos returned to Mexico City, where he fabricated a tale about the Zuñis that further fueled the Cibola rumors. As a result, in 1540 the Zuñis met their first *conquistador*, Francisco Vázquez de Coronado.

For reasons that remain unclear, Coronado stormed Hawikuh and killed twenty of its defenders. The Spaniards said that the Zuñis acted hostile and denied them entrance to the town. Some Zuñis believe, however, that the foreigners interrupted a four-day religious ceremony, when the village was closed to outsiders. To convey this, they drew a line of cornmeal on the ground, which the Spaniards were forbidden to cross until the ritual was completed. Did the Spaniards not understand this message, or did they simply ignore it? Probably, we will never know.

During the Spaniards' four-month stay at Hawikuh, the Zuñis offered no more resistance and the invaders went to other villages unopposed. Coronado's chronicler wrote that at Hawikuh the Spaniards "found what we needed more than gold and silver, and that was much corn and beans and turkeys." Still, the "little crowded village," whose alleyways were not paved with precious metals, was a bitter disappointment to them and they eventually traveled to the Rio Grande Valley.

The Zuñis' experience of 1540 initiated a diplomatic policy that served the tribe well later: to be cordial and cooperative to Europeans and to avoid further fighting. Subsequent Spanish expeditionary leaders—Espejo, Oñate, and Vargas, for example—reported on the tribe's friendliness. So too did later Mexican and American officials. In addition to their diplomatic talent, the Zuñis had a geographical advantage, being located far from the center of Spanish colonial power. This distance buffered them against outside interference and helped them keep a measure of sovereignty. Even their participation in the Pueblo revolt (1680) was minimal.

By the end of the tumultuous Pueblo revolt period in 1696, Zuñi population had declined and the Indians had deserted all but one of their pueblos, Halona. This consolidation was advantageous in fighting a new adversary, Apaches, whose raiding parties plundered their stores of corn and stole their horses. When enemies appeared—Spanish or Indian—the Zuñis, like their Anasazi ancestors, often withdrew to a place of relative safety. When Diego de Vargas reconquered New Mexico, beginning in 1692, their refuge was a pueblo on top of Dowa Yalanne (Corn Mountain), the sheer-sided mesa just southeast of town. Although relatively safe from attack, food and water had to be carried up from the valley below.

When Vargas arrived, he persuaded the Zuñi elders to let him and his two armed companies climb up Dowa Yalanne to address the people. The pueblo consisted of three multistoried, multiroomed apartments surrounding a plaza. After hearing Vargas's presentation, the Zuñis agreed to leave their refuge and return to Halona.

If Europeans bothered the Zuñis less than they did the Pueblos of the Rio Grande, Apaches and Navajos often made up for it. The Zuñis were made vulnerable by their isolation, and their herds of sheep were an enticement to these raiders. To deal with the problem, they pursued a strategy of good village defense, occasional military forays into enemy territory to regain losses, and alliances with Spaniards, Mexicans, and Americans. In 1805, for example, Zuñi warriors joined a Spanish expedition against the Navajo stronghold in Canyon de Chelly, and after 1846 their alliance with the United States helped the Anglo-Americans gain a foothold in the Southwest. New army posts, such as Fort Wingate and Fort Defiance, sometimes turned to the Zuñis for supplies of corn. Unlike many United States officials, who did not comprehend Navajo political organization, the Zuñis always distinguished between friendly and hostile Navajo bands and conducted their relations accordingly. After the return of the Navajos in 1868 from their internment at Fort Sumner (p. 258), the Zuñis even allowed one band to settle on Zuñi land in the vicinity of Ramah, New Mexico. Their descendants still live there today.

The advantage of geographical isolation vanished with the arrival of the railroad in the mid-1880s. The railroad brought in Anglo-American settlers, ranchers, and developers who coveted Zuñi land, including traditional grazing areas and water holes, for their own use. This new invasion actually threatened Zuñi life and culture more than any other in their history, except for the introduction of European diseases. As the newcomers began to appropriate Zuñi land, antagonisms sprang up, and conflicts sometimes had to be settled by U.S. troops from Fort Wingate. In addition, disagreements among the Zuñis themselves about how to deal with the Americans gave rise to internal factionalism.

Interior of a Zuñi house, c. 1890. (Photo by Ben Wittick, courtesy School of American Research collections in the Museum of New Mexico, neg. 5047.)

One important Zuñi statesman in the mid-nineteenth century was Pedro Pino, or Lai-iu-ah-tsai-lu, who traveled to the East with other tribal elders and was impressed by the potential changes that Anglo-American culture could foster. But others preferred to cling to long-held customs. In 1877, the United States established a tribal reservation, a move that opened up much traditional Zuñi land to cattle ranchers. It took another two generations before all the Zuñi people were forced onto the designated reservation. The 1880s and 1890s saw a diminishing Zuñi resource base and dwindling self-sufficiency. In addition, repressive measures were taken against the Zuñi Priests of the Bow, the traditional governing arm of the tribe, thereby weakening their influence. Economic decline, then, was compounded by political disunity, and when, in 1898–99, a final crippling smallpox epidemic struck, Zuñi's fortunes reached a nadir.

Threshing wheat on the Zuñi reservation, c. 1935. (Photo by Mullarky, courtesy Museum of New Mexico, neg. 74903.)

In the twentieth century, although the tribal council gained strength as the pueblo's governing body, various divisive issues, often involving religious versus secular viewpoints, spawned more factionalism among the leadership. One dispute revolved around the proposed reestablishment of a Roman Catholic mission at the pueblo, and another concerned freedoms to be allowed anthropologists. This latter topic was of particular concern as a result of the controversial work done here by Frank H. Cushing in the 1880s. Eventually, the factions developed into political parties, and tribal council members were elected by popular vote. After 1965, even Zuñi women were able to enter voting booths.

Over the years, Zuñi leaders persistently protested encroachments by whites and Navajos on their territory and requested the government to return illegally seized tribal land. Much of the grazing areas long used by the Indians, for example, lay outside their designated reservation, the actual boundaries of which had never been clearly marked. For many years, their efforts came to naught, for no legal means existed to pursue land claims; still, Zuñi leaders pressed their case. Finally, in 1978, after a century of land-claim agitation, the tribe achieved a measure of success in the passage of a federal bill to return tribal land surrounding Zuñi Salt Lake.

In the last several decades, the making of silver jewelry has produced considerable income for the Zuñis, and as on other reservations, federal grant projects have brought both jobs and revenue to the tribe. Schools, new housing, paved roads, and a variety of community services have projected Zuñi Pueblo into modern times. Their population has grown from a onetime low of fifteen hundred to over six thousand. The Zuñis' collective strength has not only seen the tribe through historical difficulties, but also has helped it preserve many cultural, religious, and linguistic traditions. Today, the tribe runs an active archaeological program and is considering developing the site of Hawikuh as a public monument.

Hawikuh was partially excavated between 1917 and 1923 by archaeologist Frederick Webb Hodge, with support from George Heye, founder of the Museum of the American Indian in New York City. Hodge dated the ruins to the early 1200s; however, underlying strata, which he did not penetrate, may well date to an even earlier period. If you go to this hilltop site today, you will see the remains of the Franciscan mission and a cluster of rubble mounds with a broad view over the surrounding countryside. For permission to visit ruins on the Zuñi reservation, call the Zuñi Tribal Office at (505) 782-4481.

As most of Zuñi consists of modern ranch-style homes, you will best be able to sense the community's history by strolling through the old pueblo. The old Catholic mission, dedicated to Our Lady of Guadalupe, was rebuilt and renovated in 1969 and contains a unique set of murals depicting events in the Zuñi ceremonial calendar.

TIPS FOR THE TRAVELER:
You will certainly enjoy stopping to see Inscription Rock at El Morro National Monument, thirty miles east along New Mexico 53. In addition, Chaco Culture National Historical Park, south of Farmington, is a place of special interest. At Zuñi, you will find cafés, gas stations, a market, and a public campground. Gallup and Grants have more travel services.

SUGGESTED READING:
"A Brief History of the Zuñi Nation," by E. Richard Hart, *Zuñi and El Morro: Past and Present,* edited by David Grant Noble (Santa Fe: Ancient City Press, 1993).
Cushing at Zuni: The Correspondence and Journals of Frank Hamilton Cushing, 1879–1884, edited by Jesse Green (Albuquerque: University of New Mexico Press, 1990).

THE APACHEANS

Many centuries before Europeans set foot in the Americas, groups of Apachean people began migrating south from the Mackenzie Basin in northern Canada, homeland of the Athapascans. While archaeological evidence regarding the prehistory of these people is scant, scholars believe they began their migration around A.D. 1000, possibly following a route down the eastern flank of the Rocky Mountains. Linguistic studies show that contemporary Apachean languages had begun to diverge from a common mother tongue around A.D. 1300, a time period when separate Apachean tribes probably began to form.

The earliest historical mention of Apaches in the Southwest appears in the sixteenth-century accounts by Spanish explorers. In 1540–41, Pueblo Indians told members of Coronado's army about *Querechos*, nomadic hunters on the eastern plains. The Pueblos said some *Querechos* had attacked certain of their villages around 1515. By the time of their arrival in the Southwest, the Apaches had separated into a number of tribes with distinct dialects, customs, and ranges. The Jicarillas roamed what is now northeastern New Mexico; Mescalero territory was further to the south; and the Chiricahuas lived in the mountainous region of present-day southwestern New Mexico and southeastern Arizona.

One tribe, whom the Spaniards called *Apaches de Nabajo*, had begun to practice farming as they moved into lands north and west of the agricultural Pueblos. The word *nabajo*, indeed, is thought to be derived from a Tewa term meaning "open spaces in which to plant crops." The earliest-known Navajo sites in the Southwest (now beneath the waters of Navajo Reservoir) are along the San Juan River, close to the present Colorado–New Mexico border. The *Diné*, as the Navajos identify themselves, later expanded into the Largo and Gobernador drainages, which flow into the San Juan, and still later, into what is now Arizona.

In their search to find seeds, nuts, fruits, tubers, and game, the Apaches followed a seasonal round of hunting and gathering over a wide territory. As they traveled, they would hunt buffalo on the plains, collect ripening cactus fruits in the desert, and gather medicinal plants in the mountains. When the Comanches moved down from the Great Plains in the early 1700s, they pushed the Jicarillas west into the mountains and put pressure on the Mescaleros as well. These demographic

Mescalero Apaches in line for rations on their reservation. (Courtesy Rio Grande Historical
Collections.)

changes had a major impact on Spanish colonization in New Mexico.

An integral part of the Apachean culture and economy was raiding
and warfare. Raids, conducted in stealth with the aim of acquiring
horses or other booty, usually did not result in enemy casualties. Warfare, on the other hand, was motivated by a desire to avenge enemy
attacks on one's own tribe, and killing or kidnapping were common
outcomes. To kill an enemy brought merit to an Apache warrior.

In the eyes of European Americans, the Apachean raiding and warfare complex amounted to no more than thievery and savagery, and en-
gendered strong prejudices against the tribes. In addition, the fact that
the nomads did not till the soil or live in permanent villages confirmed
biases that they were of an inferior order of humanity. To just wander
about, gathering wild plants and living in temporary shelters, was
deemed uncivilized, or, in Spanish terms, *bárbaros*.

While the Pueblo farmers were issued formal land grants by Spain
in the late 1600s, the Navajos and Apaches were not given reservations
until after the Civil War. By this time, the buffalo had been decimated,
and ranching, mining, and logging operations had encroached on traditional tribal territory. Poverty, famine, and disease were inevitable

consequences of such circumstances, and the former nomads depended on handouts from the U.S. government to survive. Even in the early twentieth century, tuberculosis was so rampant among the Jicarillas that 90 percent of school-age children were infected.

Many Navajo and Apache communities still live in relative isolation from the dominant Anglo-American society, a factor that has helped them to retain traditional values and customs. However, economic activities from the outside world, such as ranching, coal mining, oil and gas extraction, recreation and tourism, and government are now significant industries on most reservations. Even gambling is making inroads.

The present reservations of the Apaches and Navajos, of course, are not themselves historic sites in the same sense as the other places described in this book; they are included because their native inhabitants are historic peoples who have lived in the Southwest for many centuries and played a major role in its development. As you meet members of these tribes and travel over their lands, it is valuable to have as much understanding as possible about their history and culture.

SUGGESTED READING:

Handbook of North American Indians, vol. 10, edited by Alfonso Ortiz (Washington, D.C.: Smithsonian Institution, 1983).

Navajo Wars: Military Campaigns, Slave Raids, and Reprisals, by Frank McNitt (reprinted; Albuquerque: University of New Mexico Press, 1990).

THE JICARILLA APACHES

The Jicarilla Apaches live on a reservation in north-central New Mexico. From Chama, follow U.S. 64 west for twenty-six miles to Dulce, the main town and headquarters of the tribal government.

The Jicarilla Apaches were among numerous bands of Athapascan-speaking hunters and gatherers who migrated into the Southwest sometime prior to the first Spanish *entrada.* How long they had been here when members of Coronado's expedition reported the existence of "*Querechos*" (wandering people) in 1540–41 is uncertain, but probably a century or longer.

Modern Americans often mistakenly believe that European colonization of North America disrupted a patchwork of fixed tribal territories that had been stable for centuries. However, for millennia before the coming of Europeans, America's indigenous peoples had generated their own dynamic of migration and shifting territories. As our meager knowledge of Jicarilla history illustrates, this dynamic continued well into historic times.

In the seventeenth century, the Jicarillas ranged over a territory that centered in the plains of northeastern New Mexico and extended into the southern slopes of the Rockies. They used these diverse environments seasonally to gather the natural resources needed to feed themselves and make their clothing and implements. Buffalo, of course, were the main attraction of the plains and were the tribe's major source of protein.

When the Jicarilla moved from the open plains to the foothills and mountains of southern Colorado and northern New Mexico, they hunted different game—mountain sheep, deer, elk, and rabbits—and gathered a variety of seeds, nuts, fruits, tubers, and herbs. In addition, they traded buffalo hides with the Spaniards and Pueblos, with whom they usually enjoyed peaceful relations.

By the early 1700s, a new factor disrupted traditional Jicarilla patterns: the migration of Comanches to the southern plains. This powerful tribe, armed with guns acquired from the French to the east, put pressure on the various roaming bands of Apaches. The Jicarillas became more restricted to the mountain ranges, where they frequented traditional camping grounds near present-day Cimarron (p. 151), Taos (p. 208), and Picuris (p. 48). Northern New Mexico's mountain country was only sparsely populated by Hispanics and Pueblo Indians, and contained a wealth of resources. However, the Jicarillas still ventured out to the plains, albeit now with caution.

Through their contacts with the Pueblos, the Jicarillas began to practice limited farming and to live in *rancherías,* semipermanent communities near arable fields. Hunting and gathering, however, remained the basis of their economy. On occasion, the Jicarillas were recruited by the Spaniards to guide military campaigns deep into Comanche territory. These nomads continued to raid northern New Mexico pueblos, *rancherías,* and villages at will until they were defeated in 1776 by Governor Juan Bautista de Anza and combined Pueblo and Hispanic forces.

The 1800s brought changes that seriously affected the Jicarillas and their way of life. New Mexican citizens were issued land grants in the heart of their territory; one of these, the controversial Maxwell Land Grant, eventually covered over a million acres. After 1848, settlers from the United States began moving onto traditional Jicarilla lands, establishing cattle and sheep ranches, mining minerals, and developing com-

James Garfield Velarde, Chief of the Jicarillas, c. 1904. (Photo by Edward S. Curtis, courtesy Museum of New Mexico, neg. 71230.)

mercial roads and other ventures, all of which were incompatible with the Jicarillas' way of life.

In 1849, as Kit Carson recorded in his autobiography, "[Lucien B.] Maxwell and I concluded to make a settlement on the Rayado. We had been leading a roving life long enough and now was the time, if ever, to make a home for ourselves and our children." The two established a ranching operation in the Rayado valley, which was deep in the Jicarillas' home country, and in a year's time, they had brought in dozens of Hispanic families, were cutting timber, raising sheep, horses, and mules, and selling hay to the government. For a year or two, army troops stationed at the Rayado ranch chased Apaches whenever their elusive bands could be located. The Jicarillas, in turn, attacked whites and ran off livestock whenever possible. By 1850, the Jicarillas were unable to hunt and forage freely and faced starvation. They had become trespassers on their own land. Darkening their prospects for survival were U.S. troops at Fort Union (p. 264), near Cimarron, and Fort Burgwin (p. 232), near Taos.

For several decades, United States policy toward the Jicarillas was confusing and contradictory. A peace treaty, made in 1851 with Francisco Chacón and other headmen resulted in the army starting an agricultural program for the Indians near Abiquiu; however, funding for it was soon cut off and the embittered Indians had to fend for themselves. In March of 1854, they clashed with a troop of dragoons from Fort Burgwin, dealing a humiliating defeat to the Americans. After that, they were kept on the run, with many camping in the upper Chama Valley near present-day Tierra Amarilla (p. 213).

In the mid-1870s, New Mexico's Indians all had reservations save the Jicarillas, who remained landless; then, in 1883, they were removed far from their homeland to live with the Mescaleros (p. 120) in the Sierra Blanca. Finally, in 1887, the government gave the Jicarillas their own reservation in north-central New Mexico. Even though the soil was poor and the growing season too short for farming, it was a place to live.

The Jicarillas initially gained some revenue through timber sales; then, in 1907, a southern addition to the reservation allowed them to begin cattle ranching. Still, they suffered greatly from poverty, malnutrition, and diseases. The worse scourge was tuberculosis, which infected 90 percent of boarding-school children in 1921 and caused an alarming decline in population. In 1925, there were only 625 Jicarilla Indians.

From this low point in their history, conditions among the Jicarilla began slowly to ameliorate. The reservation's faltering educational program was contracted to the Dutch Reformed Church of America; health services were put in place; and a sheep-ranching business began to prosper. After passage of the Indian Reorganization Act in 1934, the tribe adopted a constitution and began to govern its own affairs through elected representatives. By 1940, the tuberculosis sanitarium in Dulce was able to close its doors.

In the 1950s, tribal revenues rose dramatically through income from oil and gas leases, and various other small business ventures began to contribute to the Jicarillas' economy. In 1970, the tribe received more than eight million dollars from the United States in compensation for the approximately nine million acres of land they had lost use of over a century earlier.

The spread-out town of Dulce forms the Jicarillas' main community and the center for social services, schools, churches, tribal police, and various government agencies. The Jicarilla Inn provides lodgings and a restaurant, and the Jicarilla Arts and Crafts Museum offers impressive displays of hand-woven baskets and beadwork, some of which are for sale. The inn is located at the main intersection in town; and the museum is found along the north side of the highway, about three blocks to the west.

Dulce is not a tourist center; however, the hunting and fishing is excellent on the 850,000-acre reservation, and there are opportunities to take scenic hikes, to go camping, and to visit Anasazi Indian ruins. Further information on these activities can be obtained by calling the Jicarilla Inn at (505) 759-3663, or Jicarilla Natural Resources at (505) 759-3255. The tribe holds two annual public festivals: the Little Beaver Roundup, which includes a parade, rodeo, and public dances, is held over a weekend in mid-July; and on September 15, footraces take place between the two Jicarilla clans.

TIPS FOR THE TRAVELER:
The historic narrow-gauge Cumbres & Toltec Scenic Railroad (p. 300) runs from nearby Chama to Antonito, Colorado. In the Chama Valley, you can also tour a group of Hispanic villages surrounding Tierra Amarilla and visit Tierra Wools in Los Ojos, where traditional textiles are woven by local artisans. If you are driving west from Dulce, you may be interested in visiting the ancient Indian ruins at Aztec National Monument in Aztec.

SUGGESTED READING:
The Jicarilla Apache Tribe: a History, by Veronica E. Velarde Tiller, (Lincoln: University of Nebraska Press, 1992).

THE MESCALERO APACHES

The Mescalero Apache reservation is located in the Sacramento Mountains of south-central New Mexico, between Ruidoso and Cloudcroft. From Ruidoso, follow U.S. 70 south to the town of Mescalero.

Among the most scenic areas of New Mexico are the Sacramento Mountains with the majestic Sierra Blanca, which rises to twelve thousand feet and looks out over the brilliant white sands of the Tularosa Valley. In this high country lies the 1,278-square-mile reservation of the Mescalero Apaches.

Mescalero Apache culture differed sharply from that of the Pueblo farmers, whose tightly built pueblos dotted the banks of the Rio Grande and its major tributaries. Relying originally on hunting and gathering for their subsistence, the Mescaleros were a nomadic people, organized in bands led by a chieftain. The men hunted buffalo, which roamed the southern plains in vast herds, and smaller game such as deer, antelope, and cottontail rabbits. The women gathered the wide array of seeds, nuts, and fruits that ripened seasonally in the deserts, plains, mountains, and river valleys throughout their territory. One important staple of the Mescaleros was the agave, or *mescal,* plant, whose large crowns were dug up and roasted in pits, then feasted upon or dried for later consumption. The tribe's name derives from the people's use of this plant.

Mescalero territory lay between the Rio Pecos and Rio Grande, on the east and west, and extended far south into Coahuila and Chihuahua, Mexico. Buffalo-hunting parties ranged eastward into the Texas Panhandle. The Indians were at home in virtually every southwestern environment, making their summer camps in the mountains and moving into warmer desert climes in winter.

In the seventeenth century, as Spaniards migrated up from Mexico, the Apaches came into possession of horses, which greatly facilitated their nomadic life-style and practice of raiding and warfare. Raiding, in fact, became a significant part of their culture and economy. Requiring skill and courage, this activity could bring accolades and status to successful warriors. In the mid-1600s, the Mescaleros repeatedly raided Pueblo and Spanish settlements in the Salinas Basin and Middle Rio Grande Valley. The Indians also struck settlements in Mexico, with their main objective the acquisition of horses, booty, and occasionally captives. The Spaniards, in turn, raided the Indians, also seizing captives, whom they transported south to labor in silver mines or become house-

Mescalero Apache camp in winter, c. 1915. (Courtesy Museum of New Mexico neg. 21553.)

hold servants. Although the Mescaleros traded with the Pueblos and Spanish, particularly at Pecos (p. 42) and Gran Quivira (p. 55), an intermittent state of warfare existed between them throughout the colonial period.

In the eighteenth century, the Mescaleros and other Eastern Apache tribes became caught in a squeeze between a newly arrived aggressive tribe from the northeast, the Comanches, and the Spaniards and Pueblos along the Rio Grande. Even their heartland on the slopes of the Sierra Blanca came under attack by the fierce newcomers. In reaction, the Mescaleros intensified their own raids on Spanish settlements to the west and down the Camino Real (p. 293) into Mexico, even establishing a base in the Organ Mountains (near present-day Las Cruces), from which they raided weakly defended caravans crossing the Jornada del Muerto.

After Texas joined the Union in 1845 and the United States took possession of New Mexico in 1848, the Mescaleros found themselves confronting a better-organized, better-equipped foe than ever before. In addition, their lands came under pressure from cattle ranchers and miners. Although they enjoyed a brief respite at the outbreak of the Civil War, the tribe was soon overwhelmed by U.S. Army units commanded by Kit Carson.

Chief San Juan with followers, c. 1883. (Photo by Edwin A. Bass, courtesy Museum of New Mexico, neg. 90634.)

General James H. Carleton ordered the Mescaleros, who numbered about 450, interned on a newly established reservation at Bosque Redondo (p. 258). Members of the tribe initially worked on the construction of Fort Sumner at the Bosque. When thousands of Navajos were later interned here and the army was unable to provide adequate food, clothing, or living quarters, the Mescaleros began to suffer and die. To make matters worse, Carleton's agricultural program also failed. Finally, the Mescaleros fled, returning to their home country in the Sierra Blanca. The federal government then established an agency at Fort Stanton (p. 254) to deal with them.

The Mescaleros' present reservation was established in 1872, when, by executive order, President Ulysses S. Grant set aside land for use by the tribe. Although now living in their homeland, they experienced a new series of misfortunes: epidemics and malnutrition; the extermination of the southern buffalo herd; land losses to outsiders; settlement of other Apache tribes on their limited reservation; and the imposition of Anglo-American education and religion on their children. Underlying specific problems was the trauma, experienced by so many Native American tribes, of a lost way of life and an eroded culture. For many years, their reservation could have been taken away by presidential decree, and as late as 1912, legislative efforts were ongoing to convert their land into a public park. Happily, in 1922, Congress confirmed the tribe's title to its reservation.

In 1883, American authorities ordered the Jicarilla Apaches (p. 115) to move from their northern lands to the Mescalero reservation. The Jicarillas stayed here until 1886–87, when the government allotted them a reservation of their own in northern New Mexico. Fifteen years later, the Lipan Apaches were ordered to join the Mescaleros, and in 1913, when the Chiricahuas were freed from their prisoner-of-war status, the majority of that tribe moved to Whitetail, on the Mescalero reservation. Over subsequent generations, the three groups have intermarried and merged culturally. Although individuals and families are aware of their original tribal affiliations, they all joined the dominant Mescalero tribe.

The twentieth century has seen many improvements in the status and condition of the Mescaleros as well as the emergence of a new tribal economy. Gaining title to their reservation was a landmark that allowed the tribe to invest in various economic enterprises such as cattle raising, logging, recreation, and tourism. The Inn of the Mountain Gods, for example, is a tribally owned luxury resort with a golf course and artificial lake, and the Ski Apache area draws people from many miles around. Under the long leadership of chairman Wendell Chino, the tribe has developed an increasingly stable economy. In addition, major improvements in diet and health services have brought about a steady increase of population, which stood at around twenty-five hundred in 1850, dropped to under five hundred by 1888, and now numbers over three thousand people.

Mescalero culture today combines native values and customs with elements from the surrounding non-Indian society. You may visit a small Mescalero cultural center and museum adjacent to the tribal offices in Mescalero. If you would like to learn more about Apache customs, you may attend parts of the girls' Coming of Age Ceremony, a four-day annual event that takes place over the Fourth of July weekend. This sacred ceremony marks the initiation of Apache girls into womanhood.

Navajo horsemen, c. 1920. (Photo by J. R. Willis, courtesy Museum of New Mexico, neg. 98187.)

Recreational opportunities on the Mescalero reservation include skiing, fishing, hunting, camping, hiking, and staying at the Inn of the Mountain Gods (call 1-800-545-9011). If you are a Billy the Kid aficionado, you will be interested to know that the site of Blazer's Mills—where the famous shoot-out between Bonney's Regulators and Buckshot Rogers took place on April 4, 1878—lies one mile east of Mescalero in the Tularosa River Canyon. An adobe ruin along the highway marks the spot.

TIPS FOR THE TRAVELER:
The historic town of Lincoln (p. 166), now a state monument, also focuses on Lincoln County War history and the Kid. The once rowdy mining town of White Oaks is another place where this outlaw hung out. A place where the Mescaleros once lived and fought numerous battles with the U.S. cavalry is Dog Canyon. It is part of Dog Canyon–Oliver Lee Memorial State Park, located south of Alamogordo. The park has a visitor center with historical exhibits and interpretive and hiking trails. For further information, call (505) 437-8284. Other places of more modern historical interest in the Alamogordo area are the Trinity Site (p. 279), and the Space Center.

SUGGESTED READING:
The Mescalero Apaches, by C. L. Sonnichsen (Norman: University of Oklahoma Press, 1958).

THE NAVAJOS

The Navajos live on the largest Indian reservation in the country, covering a block of northwestern New Mexico, much of eastern Arizona, and a small segment of southern Utah. The capital of the Navajo Nation is in Window Rock, Arizona.

There is a region in northwestern New Mexico, concentrated around the tributaries of the San Juan River northeast of Farmington, that Navajos call the *Dinetah* ("among the People"). Here are found the remains of forked-stick hogans, the earliest Navajo dwelling sites in the Southwest. In 1582, the explorer Antonio de Espejo encountered Navajos near Mount Taylor, at the southern edge of this region, and later Spanish observers described them as a semisedentary people who lived by hunting and gathering, cultivating corn, and trading with the Pueblos. Although the Navajos have long since moved away from the original *Dinetah,* they still regard the region as a sacred ancient homeland.

After they moved into the Southwest, the Navajos had many contacts with the Pueblos, a factor that probably contributed to their early adoption of agriculture. Historically, they had fluctuating relations with their Puebloan neighbors; whether they traded peaceably with them or raided their villages probably reflected their changing needs. In the 1600s, Navajo raids on northern Rio Grande Pueblo and Spanish villages were common, but during the Pueblo-Spanish wars many Pueblos found refuge among the Navajos in the labyrinthine canyons of the *Dinetah,* and the two groups collaborated in defense. They lived in harmony, shared their cultures, and sometimes intermarried.

The Navajos eventually moved away from the constrictive environment of the *Dinetah,* and by 1800 they had settled western lands all the way to the Colorado and Little Colorado rivers.

Over the same period, Spanish colonists were expanding westward from the Rio Grande Valley, encroaching on traditional Navajo territory. In the conflicts that ensued, many Hispanic settlers were driven back. Later, however, when American rifles became available through trade over the Santa Fe Trail, warfare between New Mexicans and Navajos intensified. Of even more concern to the Navajos than retention of their lands was the protection of their women and children, many of whom were taken captive and sold into a life of servitude in New Mexico.

After 1846, the Navajos also had to deal with the United States army, whose commander, General Stephen W. Kearny, had promised to protect New Mexicans from the depredations of the nomadic tribes.

The Americans also knew that the Navajos' territory would soon be needed for ranching, mining, and the development of transcontinental travel.

Beginning in 1846, the U.S. government negotiated treaties with the headmen of various Navajo bands, but these were seldom honored by either side. In 1851, the tribe found itself confronted by a new military post, Fort Defiance, located in its very heartland. In addition, a series of unfortunate incidents occurred that damaged any hopes for mutual trust between the opposing sides. Into this unstable situation in 1862 stepped Brigadier General James H. Carleton, commander of a column of California volunteers who had expected to defend New Mexico from Confederate invaders. Arriving too late for that purpose, he placed New Mexico under martial law and turned his attention to the pacification of the Navajos and Apaches.

Carleton pressured a reluctant Kit Carson to head a military campaign to pacify these independent tribes and place them on a new reservation at Bosque Redondo (see p. 258) on New Mexico's eastern plains. Using New Mexican irregulars, Carson began the Navajo roundup in late 1863. In January of the following year, he set out for Canyon de Chelly, a Navajo stronghold, where he pursued a scorched-earth policy that gave the Navajos two options: surrender or starve. Throughout that winter, droves of starving Navajos straggled into Fort Canby and Fort Wingate (p. 267), where they were treated as prisoners of war. In February, the first contingent began their Long Walk to Fort Sumner, to be followed by twenty-five hundred more in March, and more still as time went on. An estimated two thousand, who fled west to take refuge in remote canyons, remained free.

Many Navajos had perished before the Long Walk began, and more died along the four-hundred-mile trek or were shot or kidnapped by Ute and Hispanic pursuers as they straggled behind the column. Conditions at Bosque Redondo were atrocious and the dying continued. It was General Carleton's zealously held belief that the Bosque Redondo would be a "spacious tribal reformatory" where the "old Indians will die off and carry with them all latent longings for murdering and robbing," while a new generation of Navajos would learn the benefits of Western civilization and "become a happy and content people." Instead, his experiment became a subject of national controversy and scandal, certainly not an experience to inspire the Indians to adopt Anglo-American ways.

The Bosque Redondo ordeal ended in 1868, after their spokesman, Barboncito, negotiated a new treaty with U.S. representatives General William T. Sherman and Colonel Samuel F. Tappan. There were many

Barboncito. (Courtesy Smithsonian National Anthropological Archives.)

stipulations in the agreement, but key among them, at least for the present, was an end to war between the two sides and a return of the Navajos to their home country. For the Navajos, this was cause for great rejoicing. The journey home began in June and, as Manuelito expressed it, when they saw the familiar landscape of home, "we felt like talking to the ground, we loved it so."

After 1868, the Navajos entered a new era in their history. The Bosque Redondo experience had forged a collection of separate bands

Navajo home. (Courtesy Museum of New Mexico, neg. 44177.)

into a unified nation, and a series of land additions eventually much extended the limits of their reservation in a region that was still mostly uninhabited by whites. The challenge now was to rebuild a shattered society in a way that would perpetuate deep cultural traditions while adapting to the demands of the surrounding Anglo-American world. On the one hand, the Navajos had to accept Christian missionaries and boarding schools for their children and allow railroads and highways to cross their sacred lands. On the other, they had to develop a new centralized system of self-governance that would allow the nation to regain strength and sovereignty and recover a sense of cultural pride. This, too, would be a long journey.

By the 1930s, the original reservation had more than quadrupled in size and the tribe's population had risen from around ten thousand after Bosque Redondo to forty-two thousand. The fifteen thousand sheep and goats received in the 1868 treaty multiplied to well over a million, generating healthy wool exports but resulting in such environmental degradation that the government instituted a drastic and controversial livestock-reduction program.

As the twentieth century progresses, hunting and gathering have declined, but sheep herding, cattle raising, and farming continue to play a part in the economy of Navajo families, and craft arts, especially jewelry making and rug weaving, help to communicate Navajo culture far beyond the borders of the reservation. Other types of employment have become available through enterprises brought in from the outside world: ranching, mining, logging, energy extraction, electrical generating plants, and government agencies. Still, despite these examples of economic progress, unemployment on the reservation has remained consistently high.

In 1992, a group of distinguished Navajo patriots celebrated their fiftieth anniversary. They were the survivors of the approximately four hundred Code Talkers of World War II. These soldiers, who participated in every major assault in the Pacific, from Guadalcanal in 1942 to Okinawa in 1945, contributed an invaluable service by transmitting radio messages in the Navajo language, a "code" the Japanese never deciphered.

The author has a Navajo acquaintance who makes his living as a computer programmer but dedicates much of his life to studying to be a medicine man. In Navajo country, you will meet many people involved in both traditional Navajo culture and the modern "non-Indian" world; they will help introduce you to their heritage.

TIPS FOR THE TRAVELER:

Navajoland is a region of varied and ever-changing beauty. As you travel here, view it as the sacred land that has nurtured a people with a rich cultural history. Across its deserts and mountains and through its canyons, there are many places of historical significance, most known only to the Navajos themselves. As most reservation land is allotted to private families, you will need permission or a tribal permit and perhaps a native guide before exploring. Some sites, however, are public; you can stroll around old Fort Wingate, where the People stayed before and after the Long Walk, or explore the *Dinetah,* with its fortlike ruins from the Pueblo refugee period. Here, you will need a topographical map, and a four-wheel-drive vehicle is recommended. For further information, call the Bureau of Land Management in Farmington at (505) 761-4504 or 327-5344.

In Arizona, you can visit the Navajo Tribal Museum in Window Rock and Hubbell's Trading Post in Ganado. You can also take guided tours of Canyon de Chelly in Chinle and Monument Valley near Kayenta, where Navajo families have long lived and the Anasazi before them.

SUGGESTED READING:

A History of the Navajos: The Reservation Years, by Garrick Bailey and Roberta Glenn Bailey (Santa Fe: School of American Research Press, 1986).

Chiefs, Agents, and Soldiers: Conflict on the Navajo Frontier, 1868–1882, by William Haas Moore (Albuquerque: University of New Mexico Press, 1994)

NEW MEXICAN TOWNS

New Mexico's first villages were built in the hilly southwestern corner of the state by Mogollon Indians more than fifteen hundred years ago. Mogollon communities usually were composed of a cluster of separate, semisubterranean dwellings with earth-covered wood roofs. A thousand years later, when Europeans arrived in New Mexico, they found Pueblo Indians along the Rio Grande and its tributaries living in villages consisting of multistoried communal houses built of adobe or stone and wood. Taos Pueblo (see p. 89) today gives some idea of how the larger of these communities might have looked.

During the first colonial period (1598–1680), Hispanic settlers were influenced by the construction methods and village layouts of the Pueblos. Two early expeditions even appropriated entire pueblos to live in. But the newcomers also brought their own architectural traditions with them from Spain. The use of stone, adobe, and wood was common to both traditions, as was a need to design villages to be secure from outside attack.

If history and culture influenced the style of colonial towns, so too did the natural environment. The basic building material of houses, for example, was the earth itself, and settlements needed to be near a source of water. The Pueblos typically mixed clay soil and water to make adobe and coursed it by hand on house walls. The Spanish chose to make sun-dried bricks, which were handy to carry, at least for short distances. They found that adobe had numerous advantages as a building material. Massive earthen walls moderated summer's heat, precluded drafts in the region's cold winters, and provided a degree of security against marauding nomadic Indians. You can see a good example of this at Rancho de las Golondrinas (p. 325) in La Cienega.

Following established law, towns on the frontier were designed defensively. Residences and other buildings, usually including the church and a *torreón* (tower), formed a contiguous rectangle around an interior plaza that was entered by a single entranceway. Doors and windows opened to the interior. When raiders threatened, the inhabitants corralled their livestock in the court, closed the gate, and felt some measure of safety. You can still see this layout around the plazas of Santa Fe (p. 89) and Taos (p. 208) and in Chimayo's Plaza del Cerro (p. 148).

Village of Los Ojos in the Chama Valley. (Photo by David Grant Noble.)

Interior court of the Martinez Hacienda in Taos. (Photo by David Grant Noble.)

In the eighteenth century, as the capital grew crowded with new-comers from Mexico, outlying settlements were founded by small groups of colonists, usually under the leadership of one or two prominent citizens. Three such communities were Santa Cruz de la Cañada (p. 184), in the Santa Cruz Valley; Abiquiu (p. 137), on a terrace overlooking the Rio Chama; and San Miguel del Vado (p. 179), along the Rio Pecos. When the limited fields of a village were unable to support its growing population, a group of younger members would split off to found a new satellite community; Chimayo, Cordova, Truchas (p. 218), and Las Trampas (p. 157), for example, were upriver extensions of Santa Cruz.

From the time of New Mexico's settlement (1598) until after it became part of the United States (1846), the main factor determining the character of villages and community life was economic. In a region where the climate is harsh, rainfall unpredictable, and soils poor, it was a challenge just to survive. In order to make a living, fertile lowlands not already belonging to Pueblo Indians soon were claimed by Hispanos, who then petitioned the crown for a land grant.

Spanish land grants for new towns included three types of land. An appropriate area was set aside for the village center, including public lots for a church, plaza, and possibly civic buildings. In addition, families were allotted limited private parcels for their homes and fields. To

Religious procession to the Santuario de Chimayo, c. 1912. (Courtesy Museum of New Mexico, neg. 14379.)

accommodate the irrigation system, these lots ran upgrade from the river. Finally, there were the *ejidos,* or commons, which were an extensive community-use area often composed of woods and meadows. The *ejidos* were a key resource, for here the *vecinos* and their heirs supposedly forever would be able to hunt and fish, to gather wood and medicinal herbs, and to pasture their livestock.

Another central factor in colonial village life was religion. The strong Christian faith of the immigrants from Mexico and Spain, combined with a compelling urge to proselytize, was the foundation on which New Mexico was colonized. Missionary work was heavily subsidized by the crown. Church officials were powerful, even more so at times, than civil authorities. Catholicism's importance in these times is visually evident in the missions of Salinas (p. 55) and the monumental churches at Acoma Pueblo (p. 9), Pecos Pueblo (p. 42), and Las Trampas.

The inhabitants of New Mexico's colonial towns, then, valued a mix of elements: the earth and landscape; a necessary work ethic; cultural traditions from Spain and Native America; and religion. A new factor influenced their fate after the United States took over New Mexico. Most Hispanos had a different attitude toward the land and its use than that of most Anglo-American newcomers. The concept of *ejidos,* for example, so natural and appropriate to one culture, was completely foreign to the other. Anglo-Americans emphasized individual enterprise over communal economic activities and sought opportunities to exploit natural resources rather than share them. The stories of how Hispanic communities lost their commons more than a century ago reveal one way in which Anglo-American culture affected traditional life in New Mexican villages. Indeed, the militant stands taken in recent years by such activists as Reies Tijerina and Amador Flores (p. 215) were borne out of that past experience and prove that history is not dead and buried.

As you travel around New Mexico and visit towns with an Hispanic heritage, remember that history, like beauty, is in the eye of the beholder. Some towns appear to be nearly deserted or in dire economic straits, and they may well be. Others seem to have been overwhelmed by tourism, and they are. But still present in their plazas and buildings, and in the eyes and words of their native inhabitants, is a rich heritage. To understand and appreciate this will enrich your experience in New Mexico.

SUGGESTED READING:

The Spanish-Americans of New Mexico: A Heritage of Pride, by Nancie L. Gonzales (Albuquerque: University of New Mexico Press, 1967).

Hispanic Arts and Ethnohistory in the Southwest, edited by Marta Weigle (Santa Fe: Ancient City Press, 1983).

ABIQUIU

Abiquiu is located along U.S. 84, eighteen miles north of Española. The village plaza is just north of the highway.

Just over two and a half centuries ago, a handful of Spanish families, led by Bartolomé Trujillo, began building their homes along the south bank of the Rio Chama, some forty miles north of Santa Fe. They had chosen a promising village site on a terrace where the river makes a gentle bend on its southeastward course toward the Rio Grande.

Spanish officials sanctioned the new settlement in 1734, and soon thereafter the Bishop of Durango authorized construction of a chapel. At the time, this was New Mexico's northwesternmost outpost, a place

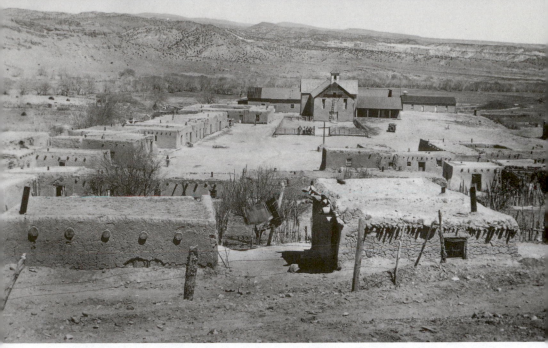

View of Abiquiu as it appeared in the early twentieth century. (Photo by T. Harmon Parkhurst, courtesy Museum of New Mexico, neg. 13698.)

on the fringe of Ute Indian country, where settlers had to depend entirely on their own resources to survive. Even though they did not finish their chapel for another decade, the colonists gave the name of its patron to the community—Santa Rosa de Lima.

In their first years here, the Santa Rosa colonists put all their energies into the challenges of living in what, from their perspective, was a virtual wilderness. In 1747, Comanches killed two among them and abducted twenty-three women and children. Fearful and discouraged, the remaining colonists were granted permission to abandon Santa Rosa until the situation improved. They returned in 1750, bringing with them a group of *genízaros,* former captives of various nomadic tribes who had lived as servants in Spanish families and adopted many aspects of Hispanic culture. In 1754, the *genízaros* moved three miles upriver to found a new village on a higher, more defensible site overlooking the Chama Valley. Here, near the mounds of a long-abandoned Indian pueblo, they built *Santo Tomás de Abiquiu. Abiquiu* probably is a Spanish corruption of the Tewa name for this site.

Ancestors of the Tewa Indians had migrated here from the north over four hundred years before and stayed in the Chama Valley for at least a century, building large adobe and stone villages on the river terraces, where they also cultivated gardens. Shortly before the first Spanish *entrada* (1540–41), they continued down the Chama to the Rio

Grande Valley, where they still reside. The people of Santa Clara and San Juan pueblos are their descendants.

Abiquiu's early settlers were a mixed lot; adventuresome pioneers, who had ventured to the northern frontier from Mexico, soon joined the original *genízaro* grantees. Abiquiu offered an attractive opportunity to the *genízaros*; stuck at the lower echelons of the highly structured Spanish society, they experienced prejudice and economic limitations in a place like Santa Fe. But in Abiquiu, far from the capital, they found new independence. Their needs happened to tie in nicely to the government's wish to establish new settlements to buffer the impact of hostile nomadic tribes.

Abiquiu thrived. By 1760, its *genízaro* population had reached 57 families, or 166 persons, and more than triple this number lived at Santa Rosa de Lima. Abiquiu's *genízaros* followed some customs from their Plains Indian heritage, a factor that occasionally brought them into conflict with Roman Catholic officials. In colonial New Mexico, superstition thrived and witchcraft sometimes served as a handy explanation for unusual, unexplainable, or mysterious occurrences. From the 1760s through the 1780s, charges of sorcery were brought against several Abiquiu *genízaros*. On one occasion, a priest even accused a villager of placing a hex on him, causing stomach-ache symptoms.

In 1776, an exploratory expedition led by Fathers Francisco Atanacio Domínguez and Silvestre Vélez de Escalante spent a day and night in Abiquiu before setting out to find a northern route to the missions of California. Although the friars failed to reach their destination, the fathers trekked more miles than Lewis and Clark and explored vast regions never before seen by Europeans. In his report, Domínguez included an interesting description of Abiquiu:

> Every year, between the end of October and the beginning of November, many heathens of the Ute nation come to the vicinity of this pueblo. They come very well laden with good deerskins, and they celebrate their fair with them. This is held for the sole purpose of buying horses. If one is much to the taste and satisfaction of an Indian (the trial is a good race), he gives fifteen to twenty good deerskins for the horse; and if not, there is no purchase. They also sell deer or buffalo meat for maize or corn flour. Sometimes there are little captive heathen Indians (male or female) as with the Comanches, whom they resemble in the manner of selling them.

Between 1760 and 1793, the population of Abiquiu grew from 733 to 1,363, thereby becoming New Mexico's third largest town after

Santo Tomás church, Abiquiu. (Photo by David Grant Noble.)

Santa Fe and Santa Cruz (p. 184). By the 1820s, it had swelled to over 3,500; by this time, however, the *genízaros* had nearly blended with the general Hispanic population and Mexico's democratic reform laws even prohibited use of the term. In 1846, when the United States invaded New Mexico, Abiquiu's residents perceived their *genízaro* heritage only as a distant ancestry.

In 1829, Antonio Armijo succeeded in blazing a northern route from Abiquiu to the Pacific Coast—the twelve-hundred-mile Spanish Trail. After that, many parties organized and outfitted themselves here before trailing their mule trains north through the Rockies and west across the deserts toward Los Angeles.

In the mid-1800s, the traffic of traders and trappers at Abiquiu equaled that of Taos (see p. 208), and Indians continued to barter their wares in the marketplace. One store was owned by the well-known New Mexico figure, Cerán St. Vrain, an entrepreneur and former mountain man who commanded a company of New Mexico volunteers in the

Mexican War period. For a time, a detachment of U.S. troops rented quarters here in order to patrol the surrounding area in defense against Navajos, Utes, and Jicarilla Apaches (p. 115). In addition, the town was headquarters for a Ute Indian agency and trading post from 1852 to 1873.

Abiquiu's glory days began to fade as other towns replaced it as major trading centers and new routes, capable of carrying wagon traffic, were blazed to California. As the world began to pass Abiquiu by, the town's formerly quiet, pastoral character returned.

Today, Abiquiu is probably best known as the home of the late American painter Georgia O'Keeffe, who lived for many years in the beautiful José María Chávez house overlooking the Chama Valley. Another distinguished New Mexico figure with Abiquiu roots is Padre Antonio José Martinez, who was born here in 1793 and briefly served its parish before moving to Taos, where he gained renown as a priest, educator, and champion of his people.

Although the homes surrounding Abiquiu's plaza today are much modernized, the historic ambience of the village still prevails and one immediately feels the continuing strength of its church, Santo Tomas. The village has an active *penitente* organization and two historic *moradas* (meeting houses), which are private. The residence of the late Georgia O'Keeffe, along a lane just south of the plaza, has been preserved just as it was when she died, and it now houses a private research foundation. It is not open to the public.

TIPS FOR THE TRAVELER:
It was residents of the Abiquiu area who founded Tierra Amarilla (p. 213) and other upper Chama Valley hamlets in the 1860s. If you are heading north, be sure to explore this part of New Mexico and, perhaps, take the Cumbres & Toltec Scenic Railroad (p. 300). For a glimpse of the lower Chama Valley's Indian past, you may visit the ruins of Po-shuouinge, two and a half miles south of Abiquiu along New Mexico 84. A National Forest Service sign and parking area clearly mark the access trail to this large prehistoric site. You will also enjoy visiting Bandelier National Monument, near Los Alamos. The nearest center for travel services is Española.

SUGGESTED READING:
Miss O'Keeffe, by Christine Taylor Patten and Alvaro Cardona-Hine (Albuquerque: University of New Mexico Press, 1992).
The Penitente Moradas of Abiquiu, by Richard E. Ahlborn (Washington, D.C.: Smithsonian Institution Press, 1968).

ALBUQUERQUE

Albuquerque is located at the intersection of Interstates 40 and 25 in north-central New Mexico.

Today, Albuquerque is a major modern American metropolis, a sprawling businesslike city whose residents sometimes view Santa Fe as a quaint, expensive, older cousin to the north. Many Santa Feans, on the other hand, enamored with their narrow, winding streets and Spanish Pueblo–style adobe homes, shun Albuquerque's freeways, traffic jams, and faster-paced life-style. Still, they are lured to the bigger city's shopping malls, discount chains, and annual State Fair.

Since its founding in 1706, Albuquerque has straddled major regional trade and travel routes. The first of these was the Camino Real (see p. 293), which linked Mexico City to Santa Fe. After 1821, the Santa Fe Trail became a conduit of commerce between Independence, Missouri; Santa Fe; Albuquerque; El Paso; and the city of Chihuahua. Later, when a new travel route was traced westward from Albuquerque to California, Albuquerque found itself at a prosperous crossroads. This prosperity has culminated in the city now having nearly half a million residents or a third of the state's entire population.

By the time Governor Francisco Cuervo y Valdés issued orders to found Albuquerque, the town already enjoyed an informal existence as a scattering of farms and ranches in the Rio Grande's Central Valley. The governor's efforts to give this dispersed community an official center were only partly successful as most landowners, understandably, preferred to reside close to their fields and flocks. To do so was a necessary tactic to survive, and each *rancho* was responsible for its own defense against Indian attacks. But with Albuquerque's founding, the Central Valley acquired a cultural and military center, tangibly symbolized by the building of a church and the assignment of ten regular soldiers to assist citizens in their defense needs. A number of single-story adobe houses soon appeared around the church to create an informal sort of plaza, the genesis of present-day Old Town.

To understand what life in Albuquerque and its environs was like in the early days, you must realize that throughout the eighteenth and much of the nineteenth centuries parts of New Mexico comprised a near war zone. To the north, settlers knew the terror of attacks by Ute war parties and better-armed bands of Comanches. In the Central Valley, farmers and ranchers were hard pressed to protect their livestock and harvests from marauding Apaches and Navajos. Periodically, New

San Felipe de Neri church, Old Town plaza, Albuquerque, c. 1882. (Photo by George C. Bennett, courtesy Museum of New Mexico, neg. 13700.)

Mexico's authorities in Santa Fe would organize brief campaigns against their Indian foes, and by midcentury Albuquerque came to serve as a staging point for offensive actions in the Rio Abajo, or Lower Valley. These forces usually included regular troops from Santa Fe reinforced by volunteer militia from the countryside, including Spanish colonists and Pueblo warriors. Now these former adversaries joined ranks to oppose new invaders from the outside. The campaigners, however, maneuvered slowly, compared to the hit-and-run nomads, and they were poorly armed; their basic weapons were bows and arrows and spears. They seldom came home victorious over an enemy adept at guerrilla tactics.

Albuquerque's plaza was unconventional from the outset and never included either perimeter walls or defensive towers. As late as 1776, there were only twenty-four houses in the *villa,* some of which, apparently, were only used as a convenience when attending church services. The church, for that matter, collapsed through neglect in 1792, suggesting that many people were not fully committed to Albuquerque as their cultural center. Still, while the town itself was slow to form, the population of the area reached 1,347 by 1789, and 2,302 by 1822. One outlier, Ranchos de Atrisco, consisted of a cluster of farms and ranches across the river to the west. Another, Alameda, was located near the site of an abandoned Tiwa pueblo to the north, and still another, Pajarito, thrived to the south of town. Most people survived by raising sheep or by farming the rich bottomlands along the Rio Grande. Attempts to establish a hamlet in the hills to the east were initially stymied by Apache Indians, who claimed this area as their own. Conflicts with the Navajos continued to impede the westward spread of colonization from the Albuquerque area until after 1863, when this tribe was defeated by the United States army and imprisoned at Fort Sumner (p. 258), in the eastern plains.

Major changes began to come to Albuquerque after the opening of the Santa Fe Trail and commerce with the United States. For the first time, Anglo-American culture began to have an influence in what had long been a culturally isolated Hispanic community. Some local families, such as the Chávezes and Armijos, joined in the booming trade and acquired new wealth and power. Manuel Armijo, whose ancestors had immigrated to New Mexico more than a century earlier, entered politics and the military and served three terms as governor before the events of the Mexican War ended his power in 1846. The United States' occupation of New Mexico initially did not have much impact on Albuquerque's way of life, but it set in motion a series of developments that eventually transformed the town's character. The city's early slow pace as a rural supply center quickened as merchants and entrepreneurs from the East introduced a capitalistic spirit and U.S. soldiers mingled with local Hispanos. By the mid-1850s, however, most troops had been transferred to remote frontier outposts that were better situated to deal with the "Indian problem."

Albuquerque played only a minor part in events surrounding the Civil War in New Mexico. Confederate troops from Texas occupied the city in early March of 1862, and were welcomed by a small contingent of Southern sympathizers. However, they were soon defeated at Glorieta Pass (p. 271), east of Santa Fe, and withdrew to the south. As they

Railroad Avenue, Albuquerque, 1881. (Photo by Ben Wittick, courtesy Museum of New Mexico, neg. 86866.)

approached Albuquerque, federal forces from Fort Craig (p. 235) briefly bombarded the city's Confederate defenders, then silenced their guns in deference to the safety of the civilian population. The Rebels, including both the Albuquerque contingent and main army, were allowed to retreat south to Texas.

The main impact of Anglo-American culture on Albuquerque began in April 1880, with the arrival of the Atchison, Topeka, and Santa Fe Railroad. The railroad tracks passed just over a mile east of the town's old plaza, stimulating a frenzy of real estate and commercial activity and creating a rowdy "New Town," not dissimilar to the one in Las Vegas (p. 161). Now life around the old plaza quieted down, a fact that probably contributed to much of that neighborhood's preservation. The railroad brought more goods from the East and a new influx of people with schemes for commercial and industrial development or for just making a fast buck. The English language, Protestantism, and capitalism all began to have an impact on Albuquerque's traditional Hispanic culture. The new and old values were vividly contrasted in the architecture and ambience of Old Town, to the west, and New Town, which sprawled around the railroad tracks. The two areas were linked by little more than the horse-drawn trolleys that carried folk from one to the other. Old Town was a neighborhood of longtime residents who, as remains apparent today, lived in adobe homes surrounding the plaza and the San Felipe de Neri Church. New Town, on the other hand, was primarily a frame-construction business district, replete with hotels, gambling halls, opium dens, and saloons whose doors seldom stopped swinging. As with many boomtowns, elected peacekeepers could scarcely manage the brawls, thefts, shootings, and other disorders, and ad hoc vigilante groups sometimes stepped in to mete out irreversible punishments to suspected offenders. Soon, however, civilizing elements, exemplified by the University of New Mexico, founded in the late 1880s, began to create a balance in the city's character.

Albuquerque's modern decades have witnessed population growth and accelerating economic development. The city has extended itself far beyond any limits that its old-time residents could have imagined possible. The gap between Old and New Towns eventually closed to form a single sprawling metropolis whose margins eventually crawled up the western slopes of the Sandias, spanned the Rio Grande, and pressed against Indian lands to the south and north. Beyond its borders, thriving industries in cattle, mining, wool, and agriculture all contributed to Albuquerque's prosperity. The advantages of location and climate continue to attract more business, industry, and people, and their combined energies have given birth to a variety of cultural institutions.

When you visit Albuquerque, you should stroll around Old Town, near Central Avenue and Twelfth Street. San Felipe de Neri Church, rebuilt in 1792, still fronts the plaza, which has kept an historical ambience. In Old Town, you will find many tourist shops, art and craft galleries, and restaurants. Close by are the New Mexico Museum of Natural History and the zoo. The campus of the University of New Mexico is another area you will wish to explore, stopping to see the Maxwell Museum of Anthropology on University Boulevard.

TIPS FOR THE TRAVELER:
The Indian pueblos of Isleta (p. 25) and Sandia (p. 59) are located near Albuquerque, and Coronado State Monument (p. 20) is in Bernalillo, less than half an hour's drive to the north. Around Mountainair, to the

south, is Salinas Pueblo Missions National Monument (p. 55), featuring three Spanish Colonial church ruins and Pueblo village sites. On Albuquerque's West Mesa is the newly formed Petroglyph National Monument, which is worth investigating (call 505-766-8375 for information). The Sandia Mountains, which are sacred to the Pueblo Indians, offer recreational opportunities, including hiking in summer and skiing in winter.

SUGGESTED READING:

Albuquerque: A Narrative History, by Marc Simmons (Albuquerque: University of New Mexico Press, 1982).

CHIMAYO

Chimayo is located along New Mexico 76 between Truchas and Española, approximately thirty miles north of Santa Fe.

An always popular excursion for visitors to Santa Fe and northern New Mexico is to take the so-called High Road to Chimayo, via Pojoaque (p. 52) and Nambe (p. 39), stopping at the famous Santuario de Chimayo, Ortega's Weaving Studio, and the Ranchos de Chimayo restaurant. The striking badlands and mountain scenery, the historic church, the Chimayo rugs, topped off by a platter of *enchiladas* with *sopapillas* make an experience offering insight into, and enjoyment of, regional Hispanic traditions.

Chimayo, from the Tewa word *tsimayo* (good flaking stone), lies in the fertile Santa Cruz Valley. It was one of several farming hamlets that sprang up as the growing Santa Cruz colony expanded up and down the river valley after 1695. It was established on or near the site of an Indian pueblo that itself was founded after 1680 by the inhabitants of San Cristóbal Pueblo, south of Santa Fe. (To read more on Santa Cruz Valley settlement, please refer to the section on Santa Cruz, p. 184.) Unlike Truchas (p. 218) and Las Trampas (p. 157), the Chimayo community consisted of a series of plazas, including La Puebla, Potero, Plaza Abajo, Los Ranchos, El Llano, and Plaza del Cerro. The decentralized character of the town is still apparent today as one drives east from Santa Cruz along Highway 76. Perhaps the most central of these communities was Plaza del Cerro, still intact today and located near Ortega's Weaving Studio at the junction of Highways 76 and 520.

Plaza del Cerro in Chimayo. (Photo by David Grant Noble.)

Visitors often miss Plaza del Cerro as it is tucked away off the highway, a fact to which we can probably attribute its preservation. The old plaza exemplifies how many northern New Mexican village compounds were planned in the eighteenth century. In those days, it was a veritable "strategic hamlet," protecting the colonists, their livestock, food supplies, and church against attack by marauding Comanches, Apaches, and Utes. In emergencies, the inhabitants could lock the gates across the plaza's narrow entranceways and withdraw to their solid adobe houses. These could be entered only from the interior quadrangle; their strong exterior walls further enhanced the fortlike character of the hamlet. When necessary, the plaza also functioned as a corral to secure livestock, or as a space for home gardens.

Today, many of the houses surrounding the plaza still are made of adobe, and the state of disrepair of some illustrates the vulnerability of this native style of building to the effects of weathering. Although much of the quadrangle is unused and overgrown, some residents of Plaza del Cerro cultivate small garden plots here. An historic *acequia* (ditch) from the Rio Quemado still flows through the compound, evidence of how water was originally brought to residents.

Although Plaza del Cerro is a tribute to preservation, it has waged a long and continuing battle against deterioration. Some old houses bordering the plaza have been restored or rebuilt using modern materials, and today, the old *torreón* (defensive tower) is covered by a barn. The best preserved structure is the Oratorio de San Buenaventura, the private chapel of the Ortega family, whose weaving studio is at the plaza's northeast corner.

Chimayo has been known for its fine weavers for a long time; in fact, the very name has become synonymous with Spanish-American blanketry. The Spaniards apparently brought looms to New Mexico within a generation or two of the founding of the San Gabriel (p. 73) colony in 1598, and practiced a weaving tradition that derived from their own European roots and without influence from the Pueblos, who also had been weaving for many centuries. By 1638, New Mexico was exporting textiles, much of them apparently fabricated in Governor Luis de Rosas's *obraje* (workshop) in Santa Fe, using captive Apaches and Utes for labor. In the eighteenth and nineteenth centuries, Hispanic weavers were probably active in most villages, including Chimayo, and using the treadle loom. By the 1940s, however, weavers in Chimayo and other villages were producing inferior textiles suitable only for the tourist trade. Although the future of this art form seemed bleak then, a revival occurred, beginning in the 1970s, in which weavers became reinspired by the fine products by their nineteenth-century forebears. Some of the finest textiles today are being woven, not just in the Santa Cruz area but at a weaving cooperative in Los Ojos (p. 217), in the Chama Valley.

By far the best-known historic landmark in the Chimayo area is El Santuario de Chimayo, located along New Mexico 520, a few minutes drive from its junction with Route 76. The Santuario is a church of serene and simple beauty and a site which devotees believe contains miraculous healing powers. Completed in 1816, the Santuario was originally the private shrine of the Abeyta family and dedicated to the manifestation of Jesus Christ as Our Lord of Esquipulas. Esquipulas is a town in southeastern Guatemala, also noted for its miraculous cures and where the image of the Black Christ is housed in a massive white baroque sanctuary.

The Santuario de Chimayo, like that of Esquipulas, is a place of regional pilgrimages for people wishing to express their faith and partake of the holy earth, with its curative attributes. At the Santuario, handfuls of earth may be obtained from a small round hole in the floor of a back room to the left of the altar. In the adjoining room, pilgrims

El Santuario de Chimayo. (Photo by David Grant Noble.)

attach handwritten testimonies and expressions of gratitude to the sacred images, especially that of Santo Niño de Atocha. The holy child, a favorite of New Mexico colonists and their descendants, is believed to wander through the countryside on nocturnal errands of mercy. For this reason, the devout bring him new pairs of shoes as gifts.

Many Hispanos make pilgrimages to the Santuario, especially at Easter time, when throngs can be seen walking along the highways, some even carrying wooden crosses on their shoulders. These pilgrimages are often the fulfillment of previous vows made in connection with answered prayers. In 1946, members of the New Mexico 200th National Guard Regiment, who had survived the Bataan Death March, made the pilgrimage, and this was repeated in the 1960s and 1970s by grateful survivors of the war in Vietnam. Others make the strenuous walk to the Santuario de Chimayo primarily to partake in a cultural tradition and test their physical endurance.

Chimayo makes a fascinating side trip from Santa Fe. To extend the experience, you can continue to Truchas and Las Trampas, or complete a circuit through Peñasco, Picuris, and Dixon, then return on New Mexico 68. For a longer trip, drive on to Taos (p. 208) and Taos Pueblo (p. 89).

SUGGESTED READING:
Spanish Textile Tradition of New Mexico and Colorado, edited by Nora Fisher (Santa Fe: Museum of New Mexico Press, 1979).

CIMARRON

Cimarron is located along U.S. 64, fifty-four miles east of Taos and forty-one miles southwest of Raton.

Decades of novels and movies have created a stereotype of the old-time western town. Familiar characters include the overbearing landowner or rancher with his entourage of rowdy cowboys; hard-working squatters being forced off their land; a hired gunslinger or two; a grizzled prospector soliciting drinks along saloon row; and stolid Indians lounging on the sidewalk. Where did this myth originate? Perhaps in Cimarron, New Mexico.

Cimarron was the creation of one man, Lucien Bonaparte Maxwell, a colorful entrepreneur who reportedly was irresistible to his friends, but feared by many living under his power. Maxwell had come west as a young man, and in 1842 he married Luz Beaubien, the beautiful young daughter of Carlos Beaubien, a successful Taos merchant. The previous year, Beaubien, with Guadalupe Miranda, had received a land grant from the Mexican government on the east side of the Sangre de Cristo Mountains; they believed it to cover about ninety-seven thousand acres. After marrying, Maxwell joined John C. Frémont's historic exploration across the West as a hunter. As an expeditionary scout, Frémont hired Kit Carson, who became Maxwell's lifelong friend.

When he returned, Lucien began managing his father-in-law's lands and, with Carson, established a ranch along Rayado Creek, twelve miles south of present-day Cimarron. As the first Anglo-American settlement in this wilderness, which had long been home to the Ute and Apache Indians, the enterprise presented a challenge to the two young men. The winters were hard and the partners frequently lost stock and other goods to the local Indians as well as to transient war parties of Comanches, Kiowas, and Cheyennes. Maxwell himself was severely wounded in an attack in 1848. For several years, the U.S. Army stationed troops at the Rayado ranch; however, this protection was discontinued in 1851, when Fort Union (see p. 264) was established about thirty miles to the south.

In the late 1850s, Maxwell realized that the broad fertile valley of the Cimarron River would better serve the requirements of his expanding business operations. In 1858, therefore, he moved twelve miles to the north, where he built his famous twenty-two-room mansion and founded the company town that would later be called Cimarron, or "wild." The town site, in the heart of the Beaubien-Miranda Grant, was ideally suited to his purposes, for not only did it have immense ranching and farming potential, but it was situated along the Taos link of the popular Mountain Branch of the Santa Fe Trail. Here, for the next dozen years, Maxwell was free to build his empire. Initially, his income was based on what he and his tenants and peons could raise from the land: sheep, cattle, horses, corn, wheat, and hay. His main clients were the U.S. Army and the Cimarron Indian Agency, which was moved here from Taos. He also made enviable profits from selling goods and services to travelers, leasing land to various tenants, and producing flour at a still-extant three-story stone grist mill. Eventually, his interests expanded into mining—gold was discovered on nearby Baldy Mountain in 1866—and into banking. Of course, the power base underlying all of Maxwell's enterprises was land, for he had bought out Miranda's interest in the grant and inherited the Beaubien share. Subsequently, a land survey (controversial, to be sure) revealed the grant's boundaries to be far wider than anyone had previously imagined: ninety-seven thousand acres expanded to nearly two million!

During Maxwell's twelve years as the patron of Cimarron, the town served as a business and ranching center, a crossroads, the site of the Ute and Jicarilla Apache Agency, and the headquarters of all Maxwell Land Grant enterprises. Like a feudal lord, Lucien Maxwell dominated every business activity in the region, and his pretentious home, which boasted fine furniture, plush carpets, and four grand pianos, was a center of social life. He was even the town's postmaster, though it is doubtful that he spent any time sorting mail. For entertainment, he offered his renowned hospitality to a parade of guests, from old friends like Kit Carson to strangers traveling the Trail and needing a place to stay. He also had a passion for breeding and racing horses.

The Old Aztec Mill Museum in Cimarron. (Photo by David Grant Noble.)

Whether Maxwell's rule was benevolent or oppressive depended upon who you were. To his Anglo-American friends and acquaintances, his friendliness and generosity were legendary. He was popular, too, among the free-roaming Utes and Apaches, who continued to live on his vast domain as they had for generations. However, if you were one of his Navajo slaves or Spanish-American peons or tenants, you had to know your place and you no doubt felt the weight of his arrogance and condescension.

After the discovery of gold, settlers poured into the area, and Elizabethtown sprang up. As life and business grew more complicated for Maxwell, he decided to make a change. In 1870, he sold out and purchased Fort Sumner (p. 258), which the army had abandoned two years earlier. Moving here with a large entourage of his Hispanic employees and their families, Maxwell concentrated on cattle raising.

With Maxwell gone and with the new owners of his grant and company, known as the Maxwell Land Grant and Railway Company, living in Europe, Cimarron's social and political fabric soon deteriorated. The new managers, insensitive to local history and customs, began a relentless campaign to evict hundreds of Hispanic people who believed themselves to be legitimate homesteaders. Cimarron soon split into pro-grant and anti-grant factions. After the Reverend F. J. Tolby, a Methodist circuit rider and outspoken pro-settler advocate, was murdered, the dispute escalated into what has been dubbed the "Colfax County War." To further complicate matters, the federal government ceased feeding and clothing the Indians, who were forced to steal cattle to survive on a land from which they had been dispossessed. Cimarron, with its saloons, dance halls, and hotels, became a hangout for disappointed prospectors, unruly cowboys, and hired gunfighters. Even military personnel on pass from Fort Union were not safe—in 1876, three soldiers of African lineage were unjustly gunned down in the St. James Hotel by thugs. Their deaths were among twenty-eight killings that took place in the hotel during Cimarron's lawless years.

In 1876, a grand jury was convened in Taos to investigate the situation in Cimarron. In his charge, the judge stated that in the past sixteen months,

> at least 16 or 18 men have come to their deaths in brawls or by assassination to say nothing of numerous shootings and woundings of which but little note has been taken. It is a matter of shameful and horrid notoriety . . . that one room alone in the Village of Cimarron, can boast that not less than 6 men have been killed within its walls, during the last 9 months. . . . It is perhaps no exaggeration to say that there is hardly a plank in its floor, but that it could speak, would tell some fearful tale of blood. . . . Yet no indictments have been found.

The judge, incidently, was pro-grant.

The St. James Hotel opened its doors in 1880, after having operated as a saloon for eight years. Its proprietor was Henri Lambert, a French-born businessman and chef who had previously cooked for Abraham Lincoln in the White House. Amazingly, after more than a century, this venerable hostelry is still operating and, as you might expect, is very popular among western history buffs. In its dining room, formerly the saloon, you can count the bullet holes in the pressed tin ceiling, some of which were made by Cimarron's own celebrity shootist, Clay Allison. You also can stay in the same rooms (the beds are new) where, according to local belief, once slept such notorious outlaws as Jesse James, Doc Holliday, and Blackjack Ketchum, not to mention a more distinguished slate of figures that included Buffalo Bill Cody, Zane Grey, and Charles Remington.

After the peak of its desperado years, Cimarron fell into decline when the Santa Fe Railroad bypassed the town. In 1882, the county seat

A pioneer's grave in Cimarron. (Photo by David Grant Noble.)

moved to Springer, and soon thereafter the town's dropping population could not even support a newspaper. To be sure, in 1906, a railway spur did come to Cimarron to service the lumber industry and it gave birth to a "new town," which still exists to some extent across Highway 64. Although the railroad here was short-lived, Cimarron carried on as a supply center for local ranching and lumbering outfits. Its most prominent rancher, after Lucien Maxwell, was Frank Springer, who founded the large CS Ranch, which is still operated by his heirs. Springer, for whom a town along Interstate 25 is named, was the attorney for the Maxwell Land Grant, a successful businessman, and a noted paleontologist. In 1927, the Oklahoma oil magnate Waite Phillips, built a mansion on a large tract of land just south of Cimarron. He eventually donated his estate to the Boy Scouts of America, who use it as a summer camp for thousands of scouts.

A complete Cimarron experience today should include staying at, or at least having a meal at, the St. James Hotel. The massive stone Aztec Mill, now an historical museum, also should be a priority stop. Here, you can pick up a walking-tour booklet of the town's historic district, which will lead you to several other nearby preserved buildings as well as the old cemetery and a pioneer's grave.

San José de Gracia Church, Las Trampas. (Photo by David Grant Noble.)

TIPS FOR THE TRAVELER:

At the nearby Philmont Scout Ranch, you can see Villa Philmonte, the restored Phillips home, the Philmont Museum, which houses art and local history exhibits and Ernest Thompson Seton's library, and the Kit Carson Museum, which focuses on the early history of the area.

The Cimarron environs offer more than historical sites; you can use Cimarron as a base from which to hike, camp, hunt, or fish, all in a beautiful natural setting. A hike up Turkey Creek Canyon will lead you to Black Jack's hideout, where, after a July 1899 train robbery, the gang was surprised and scattered by a sheriff's posse. Other historic sites in the area are Taos (p. 208), Taos Pueblo (p. 89), and Fort Union. More travel services can be found in Taos, Raton, and Las Vegas (p. 161).

SUGGESTED READING:

Maxwell Land Grant: A New Mexico Item, by William A. Keleher (reprinted; Albuquerque: University of New Mexico Press, 1983).

Philmont: A History of New Mexico's Cimarron Country, by Lawrence R. Murphy (Albuquerque: University of New Mexico Press, 1972).

LAS TRAMPAS

Las Trampas is located along New Mexico 76, twenty-five miles northeast of Española.

If ever there was a frontier outpost, it was Las Trampas or *Santo Tomás Apostal del Río de Las Trampas* (Saint Thomas the Apostle of the River of Traps), as early Spanish colonial records refer to the hamlet. In 1751, when the colony was founded on the uplands above Santa Cruz (p. 184), its members were in as precarious a situation as any group in New Mexico. Above Las Trampas, a mountainous pass allowed Comanche warriors from the buffalo plains to raid settlements in the Rio Grande Valley. Fortified hamlets such as Las Trampas were buffers against these war parties and helped to defend against Apaches and Utes, too.

The initial Las Trampas colony was composed of twelve families, most of whose heads had been attached to the presidio in Santa Fe and who were related to its leader, the aging Juan de Arguello. Who among us, at the age of seventy-four, would take on such a venture? Arguello not only did, but reportedly survived beyond his centenary, time enough to taste the fruits of his efforts. Another of the pioneers was Sebastian Rodriguez, of African heritage, who had served as Diego de Vargas's drummer boy when the latter had reconquered New Mexico almost sixty years earlier.

Given the Comanche threat, a priority of the colonists was to make their new mountain settlement a veritable stronghold. They accomplished this by building their thick-walled adobe houses contiguously around a square plaza that was spacious enough to hold their livestock in times of danger. The plaza probably had only two narrow entrances, which villagers could securely lock as needed. It was a standard design, shared by many Indian pueblos. Of course, their refuge of last resort, physical and spiritual, was the church, *San José de Gracia de Las Trampas,* but construction of this edifice was not even begun until the early 1760s and not completed until 1776. Therefore, for more than a decade, the Las Trampas faithful trudged nine miles to Picuris Pueblo (p. 48) to attend Mass. This trek was inconvenient enough in summer, and often impossible through winter snows.

The challenges of survival and the hardships of daily life were formidable for the Las Trampas colonists. At an altitude of over eight thousand feet, snow sometimes lay deep beyond the winter months, and frosts could nip garden crops soon after summer's end. From April to October, the settlers toiled long days to build and repair their homes, stables, barns, and corrals; to clear fields; to dig irrigation ditches; to cultivate crops; to care for livestock; to hunt game; and to gather fuel wood. In addition, there were Indian raids and epidemics to contend with. Still, by 1776, the hamlet had grown to 63 families—276 people.

By the nineteenth century, life at Las Trampas had eased somewhat, the community had grown, and most tillable land was being used. A new generation of *Trampaseños* expanded into nearby valleys to found new hamlets such as Chamisal, Ojo Sarco, and El Valle. The Indian danger rose and subsided into the 1800s; in 1844, for example, Las Trampas contributed a force of a hundred men to a military campaign against this foe.

When Anglo-Americans began moving to New Mexico after 1846, the residents of Las Trampas and other New Mexico communities faced a new problem. For these rural farmers and herders, Santa Fe was far away and trips there were only rarely made. By the 1870s, a clique of Anglo-American entrepreneurs that included businessmen, judges, and politicians had acquired power in the capital city and even considerable influence in Washington, D.C. Members of this group, who were known as the "Santa Fe Ring," understood that profitable opportunities awaited them in the field of real estate, if only they could exploit the nebulous legal status of ancient Spanish land grants. How they gained possession of most of the Las Trampas grant is a well-documented story whose key factor was the concept of the *ejidos,* or commons.

The Las Trampas land grant had a core area for the community's plaza and church. Added to this were small private parcels for homes around the plaza and allotments of bottomland for cultivation. The rest consisted of extensive lands dedicated to communal use. Encompassing upland meadows and woods, this portion was the *ejidos*. It was available to the grantees and their descendants for such purposes as grazing stock, hunting and fishing, and gathering wood, plants, herbs, and minerals.

The *ejidos* concept was foreign to the American system of private ownership, and it did not take long for the Santa Fe cabal to devise ways to acquire title to the Las Trampas grant. Through legal shenanigans, speculators dispossessed the descendants of the Las Trampas grantees of their commons. Eventually, they then went into bankrupty themselves and sold out to the U.S. Forest Service, which assumed management responsibilities for the land. As recently as 1982, residents of Las Trampas were apprehended by a ranger for gathering wood near their village; in fact, they were on the *ejidos* which the king of Spain had long ago granted to their forebears.

Since the turn of this century, many of Las Trampas's younger generation have been drawn to the outside world, leaving the town with a smaller, more elderly population. Two world wars accelerated the exodus, which was further stimulated by the decline of small-scale farming. When a new highway was built to Las Trampas, it allowed access to better education and medical facilities and helped to reduce the community's sense of isolation. However, it also cut through the side of the plaza near the church. In 1967, plans to widen the road, which would have further compromised the integrity of the church and plaza, were modified after a controversy that focused wide public interest on historic preservation.

It is a tribute to the efforts of generations of Las Trampas residents that the San José church survives in such fine condition. In a town that has few shops, it is the main attraction to outsiders. A noted architecture historian described it as "the most perfectly preserved Spanish colonial church in the United States." To enter it, you step through a small door, which is set in one of two massive, handsomely carved doors. This brings you into the dark entranceway under a choir loft supported by heavy hand-adzed wooden beams. On a bright day, sunlight from a transverse clerestory window floods the sanctuary ahead, illuminating a fine painted *retablo*, in which is set a figure of the community's patron, St. Joseph—it was the creation of Friar Andres García in the mid-1700s. On the right stands an unusual pine pulpit carved with floral reliefs, which the priest mounts with the aid of a small ladder. Unlike other early New Mexico churches, San José de Gracia has a plank floor, probably added in the 1860s, under which parishioners who died in winter were interred.

When you visit Las Trampas, you may find San José de Gracia locked. In this case, inquire locally who is serving as custodian and see if this person is free to show you inside. Donations to the church maintenance fund are appreciated.

The church borders the village plaza, whose extent, except on the highway side, is still discernible by house alignments. Beyond the plaza, along the highway, you can still get a sense of the area's agricultural and pastoral traditions. Horses and sheep graze in lush meadows in summertime, and a wooden flume north of town still carries water. While the residents of Las Trampas remain somewhat isolated, at least by modern standards, some commute to Española or Los Alamos to work, and all are familiar with the world beyond their valley. With their feet planted in both past and present, they are owed a debt of gratitude for preserving a place of grace for everyone's appreciation.

Interior of San José de Gracia. (Photo by David Grant Noble.)

TIPS FOR THE TRAVELER:

Las Trampas is situated along what is popularly called the "High Road" to Taos. Other points of interest along the route are Chimayo (p. 147) and Truchas (p. 218), to the south, and Picuris Pueblo and Taos (p. 208), to the north. You may also enjoy seeking out other hamlets in these foothills—Cordova, Cundiyo, and El Valle, for example. Travel services are available along Route 76 in Chimayo and in Española and Taos.

SUGGESTED READING:

Enchantment and Exploitation, by William deBuys (Albuquerque: University of New Mexico Press, 1985).

River of Traps: A Village Life, by William deBuys and Alex Harris (Albuquerque: University of New Mexico Press, 1990).

LAS VEGAS

The city of Las Vegas is along Interstate 25, sixty-five miles east of Santa Fe and 106 miles south of Raton.

On August 15, 1846, Juan de Dios Maese, the forty-six-year-old *alcalde* (mayor) of Las Vegas, stood beside General Stephen Watts Kearny, commander of the Army of the West, on a rooftop along the town plaza and swore allegiance to the United States of America. Although Maese had lived his entire life within a few miles of where he stood, this was the third country in which he held citizenship.

In 1821, when Mexico gained independence from Spain, Maese lived in San Miguel del Vado (see p. 179), about twenty-five miles west of the future site of Las Vegas. As a young man, he saw San Miguel's population bursting beyond the carrying capacity of surrounding farm and grazing lands. With several partners, he petitioned for a grant of land along the Gallinas River, where the eastern foothills of the Sangre de Cristo Mountains meet the western edge of the southern Great Plains. This appeared to be a fine area for farming and grazing and was served by a clear stream flowing out of the hills. Dangers posed by nomadic Indians had heretofore inhibited settlement. The petitioners, who also represented twenty-five other San Miguel residents, received permission to establish a new town, for which they chose a site on the west bank of the river, naming it *Nuestra Señora de los Dolores de Las Vegas,* "Our Lady of Sorrows of the Meadows." The major part of the half-million-acre grant was commons, for the shared use of all members of the community, but each member was allotted a plot for his house and garden. The colonists planted crops the first spring, but apprehensive of Indian attacks, they did not move here until the following spring.

The original village of Las Vegas was laid out according to a standard formula, with single-story adobe homes and a church girdling a rectangular plaza. The design fostered community cohesiveness and provided a degree of defensibility, and the location of the church expressed this institution's centrality in the settlers' lives.

Las Vegas lay along the increasingly active Santa Fe Trail and replaced San Miguel as New Mexico's port of entry. Seventy-five wagons passed through town in 1835, but within a generation that number had risen to several thousand. When freight caravans pulled up around the dusty (or muddy) plaza, they generated a frenzy of buying, selling, hiring, and general excitement. The trade also drew more people here—

farmers, ranchers, laborers, businessmen, merchants—and within a decade, the town had more than a hundred dwellings.

Until the 1870s, anyone riding east from Las Vegas soon encountered buffalo, sometimes in numbers that seemed infinite. Hunters, known as *ciboleros,* ventured out to meet the herds, returning with loads of jerked meat and hides to sell in Santa Fe, Taos, and other New Mexico markets. Another commerce flourished out of Las Vegas—bartering with the Comanches and other Indian tribes who roamed the southern plains. Hispanic traders, or *comancheros,* loaded their mules with trinkets, grain, arms, and liquor to exchange with the Indians for meat, hides, horses, and cattle, with the last often having been stolen from ranches in Texas.

On August 14, 1846, the United States' Army of the West, trekking west from Missouri on a mission of conquest, was camped outside Las Vegas. The next morning, Brigadier General Stephen Watts Kearny, rode into town with several staff officers and, accompanied by the mayor, Juan de Dios Maese, addressed the assembled populace from a rooftop on the north side of the plaza. Dire rumors had created anxieties among the people, especially as regards the safety of women and the freedom to continue practicing their Roman Catholic faith. Kearny allayed their fears, promising to act as the people's protector rather than as their conqueror and to respect their faith, which was shared by many of his troops. "We come among you for your benefit—not for your injury," he declared. But the commander also made it clear that the citizens of Las Vegas were now United States subjects. However much they might oppose the occupation of their country, they should "remain peaceably at home." He added a warning: "He who promises to be quiet, and is found in arms against me, I will hang!"

Las Vegas's boom years continued with the building of nearby Fort Union. Now, the Trail was both a commercial and military road, although ordinary travelers used it too, with the Independence-to-Santa Fe fare by wagon being two hundred dollars. Las Vegas's citizens became entrepreneurs, setting up new businesses, founding trading companies, and working in a myriad of transportation-related jobs.

While the United States' seizure of New Mexico had occurred virtually unopposed, some New Mexicans deeply resented the occupation of their land. In January of 1847, residents of Taos (p. 208) and Taos Pueblo (p. 89) formed a rebellion that quickly spread to Mora (p. 175), a mountain village near Las Vegas. United States troops clashed with the insurgents at both places. Reinforced by Las Vegas volunteers, they razed most of Mora and routed the rebels, some of whom

The "Dice Apartments," from whose roof General Kearny addressed the Las Vegas populace in 1846. (Photo by David Grant Noble.)

fled to the region northeast of Las Vegas. From here, for a short time, they raided army grazing camps and even killed some soldiers. Ultimately, the diehards were overwhelmed and driven away, but not until forty were taken captive, among whom six were convicted of treason and executed in the Santa Fe plaza.

The coming of the railroad in 1879 truly transformed Las Vegas. To the consternation of old-time residents, the station was located a mile east of the plaza, giving birth to East Las Vegas, or "New Town." This division was more than geographical for, in effect, it separated the old Hispanic residents from the Anglo-American newcomers and created a gulf between Spanish and English, Catholic and Protestant, and differing cultural values.

With the arrival of the railroad and the building of New Town, the population rose again and surpassed five thousand by 1890. New classes of people came to town, from respectable German Jewish merchants to rowdy drifters and outlaws. All-night saloons and gambling houses proliferated, attracting everyone from hoodlums to district judges, and a libertine atmosphere fostered alcoholism, robberies, and even murders. The inability of local law officers to stem the crime rate gave rise to a vigilance committee, whose members took matters into their own hands, hunting down and shooting suspects or stringing them up by the neck from a windmill on the plaza.

Some of Las Vegas's unsavory characters eventually gained immortality in Western folklore. One was "Doc" Holliday, who briefly opened a dental practice on Center Street before local citizens forced him to return to Dodge City. Another was Lincoln County's famous sheriff, Pat Garrett, who once locked up Billy the Kid in the town jail. Most of Las Vegas's wrongdoers, however, were of a less romantic caliber—little-known vagrants, thieves, and gamblers whose violent acts usually were unleashed while inebriated.

Like so many northern New Mexico communities, where land tenure derived from old Spanish or Mexican grants, Las Vegas saw conflicts between Hispanics and Anglo-Americans over real estate dealings and political power. In the 1880s, an Hispanic group, known as *Las Gorras Blancas,* or White Caps, formed to deal in extralegal fashion with such problems. Wearing long white masks, members of this loose organization enjoyed considerable local support, which allowed them to hold intimidating public demonstrations and to carry out mild acts of vandalism.

Las Vegas's boom days slowly came to an end. The closing of nearby Fort Union (p. 264) in 1891 was the first economic blow, soon to be followed by the Panic of 1893, railroad layoffs, and a decline in the wool market. The town's attempts to find new sources of revenue did not always bear fruit, as witnessed by the fluctuating fortunes of the Montezuma Hotel, a nearby health resort for a growing number of tourists. In addition, as the upcoming city of Albuquerque became New Mexico's new commercial center, business activity in Las Vegas stagnated even further. Two enterprises, however, a state mental asylum and a university, both founded in the 1890s, provided the town with needed economic anchors. Even so, a local agricultural depression in the 1920s and the Great Depression in the thirties were setbacks from which Las Vegas never fully recovered. Interestingly, many members of Theodore Roosevelt's Rough Riders of Spanish-American War fame were recruited in Las Vegas, and the group long gathered here in later years for its reunions.

Las Vegas has many houses listed on national and state historic registers. They reflect a myriad of architectural styles, including Territorial, Queen Anne, Romanesque Revival, Neo-Classical, Renaissance,

The Castañeda Hotel by the Las Vegas railroad station. (Photo by David Grant Noble.)

and New Mexico Folk. When you visit the city, you will enjoy driving and walking around its several historic districts. The Plaza and Bridge Street district is one; it includes the Plaza Hotel, the First National Bank of Las Vegas, and the Charles Ilfield Building, all dating to the 1880s. Also on the plaza are the pre–Mexican War Dice Apartments, on whose roof General Kearny spoke to the town's citizens. Along Railroad Avenue, in New Town, you will certainly be impressed by the old Castañeda Hotel, which reflects the elegance of Las Vegas's affluent era. Tour brochures, published by the Las Vegas Citizens' Committee for Historic Preservations, are available at many downtown locations or may be ordered by writing P.O. Box 707, Las Vegas, New Mexico 87701, or by calling (505) 454-1401, extension 77.

TIPS FOR THE TRAVELER:
Other historic points of interest in the area include the Montezuma Hotel, now the Armand Hammer United World College; the Rough Riders Museum at 727 Grand Avenue; Fort Union National Monument; and Pecos National Historical Park (p. 42). In addition, you will find a side trip to the Mora Valley of both historical and scenic interest.

Travel and tourist services are abundant in Las Vegas, and the Plaza Hotel, which was renovated in recent years, is recommended for history buffs.

SUGGESTED READING:

Wildest of the Wild West: True Tales of a Frontier Town on the Santa Fe Trail, by Howard Bryan (Santa Fe: Clear Light Publishers, 1988).

From Hacienda to Bungalow: Northern New Mexico Houses, 1850– 1912, by Agnesa Lufkin Reeve (Albuquerque: University of New Mexico Press, 1988).

LINCOLN STATE MONUMENT

Lincoln State Monument is located in Lincoln, along U.S. 380, thirty-two miles east of Carrizozo and fifty-seven miles west of Roswell.

The troubles in Lincoln County in 1878, commonly referred to as the Lincoln County War, have come to symbolize the lawlessness that sometimes reigned in pockets of the American West. Indeed, the anarchic state of affairs in Lincoln fascinated a national audience and even had incipient international repercussions. Lincoln's violent events immediately generated governmental investigations and later inspired historical studies and a spate of novels and movies, which continue. In addition, out of the smoke rose a mythic American figure—William H. Bonney, better known as Billy the Kid.

Many old-time western towns have been reduced to ruin and rubble or have disappeared altogether. Not so Lincoln. By good fortune, the town and many of its old buildings have survived or have been restored. Today, thanks to the preservationist efforts of the Lincoln County Historic Trust and the Museum of New Mexico, the town is a living public monument.

As a community, Lincoln dates to a time before its infamous years in the 1870s. In 1855, the Rio Bonito Valley attracted Hispanic farmers, who called their settlement *La Placita.* Living in single-storied adobe houses along the road, the settlers built a *torreón,* or stone tower, where they could gather for safety when threatened by marauding Apaches. The old *torreón* still stands along the main street. In 1869, when Lincoln County was formed, the town's name was changed to commemorate the country's late president. At the same time, Major William Brady was sheriff.

The ancient fortified tower in Lincoln. (Photo by David Grant Noble.)

In 1873, L. G. Murphy & Company, which had been operating a store at nearby Fort Stanton, moved into a two-story adobe building in town. Its owner, Lawrence Murphy, had James J. Dolan and Emil Fritz as his representatives, but after Fritz died in 1874, Dolan took over the store along with a new partner, John H. Riley. Murphy and Dolan were more than simple traders and shopkeepers. It was no secret that their business practices, especially in fulfilling government contracts, were less than honest. Flour, for example, often was below standard, and cattle supplied to the Mescalero Apaches (p. 120) frequently included scrawny steers that outlaws in the company's employ had rustled off the open range. Murphy and Dolan, however, had well-placed friends such as Governor Samuel B. Axtell, U.S. District Attorney Thomas B. Catron, and Sheriff William Brady. With such contacts, they were able to operate with relative immunity from prosecution.

Enter upon the scene a young, wealthy, cultivated Englishman, John H. Tunstall, who had left his homeland to travel around North America in search of a fresh life and innovative business opportunities. Tunstall had been persuaded to come to Lincoln by Alexander A. McSween, an attorney with business ambitions whom he had met in Santa Fe. Together, McSween and Tunstall opened a merchandising business in Lincoln in competition with Dolan and Riley. Tunstall also purchased a cattle ranch outside town and hired ranch hands and wranglers to help in running it. Soon included in the Tunstall-McSween circle was John S. Chisum, a major stockman along the Pecos near Roswell.

Conflict between the Murphy-Dolan-Riley-Brady clique and the new McSween-Tunstall partnership was predictable, but it was made inevitable by other factors. One of these factors was a dispute over the estate of the late Emil Fritz, which Murphy had hired McSween to settle; and another factor was the publication of a letter by Tunstall, naively (though probably accurately) accusing Sheriff Brady of mismanaging public tax funds. "A delinquent tax payer is bad; a delinquent tax collector is worse," he pontificated. The letter, published in the January 26, 1878, issue of the Mesilla *Independent,* seems to have sealed the Englishman's fate, for a month later he was assassinated by a Brady "posse" while riding unarmed from his ranch to Lincoln. Just out of sight of the murder were several of Tunstall's own ranch hands, including the young William Bonney.

Tunstall's death touched off the six-month-long spate of killings that won Lincoln County its everlasting notoriety. In March, a "posse" of Tunstall supporters killed two of the slain Englishman's alleged murderers. Soon after, at Blazer's Mills, a furious gun battle resulted in the death of Andrew A. "Buckshot" Roberts and a member of the Tunstall posse, which now called itself "The Regulators." In April, Sheriff Brady and his deputy were gunned down in a hail of bullets as they walked down Lincoln's main street in broad daylight. The slayers were Billy "The Kid" Bonney and several cohorts. And so it went. In an April 13 letter to the Las Vegas *Gazette,* one dismayed visitor to Lincoln observed that "killing people in Lincoln is the leading industry at the present time."

The feud reached a climax in mid-July 1878, when the two factions, resigned to having a showdown, raised small militias of gun-toting henchmen and headed for Lincoln. The shooting began on the fifteenth when the groups took shelter in buildings and houses along the town's main street and sporadically sprayed bullets at each other. On the nineteenth, with neither side having gained an advantage, the Dolan forces persuaded Colonel Nathan Dudley, the commanding officer at Fort Stanton (see p. 254), to intercede to defend the public safety. Dudley, who had heretofore considered the Lincoln chaos a civil affair, brought four officers, eleven cavalrymen, and twenty-four infantry to town, backed up by a Gatling gun and howitzer. The troop marched smartly into Lincoln and broke the stalemate. It was soon apparent which side the army

The old Lincoln County Courthouse from which Billy the Kid escaped. (Photo by David Grant Noble.)

favored; by nightfall, the McSween house was burned to ashes, Mc-Sween and several henchmen lay dead on the ground, and the rest of his cohorts, including Billy, had fled into the darkness. The war was over.

As might be expected, the aftermath of the battle saw a series of inquiries in which witnesses and participants gave varying accounts of what had happened and why. The scandal did bring about changes: Governor Axtell was replaced; Catron resigned his position as U.S. attorney; Dudley was relieved of his command; and Lincoln got a new sheriff, Patrick F. Garrett. John Tunstall's father, using influential contacts and diplomatic channels, tried unsuccessfully for six years to obtain redress for his son's murder. Alex McSween's widow, Susan, became a successful cattle rancher, eventually retiring to White Oaks, where she is buried.

William Bonney pursued his outlaw career for three more years, building his own legend by repeatedly eluding capture, escaping from jails, and shooting or humiliating lawmen. It was on April 28, 1881, that, shackled in an upstairs room of Lincoln's courthouse and awaiting execution, he made his most daring breakout. In the course of the escape, he killed both of his guards, then almost casually, under the gaze of townsfolk, pounded off one of his leg irons, collected arms, ammunition, blankets, and a horse, and rode out of town. The Kid remained on the lam for three more months before a bullet from the gun of Sheriff Pat Garrett ended his life at Fort Sumner (p. 258).

When you visit Lincoln, you may wish to stop first at the museum to see its regional-history exhibits and to obtain a walking-tour guide. From here, you can stroll through town; stop at the Tunstall Store, which contains much of its original stock; view the *torreón;* explore the courthouse with its bullet hole in the wall from Billy's six-shooter; and visit other historic houses. You may enjoy having a meal or staying overnight at the restored Wortley Hotel, which is open May through October (call 505-653-4500 for reservations). Several bed-and-breakfast establishments in town also offer accommodations.

TIPS FOR THE TRAVELER:
Nearby Fort Stanton is a fort site that was once active in New Mexico's Indian wars and, in the years since, has played other interesting roles. You may also enjoy a stop at White Oaks to see a number of remarkable mining-era buildings and a historic cemetery. Five miles east of U.S. 54, at Three Rivers, you can explore an ancient Indian petroglyph site maintained by the Bureau of Land Management. If you enjoy outdoor sports, including hiking and skiing, you may wish to visit Ruidoso, a major resort town at the foot of Sierra Blanca, the highest peak in southern New Mexico.

SUGGESTED READING:
High Noon in Lincoln: Violence on the Western Frontier, by Robert M. Utley (Albuquerque: University of New Mexico Press, 1987).
Merchants, Guns and Money: The Story of Lincoln County and Its Wars, by John P. Wilson (Santa Fe: Museum of New Mexico Press, 1987).

MESILLA

Mesilla is located just off New Mexico 28, in the southwest sector of Las Cruces. Its historic plaza lies between Calle de Santiago and Calle de Parian.

The Mesilla Valley is New Mexico's most fertile agricultural region. This sixty-mile-long plain along the Rio Grande produces a wide variety of vegetables as well as fruits, nuts, and cotton. Before the construction of Elephant Butte Dam (1911–1916), the waters of the great river periodically spilled over its banks, inundating farms and fields, and demolishing irrigation gates. Each flood, however, distributed fertile deposits of silt to the agricultural lands. Today, the river is harnessed and its silt-free waters are carefully apportioned to farms along the way.

The valley's recorded history goes back more than four centuries. It was in 1581 that the Spanish friar Agustín Rodríguez charted a more direct route to New Mexico than the westerly trail used by his predecessors. Rodríguez descended the Rio Conchas to the Rio Grande, which he then followed northward into the land of the Pueblos. He was followed in 1598 by New Mexico's first colonizer, Juan de Oñate. A member of his expedition, Pedro Robledo, died at a camping spot at the north end of the valley; nearby Robledo Mountain still bears his name. But while expeditions, trade caravans, and ordinary travelers on the Camino Real (see p. 293) increasingly passed through the valley, they stopped only to camp or forage, for this was the domain of the Apache Indians, who frequently expressed their attitude toward the newcomers in fierce attacks. Two Spanish parties, indeed, were wiped out by the Apaches as they proceeded up the valley; their bones were later discovered and buried by other travelers. The place of the tragedies was marked by a cluster of crosses, known as *El Jardín de las Cruces* (the Garden of the Crosses). Later, the name was shortened to Las Cruces.

In 1843, 261 adventurous Mexican pioneers led by Don José María Costales decided to have a try at settling the Mesilla Valley and established a farming hamlet, known as Doña Ana, at a bend in the river. They struggled, not just to build homes and to till fields, but also to defend themselves against the Indians, who repeatedly swept through the vulnerable community. The following year, many among them returned to El Paso in discouragement. The rest, however, persevered, and they were seen to be thriving three years later.

Eighteen hundred forty-six was the year the Mexican War broke out. American troops occupied Santa Fe in August. In late December, Colonel Alexander Doniphan led a regiment of buckskin-clad Missourians through Doña Ana and on southward to a place along the river called *brazito* (little arm). Here, on Christmas day, they routed a Mexican force of five hundred dragoons reinforced by El Paso militia under the command of General Antonio Ponce de León. These developments were not welcomed by all Doña Anans (now, by decree, American citizens), and in 1848, half the population decided to pack their meager belongings and found a new town at Mesilla, which they believed to be still on Mexican soil. Indeed, it was, until a new survey clouded its

Early Mesilla street scene. (Courtesy Rio Grande Historical Collections.)

status. Then, in 1853, James Gadsden negotiated a purchase by the United States of thirty thousand square miles of Mexican territory in southern New Mexico and Arizona; the following year Mesilla unquestionably became part of the United States. Once again, some residents were dismayed and moved farther south and across the new border.

Mesilla, then, was a product of the Mexican War. It was, at least initially, a small dusty (or muddy) Mexican-style village whose residents diverted the Rio Grande's waters to their fields and held off the ever-troublesome Indians. By 1850, other settlers had moved here from points south, swelling Mesilla's population to 650. A decade later, after Forts Selden (p. 249) and Fillmore introduced a measure of security to the region, Mesilla's numbers had swelled to over two thousand to make the town a major hub of activity. The army hired many Mesilla laborers to build Fort Fillmore, and more found employment as the town became a military supply center.

Old Mesilla has inspired works by a host of romantic writers and film directors, and not without reason. It was a rough and tumble cross-roads where travelers and traders, farmers and cattlemen, sheriffs and outlaws, and even Union and Confederate soldiers could be counted on to lend excitement to the town's underlying rural Mexican character.

By the late 1850s, the Butterfield Overland Stage Line (p. 287), operating between St. Louis and San Francisco, dropped off passengers and mail on Mesilla's plaza on a daily basis. Intersecting the route here was another between El Paso and Albuquerque. The stagecoach station, where road-weary travelers could eat and rest, was at the southeast corner of Mesilla's plaza; the old building is still there, though now housing La Posta, a popular restaurant.

On July 25, 1861, Confederate soldiers from Texas, under Lt. Col. John R. Baylor, marched into town and were attacked that same afternoon by Union troops from nearby Fort Fillmore. It was an odd battle. The Federals lobbed a couple of howitzer shells toward town, which had no more effect than to cause townsfolk to duck for cover. The Rebels reportedly dashed about, exposing themselves in rapid sequence in various locations to create a false impression of superior numbers. Then they sent a volley of fire into the enemy's ranks, killing three men. The ruse worked. In short order, the Federals were in full retreat; what was more, before dawn on the following day they withdrew across the Jornada del Muerto toward Fort Stanton (p. 254). Some wise troopers filled their canteens with whiskey before starting the trek. Several hours after the sun rose over the desert, the troops grew hot and thirsty. When the Confederates caught up with the bedraggled column, it was strung out for miles along the trail, with its members collapsing from dehydration and fatique.

A decade after the tragicomic surrender of Fort Fillmore, Mesilla residents witnessed a political riot. New Mexico's party politics often were heated affairs, and on August 27, 1871, inebriated members of Democratic and Republican rallies clashed on the plaza. A gun discharged and mayhem ensued. When the dust cleared, nine men lay dead and more than forty people were wounded. Army troops arrived from Fort Selden and stayed in town for two weeks to maintain order. In the wake of this violent event, some residents left Mesilla altogether to start a new life in the Mimbres Valley; others moved to Ascension in Chihuahua.

Mesilla also is associated with Billy the Kid, for it was here that the legendary outlaw was tried and sentenced to hang in 1881. The old courthouse where he was held, now a gift shop, is on the south side of the plaza. The Kid was transferred to Lincoln (p. 166), where he shot his jailers and escaped, later to be killed himself by Sheriff Pat Garrett. Even with him gone, other outlaws frequented Mesilla between raids on cattle herds in the region.

In 1881, a north-south branch of the Santa Fe Railroad was laid through Las Cruces, just missing Mesilla, and soon that settlement became a burgeoning center of business. Mesilla carried on as a rural community, with a sense of history. In recent years, as Las Cruces has grown

Mesilla street today. (Photo by David Grant Noble.)

into New Mexico's second largest city, Mesilla's romantic past and Mexican ambience have become the foundation of a modest tourist industry. If you visit, take a stroll around the plaza and surrounding streets to see many buildings and houses dating from the mid-1800s. You should see San Albino Church, on the north side of the plaza, and, perhaps, stop for a drink or meal at the historic La Posta or El Patio restaurants. The latter, on the plaza's south side, once housed offices of the San Antonio Mail and the Butterfield Overland Mail. At the outskirts of town, cotton fields and pecan groves will remind you of the economic base underlying Mesilla's longevity.

TIPS FOR THE TRAVELER:
Although Fort Fillmore was never reoccupied after its 1861 abandonment and has disappeared even as a ruins, the remains of Fort Selden are very much worth a visit. Fort Selden State Monument is only a short drive north of Las Cruces. Fort Cummings (p. 241) is a bit longer trip, but also one of historical interest; after Mesilla, it was the next stop west for Butterfield stages. You will find many nearby travel and tourist services in the Mesilla–Las Cruces area.

SUGGESTED READING:
The California Column in New Mexico, by Darlis A. Miller (Albuquerque: University of New Mexico Press, 1982).
Las Cruces: An Illustrated History, by Linda G. Harris (Las Cruces: Arroyo Press, 1993).

MORA

Mora is located along New Mexico 518, thirty-one miles north of Las Vegas and forty-two miles south of Taos.

After Governor Juan Bautista de Anza made a truce with the Comanche Indians in 1786, the New Mexico frontier became more secure and farming hamlets sprang up in areas that heretofore had been deemed too perilous to settle. Taking advantage of the relatively peaceful conditions, a group of pioneers from Las Trampas (see p. 157), Picuris (p. 48), and Embudo hauled their simple belongings over the Sangre de Cristo Mountains and built a small cluster of houses overlooking the lush meadows of the Mora Valley. It seemed an ideal place to start a new life. Grazing was good and agriculture promising; what was more, the surrounding hills abounded in deer, elk, and mountain sheep and offered an abundance of fuel and building wood.

In the early 1800s, American trappers discovered abundant beaver in Mora streams, and by 1823 a group of mountain men, including one Cerán St. Vrain, were camped in the valley and collecting pelts. It was the French trappers who, according to popular legend, originally named the valley L'Eau des Morts (the Water of the Dead), because they once came upon human bones scattered on the river bank. The name, presumably, was Hispanicized to Lo de Mora, then condensed to Mora. St. Vrain later gained wide renown in the territory as an entrepreneur, freighter, and partner of the Bent brothers in their trading empire based at Bent's Fort in southeastern Colorado. He also commanded a company of New Mexico volunteers during the Taos uprising of 1847, and later led troops against the Utes and Apaches. His early beaver-trapping days in the Mora Valley apparently stayed in his memory, for later in life he brought his family here and built a home.

The Mora Valley is situated along a once well-traveled route between the buffalo plains and Taos. While this location favored trading with friendly Indians, the easy access also attracted hostile tribes such as the Pawnees, who raided Mora in 1830.

In 1835, a pioneering individual named José Tapia brought seventy-five settlers to the Mora Valley to claim their portions of a land grant. The settlers had much to cope with, and building homes and breaking ground for crops were among the most basic survival tasks. The Tapia family's experience illustrated the inherent dangers of frontier life; Tapia himself was shot by Indians, then his son was killed by a bear. Colonial New Mexico saw waves of virulent epidemics that devastated Hispanic people as well as the Indians. In one of these, more than a hundred residents of Mora Parish, half of whom were infants, succumbed to smallpox.

Still, the Mora community persevered, and its members set down deep roots. They grew wheat, oats, and barley, and within two generations of receiving the land grant they were producing up to sixty thousand bushels of wheat each season. Underlying their success was an ingrained self-reliance, an essential attribute on any frontier. In a town like Mora, doctors were unknown and often it was hard even to obtain the services of a priest for baptisms or to give last rites to the dying. Isolated rural people like those of Mora developed their own folk medicine, a tradition usually passed from generation to generation by women, known as *curanderas,* who understood the healing arts. Such knowledge is still valuable in the New Mexico countryside.

The people of Mora built their homes entirely from native materials—adobe, stone, and wood—and raised, gathered, or hunted their own food. They hauled firewood out of the hills with burros, spun yarn and wove clothing from homegrown wool, and often settled their own disputes. When priests were too scarce to serve their needs, they developed their own lay religious order, *Los Hermanos Penitentes,* the Penitent Brothers.

Along with the people of Taos and several other northern New Mexican towns, the inhabitants of Mora retained a degree of loyalty to Mexico and resented the seizure of their land by foreign troops. In January 1847, word of a native rebellion in Taos (see p. 208) quickly spread to Mora, where a group of insurgents, led by Manuel Chávez, massacred a party of seven unsuspecting American traders. In response, Captain I. R. Hendley, who was in charge of a grazing detachment near Las Vegas, led a company of U.S. soldiers here, reinforced by Las Vegas volunteers. They attacked the town, in which some two hundred insurgents had fortified themselves, and fought a battle in the streets around the town plaza. Captain Hendley and fifteen of his volunteers were killed in the fighting, after which the troops retreated. When they later returned with a cannon, the rebels scattered into the hills, leaving the soldiers free to set fire to buildings and stores of food. As much of the grain had been grown to sell to the army, the soldiers, in effect, destroyed their own supplies.

Some of Mora's hostility toward Americans may have derived from a raid upon the town in 1843 by a renegade band of Texans, who were trying to repossess stock previously stolen from them by Comanches and sold to New Mexicans. The Texans killed five Mora citizens, took

Farm family in Mora, 1895. (Courtesy Museum of New Mexico, neg. 22468.)

eighteen more captive, and made off with seventy-five horses. In the end, the escapade turned out badly for the Texans, as they were pursued and counterattacked by a posse of outraged Morenos and forced to release not only their prisoners, but all their horses. The Texans headed home on foot.

Despite its problems with Indians, Texans, and Anglo-Americans, Mora thrived as a farming community and established satellite hamlets such as Holman and Cleveland. The Spanish-American community swelled and was reinforced by Irish and German farmers, ranchers, and merchants. When St. Vrain returned to Mora in 1853, he built a comfortable home for his family and their Indian and black servants. He also became a major supplier of grain and hay to nearby Fort Union (p. 264), set up a grist mill in about 1860, and became involved in real estate and lumbering enterprises. He died in 1870; his grave is on a hillside a short distance west of the Catholic cemetery.

Mora's fortunes eventually declined. Once a breadbasket with five active grist mills, its agricultural industry all but collapsed and its rangeland became sorely depleted by overgrazing and erosion. Today, the population is a fraction of what it was in the latter part of the nineteenth century; still, numerous old adobe houses with pitched tin roofs are still in use, conveying a sense of the town's heritage, and numerous families in the area trace their roots back to the town's pioneering era. In addition, three historic grist-mill buildings are still standing.

La Cueva Mill near Mora. (Photo by David Grant Noble.)

St. Vrain's mill, in poor condition, sits along the road one block north of Mora's main street, and another, which is well maintained, is in Cleveland. The third, which has been restored, is in the La Cueva Historic District, six miles east of town, at the junction of New Mexico 518 and 442. It was built in 1870 by Vicente Romero, who had already established the La Cueva Ranch, which he purchased from original land-grant settlers. The La Cueva Mill, which operated until 1949, is now owned and protected by the owners of the adjacent raspberry farm. You can see the old mill house with its still-revolving water wheel, adjoining adobe farm buildings, and an old corral area surrounded by a massive stone wall. There are picnic tables here, too, making the site a very pleasant place to spend half an hour.

TIPS FOR THE TRAVELER:
While in this area, you will enjoy visiting Las Vegas (p. 161) and Taos (p. 208) and the pueblos of Picuris (p. 48) and Taos (p. 89). The Mora Valley is in the scenic Sangre de Cristo Mountains, where you can explore many back roads leading to other rural Hispanic communities. There is a restaurant and gas station in Mora, but few other tourist or travel services.

SUGGESTED READING:
"Revolt at Mora, 1847," by James W. Goodrich, *New Mexico Historical Review,* vol. 47, no. 1 (1972).

SAN MIGUEL DEL VADO

San Miguel del Vado is located along New Mexico 3, two miles south of Interstate 25, approximately midway between Pecos and Las Vegas.

Today, one might drive through small rustic San Miguel del Vado (St. Michael of the Ford) with scarcely a second glance. However, this was once a bustling, fortified, Spanish colonial village—the present highway bisects its plaza—and some of its still-standing adobe structures may date well back into the 1800s. Two significant historic landmarks also survive here—the ford where the Santa Fe Trail crossed the Pecos River, and San Miguel Church, on the plaza's north side. Although renovated, the church's exterior is remarkably unchanged since it was sketched by Lieutenant J. W. Abert in 1846.

A segment of the Santa Fe Trail in San Miguel del Vado. (Photo by David Grant Noble.)

Throughout the 1700s, a steady stream of immigrants from the south arrived in New Mexico and soon outnumbered the territory's Pueblo Indian residents. Before long, Santa Fe was bursting at the seams and the settlers spread up and down the Rio Grande Valley, claiming the best farming areas. New arrivals, therefore, had to look further afield for places to colonize.

For generations, settlement along the Pecos River, some forty miles east of Santa Fe, was unthinkable for New Mexican colonists due to the depredations of Comanche Indians. These nomads of the southern plains struck both Indian and Spanish settlements until, in 1779, they were defeated by Spanish and Pueblo forces led by Governor Juan Bautista de Anza. Anza's victory, and the death of the Comanche chief Cuerno Verde (Green Horn) laid the base for an enduring peace and the possibility of expanding colonization.

In 1794, Lorenzo Márquez and fifty-one other Santa Feans successfully petitioned for a grant of land at a well-known crossing, or *vado,* of the Pecos River. The grant was allowed with certain standard stipulations; for example, the colonists agreed to bring firearms or bows and arrows with which to defend themselves and to build a fortified plaza. In addition, they would hold land in common in order to serve the best interests of all and allow the colony to grow. Márquez's pioneers took some time to organize themselves, and it probably was not until 1798 that they were permanently settled at El Vado. They built contiguous homes and a *torreón* (defensive tower) around a square, formed a citizen militia, cleared and cultivated fields, dug irrigation ditches, and planted corn and beans.

Of the original fifty-two, thirteen were *genízaros* or Hispanicized Indian captives from the nomadic tribes. Spanish colonists ransomed these unfortunates or bought them at the slave markets in Taos, Pecos, or Santa Fe. The women became household servants and their children did chores and were raised and educated within the context of Spanish frontier culture. They were instructed in Christianity, learned Spanish, and adopted some Spanish customs. From the viewpoint of the colonists, this system had multiple benefits. It provided a home for victims of what the Spanish termed *indios bárbaros,* generated converts, and produced a supply of free labor. At maturity, the *genízaros* normally were granted their independence. Still, being on the lowest rung of the social ladder, they were easily exploited. For this reason, groups of *genízaros* sometimes petitioned the governor to found new colonies on the fringes of the Spanish colonial world, where they could enjoy a measure of freedom and independence. These settlements—Abiquiu (p. 137) and Tomé are other examples—also buffered the Rio Grande Valley from the feared Plains tribes.

By 1803, after the required five-year probation period, San Miguel's fifty-eight heads of family qualified for individual allotments of land. By this time, a sister settlement several miles upstream, San Jose del Vado, also had been established. While the colonists clearly had passed the test, they still waged a struggle to survive. In 1804, a visitor described the community as "composed of one hundred and twenty families, all poor and unfortunate people with no greater resource for their subsistence than their own labor and no greater possessions than the little land with which Our Sovereign (God save him) has succored them."

The colonists, however, had to travel to Pecos Pueblo (p. 42) to attend church. While San Miguel and San José were fast growing in population, Pecos Pueblo was diminishing; soon it made little sense for so many people to travel so far to worship or to have a child baptized. Consequently, in 1804, the Pecos River settlers began construction of their own church and, when it was completed, arranged for the transfer of the priest at Pecos.

Interior of San Miguel Church. (Photo by David Grant Noble.)

In time, San Miguel became the most important town on New Mexico's eastern frontier. Apaches and Comanches rode into town to barter buffalo jerky, hides, and horses, with the last usually having been stolen from western Texas ranches. After Anza's truce, Spanish *comancheros* made San Miguel a base from which to mount expeditions out to the plains to sell cloth, hunting knives, beads, and other "civilized" items to the nomadic bands.

In November 1821, San Miguel's citizenry must have enjoyed the spectacle of a new and exotic group of visitors, Americans from across the Great Plains leading a train of pack animals laden with goods. Their leader was William Becknell, known today as "the founder of the Santa Fe Trail." Becknell's trip opened a veritable floodgate of commerce; in four years, sixty-five thousand dollars worth of goods passed over the Trail, and in 1846, when a conquering army from Missouri splashed over the Pecos River *vado* into San Miguel, this figure rose to a million dollars.

To minimize tariffs, which were charged by the wagonload, caravans from the States often would "double load" their goods before pulling up at the San Miguel customs house. No doubt, the drovers and travelers, who were by now starved for entertainment, opened their purses in the village's stores and cantinas. Business in the town also boomed as eastbound caravans stopped here for "last chance" supplies before setting out on the seemingly limitless prairies. At the peak of this era, the town's population swelled to between fifteen hundred and two thousand people, making it one of the most important towns in New Mexico. The population also expanded up and down the river valley, establishing new farming communities such as San Juan, Sena, and Villanueva, in addition to San José.

In 1841, still another unexpected group of *gringos* surprised San Miguel residents, this time it was *Tejanos* taken prisoner by Governor Manuel Armijo's militia. Texans, even though they were still officially in a state of war with Mexico, longed to play a hand in the United States–Mexico trading frenzy. The expansive new republic even made claims to New Mexico territory. When an ostensible trading expedition of four hundred armed men arrived on New Mexico's eastern frontier, Governor Armijo was there to meet it. The Texans' thirteen-hundred-mile trek across the plains had met a series of mishaps, and the ill-equipped party arrived in New Mexico in such a bedraggled state that they may have viewed their captors more as saviors than as foes. If so, they were sadly mistaken, for Armijo's soldiers treated them as prisoners of war, quickly rounded them up, disarmed them, executed two in San Miguel's plaza, and marched the rest all the way to Mexico City. Ultimately, the survivors were freed.

Although San Miguel's importance as a supply center diminished after 1835, when a group of its townsfolk founded Las Vegas (p. 161) twenty-three miles to the east, it continued to thrive throughout the life of the Santa Fe Trail. In 1879, however, the Santa Fe Railroad laid its tracks a couple of miles north of the town, and San Miguel's fortunes took a downturn. The area had no further economic potential beyond small-scale farming, which had been the genesis of San Miguel's original founding. By 1910, scarcely more than four hundred people still lived in San Miguel, and today only a few families remain here.

However depressed San Miguel may appear today, one must keep in mind the town's former importance. If you come here, see the community's beautifully maintained church, then cross the plaza (highway) and stroll down the shady lane to the banks of the Pecos River. Here, you will actually be on a remnant of the Santa Fe Trail, and you may be able to imagine Conestoga wagons splashing across the river and drivers urging their teams up its banks toward the plaza. During the heyday of the Trail, a traveler described this place as follows:

> A beautiful crystal stream rushes through this town, at no part more than four feet in depth, and so clear that the white pebbles can be seen glittering at the bottom and skipping along with the force of the current. Here in the afternoon, when the heat of the day had passed, groups of girls and children were seen plunging their bare feet into the refreshing stream and arousing echo with screams of laughter and delight.

TIPS FOR THE TRAVELER:
While in the area, you will be interested to see the nearby village of San José, whose old plaza, surrounded by adobe houses, suggests how San Miguel originally looked. You may also enjoy the drive south on New Mexico 3 to Villanueva, another old Hispanic village with traditional adobe homes and a state park along the Pecos River. Other historic sites in the area are Pecos National Historical Park, the old plaza and Victorian homes in Las Vegas, and Fort Union National Monument (p. 264). You will find travel services along I-25 and in Santa Fe and Las Vegas.

SUGGESTED READING:
The Commerce of the Prairies, by Josiah Gregg (reprinted; Lincoln: University of Nebraska Press, 1967). This book was first published in 1844.

SANTA CRUZ

Santa Cruz is located on the north side of New Mexico 76, about three miles east of Española.

Today, the village of Santa Cruz offers few visual clues to its former prominence in New Mexico's past, but this village was once New Mexico's second largest town and the administrative center for the area north of Santa Fe.

Under the onslaught of the Pueblo Indians in 1680, the original Spanish settlers of the Santa Cruz Valley had either been killed or had fled to Santa Fe, leaving behind a destroyed church. Most of their simple homes, built of adobe, had deteriorated under the effects of a dozen seasons of rains and snows. Other houses had been reoccupied since the

Santa Cruz Church, c. 1895. (Photo by Keystone View Company, courtesy Museum of New Mexico, neg. 89410.)

revolt by Tano (Southern Tewa) Indians from the pueblos of San Lazaro and San Cristóbal in the Galisteo Basin, south of Santa Fe. Why the Tanos relocated here is unrecorded, but presumably they were attracted by the agricultural potential of the Santa Cruz Valley.

Diego de Vargas's reconquest of New Mexico was an extenuated and often conflictive process that began in 1692 and was not finished until 1696. As part of his strategy to augment his authority in the territory, he recruited groups of prospective colonists in Mexico to settle the insecure hinterlands north of Santa Fe. After a thorough reconnaissance, the governor targeted the Santa Cruz Valley, thirty miles from the capital city, as the first outlying area to recolonize.

Vargas, however, recognized that the valley could not sustain the Tanos as well as a growing Spanish community; thus, in 1695, he gave the Indians notice to leave. The San Lazaros, evicted immediately to make room for Spanish settlers already en route from Zacatecas, were allowed to move to Chimayo (p. 147), a few miles away, until they had harvested crops already planted. Afterward, they were to go to San Juan or to other Tewa pueblos along the Rio Grande. Most of the San Cristóbal Indians eventually migrated all the way to First Mesa in the Hopi country of eastern Arizona.

Vargas granted land on the south side of the Santa Cruz River to sixty-six Zacatecas families, who moved into the abandoned San Lazaro pueblo and began planting crops on lands already cleared by the Indians. He accompanied the colonists to their new home and performed the formal land-transfer ceremonies for the new settlement, named *La Villa Nueva de Santa Cruz de los Españoles del Rey Nuestra Señor Don Carlos Segundo* (The New Town of the Holy Cross of the Spanish Mexicans of the King Our Master Carlos the Second). This clumsy name was soon shortened to Santa Cruz de la Cañada, later to La Cañada, and ultimately to Santa Cruz. In 1696, more families moved up from Santa Fe and occupied lands in Chimayo, where the Tanos from San Cristóbal had been living.

The Santa Cruz settlers led a precarious existence. The governor's promised support was slow to materialize, and the settlers had to fend for themselves and fashion many of their own tools. Agriculture here was only by irrigation, and rainfall was unpredictable and uncertain. Crop failures from drought and flood were one threat; another was depredations by nomadic Indians—Comanches, Utes, and Jicarilla Apaches. Still, the colony survived and even increased in numbers; within a generation, homesteads were spreading up and down the valley. As the community grew, more settlements were founded: Chimayo, Quemado (Cordova), Las Trampas (p. 157) and Las Truchas (p. 218). Santa Cruz itself was moved in 1632 to higher ground across the river, out of the path of floods.

The colonists initially attended Mass at a small church served by the priest from San Juan Pueblo; then, in 1733, they began construction of a larger church, *Santa Cruz de la Cañada,* which took them fifteen years to complete. It is this church that still dominates the village plaza. From 1765 to 1768, its priest was Fray Andrés García, who was also an artist. His decorative altar rail, several carved statues, and an altar screen still adorn the church.

When Father Francisco Atanasio Domínguez visited Santa Cruz in 1776, the church had, in his words, "eight small houses like ranchos to keep it company." Other farms were scattered along the river, which the priest described as being endowed with "delicious crystalline water." Domínguez's census for the Santa Cruz parish included a sum total of 274 families with 1,389 persons, of whom 680 lived in Santa Cruz itself. Santa Fe's population at the same time was only just over 2,000.

As New Mexico's "second city," Santa Cruz developed a reputation for its independent spirit; its residents, indeed, may have felt in some competition with the capital. In the 1800s, the town was involved in two civil disorders. The first, which erupted in 1837 and is commonly called the Chimayo rebellion, was directed against the government in Santa Fe. Against a background of hard work and poverty, passions among the common folk of the Santa Cruz countryside were aroused by rumors that the new centralist government of Mexico planned to tax New Mexicans. (Heretofore, New Mexicans' military service in campaigns against marauding Indian tribes had been accepted in lieu of monetary taxes.) In addition to the tax scare, Santa Cruz and Chimayo residents resented what they perceived as the extravagant life-style of their Mexican governor, Albino Pérez.

Open rebellion broke out in the first week in August, with the issuance of an angry proclamation against the policies of the Mexican government, taxation, and the governor's "excesses." Pérez led troops north to put down the insurrection, but the Santa Cruz–Chimayo rebels sent them scurrying back to Santa Fe, where Pérez was assassinated. Then they installed one of their own as governor, a Hispanicized Plains Indian from Ranchos de Taos named José Gonzales. Gonzales himself was soon killed and replaced by Manuel Armijo.

A decade after the Chimayo rebellion, another revolt broke out in New Mexico, this time in Taos and against the Americans, who had seized the territory from Mexico. This group of insurgents, based in Taos, assassinated Governor Charles Bent in his Taos home, killed other citizens, and headed toward Santa Fe. Poorly led and organized, the Taos rebels skirmished with better-armed U.S. troops in Santa Cruz and were routed.

Under the United States, many economic and political changes came to New Mexico, and Santa Cruz's importance diminished. When the Denver and Rio Grande Railroad laid its tracks down the west side of the Rio Grande, bypassing Santa Cruz and shifting the main route to Taos, Santa Cruz became just another small farming community, although noted for its excellent crops and apple orchards. In 1928, construction of a dam across the Santa Cruz River greatly stabilized agriculture in the valley. Today, the old Santa Cruz plaza retains much historical character, its anchor being the church.

The painted altar screen in Santa Cruz Church. (Photo by David Grant Noble.)

La Iglesia de Santa Cruz de la Cañada underwent major structural renovation and modernization in the late 1970s. In addition, its altar screen and six valuable altar paintings were professionally restored. The church is known for its fine artwork, some executed by Fray García, some by the noted *santero* José Rafael Aragon, much of whose work can still be viewed here.

other Santa Cruz area villages are much worth visiting. These Chimayo and its famous Santuario, Cundiyo, Cordova, Las and Las Trampas. In these places, you will gain a sense of northern New Mexico's Hispanic life and culture. Nearby Santa Cruz Lake has an attractive park, where you can picnic, camp, hike, and try your luck at fishing.

SUGGESTED READING:

La Iglesia de Santa Cruz de la Cañada: 1733–1983 (Santa Cruz: Santa Cruz Parish, 1983).

Rebellion in Río Arriba, 1837, by Janet Lecompte (Albuquerque: University of New Mexico Press, 1985).

SANTA FE

Santa Fe is located off Interstate 25, between Albuquerque and Las Vegas, in north-central New Mexico.

Native Santa Feans enjoy telling visitors from the East that their town was founded a decade before the Pilgrims landed at Plymouth Rock. But even their pre-Pilgrim ancestors were latecomers to this picturesque riverside site by the foothills of the Sangre de Cristo Mountains. As early as A.D. 1200, Puebloan people had built a village we call *Pindi* about five miles downriver from later Santa Fe, and for the next two hundred years other Indian communities thrived nearby. Foremost among them, with a population of over a thousand, was Arroyo Hondo Pueblo, just south of the city. It was occupied between around A.D. 1300 and 1425.

In 1610, Spaniards were drawn to the Santa Fe locality for reasons similar to those of their Native American precursors: fresh water flowed from the mountains; the adjacent hills were rich in game; and fertile soils promised good crops. In addition, they could graze their horses in nearby pastures. Santa Fe's settlers had been living since 1599 in the Tewa pueblo of *Yunge* (San Gabriel), near the confluence of the Rio Grande and Rio Chama. Having been brought to New Mexico by Juan de Oñate, they now had a new governor, Pedro de Peralta. Peralta surveyed the site on the north side of the Santa Fe River and drew up a conventional plan for the new colonial capital, including a central

square (*plaza*), a block of government buildings (*casas reales*), and a series of neighborhoods (*vecindades*). He also appointed a hierarchy of governing officials; every member of the colony, from council member to farmer, knew his responsibilities and place in the social order.

The colonists with Indian labor constructed the *casas reales,* from which civil power emanated. (Today, the Palace of the Governors is located on this site.) We know little about how the rest of the plaza area looked in this early colonial era except that it was at least twice as large as it is today, and the buildings around it included private residences, administrative offices, and a military chapel.

Santa Fe's earliest settlers included soldiers, farmers, traders, artisans, and missionaries; in addition, there was a large contingent of Mexican Indians, who also had made the trek to New Mexico with Oñate and had their own neighborhood, known as the *Barrio de Analco* (*analco* means "on the other side" in Nahuatl), on the south side of the river. It, too, has survived (though not as an Indian neighborhood) in modified form around East De Vargas Street and San Miguel Church.

Left: the Palace of the Governors and the Plaza in 1861 with a wagon train just arrived over the Santa Fe Trail. (Courtesy Museum of New Mexico, neg. 11254.)
Above: similar view in 1993. (Photo by David Grant Noble.)

Members of the colony were apportioned lots for their homes as well as parcels of land for fields, vineyards, and orchards. Although some lived in town, most chose to build their dwellings close to their fields downriver. The *casas reales* were a sprawling compound that included the offices, storerooms, defensive towers, a military chapel, stables, corrals, and even a jail. Peralta and his successors also lived here. In these buildings, policies and directives were formulated to govern the entire province. The interests of Santa Fe's civil authorities, however, soon came into conflict with those of New Mexico's clerics, who had their headquarters in Santo Domingo Pueblo (p. 85), and the policies of both church and state were deeply resented by the region's Native American inhabitants.

Long-festering grievances, on the part of the Pueblo Indians against Spanish rule, and economic hardship came to a head on August 10, 1680, when the Indians initiated a general revolt. The planning and organization of the rebellion was carried out at Taos Pueblo (p. 89) by a group of Pueblo leaders led by Popé of San Juan (p. 72). The rebels first struck rural settlements and missions north and south of the capital, killing priests and settlers and burning churches. Survivors fled to Santa Fe, where they took refuge in the *casas reales*. On August 13, Pueblo warriors arrived in the capital, occupied the Barrio de Analco, and laid siege to the *casas reales* with its thousand Spanish refugees. When Governor Antonio de Otermín failed to negotiate a truce with the Indians, they cut off the refugees' water supply, plundered the homes of Christianized Indians in the barrio, burned San Miguel Mission, and destroyed crops. For nine days, the colonists held out in their sanctuary. Then, on August 20, Otermín and a contingent of veterans broke through the Indians' ranks and led the desperate colonists into exile.

For twelve years, the Pueblo Indians were in control of Santa Fe and most of New Mexico, living in the Palace of the Governors, which they converted into a pueblo-style stronghold. In September 1692, however, they watched from its walls as a force of a hundred soldiers, armed citizens, and Indian auxiliaries came into view, led by a newly appointed aristocratic Spanish governor, Diego de Vargas. With what one historian has characterized as "extraordinary boldness and personal diplomacy," Vargas negotiated a peace with the Pueblo leaders and returned triumphantly to Mexico. This peaceful, though only symbolic, reconquest is marked at Santa Fe's annual fiesta in September. The true reconquest, however, was to wait another fifteen months, when Vargas returned, now at the head of a colonizing expedition.

This time, Santa Fe's native defenders were less cooperative. It was midwinter and the Spaniards were starving and suffering from exposure. Still, they stormed the *casas reales* the morning of December 29, and to their good fortune they were soon joined in battle by warriors from Pecos Pueblo (p. 42). Pueblo unity had disintegrated since 1680, and Vargas enjoyed the collaboration of not just Pecos but San Felipe, Santa Ana, and Zia as well. The Battle of Santa Fe lasted only a day and a half before Pueblo resistance collapsed and the capital fell back into Spanish hands. In its aftermath, Vargas executed seventy native defenders, condemned another four hundred to terms of servitude, and took possession of large stores of food.

In the eighteenth century, Santa Fe's population grew rapidly, and colonists established settlements to the north in the Santa Cruz and Chama river valleys. Albuquerque was founded in 1706 at the center of a series of farming hamlets in the Middle Rio Grande Valley. Greater Santa Fe grew in a somewhat disorganized fashion that moved one contemporary observer to describe it as "many small ranches at various distances from one another, with no plan as to their location." Most public thoroughfares were little more than ruts leading to farmsteads.

West San Francisco Street in Santa Fe, 1881. (Photo by W. H. Jackson, courtesy Museum of New Mexico, neg. 11354.)

The downtown did have one "semblance of a street," but except around the plaza it lacked orderly blocks of houses. Periodic attempts to consolidate the town in order to better defend its citizens from anticipated attacks by Plains Indians were unsuccessful. Most citizens were farmers and laborers, but some followed such trades as carpentry, blacksmithing, muleskinning, and weaving.

As in other parts of New Spain, society in colonial Santa Fe was highly stratified. At the top were persons born in Spain or who had pure Spanish blood, and below this elite were the *castas*, whose heritage included admixtures from Native America and Africa. While Santa Fe was important as New Mexico's capital and main *villa*, it never attained the impressive aspect of cities in Mexico; indeed, highbrow visitors from the south often regarded it as downright shoddy in appearance. The underlying cause for the capital's dilapidated adobe buildings was that it administered a territory many of whose residents lived at little more than a subsistence level. The proceeds of any surpluses often ended up in the pockets of corrupt officials, or were spent on overpriced essentials from Chihuahua.

In 1821, when Mexico gained its independence, Santa Fe opened up trade with the United States, and economic conditions began to turn around. Santa Fe became the destination point of traders from Missouri, who brought in an exciting inventory of trade goods and introduced a new culture to isolated New Mexico. Soon Mexican traders joined the burgeoning commerce.

One of Santa Fe's outstanding figures during its Mexican period was Manuel Armijo, a successful businessman who served three terms as governor between 1827 and 1846. Armijo received little support from Mexico City, but aggressively generated income for the state by taxing the American caravans that rumbled in growing numbers over the Santa Fe Trail.

When the United States invaded New Mexico in 1846, Armijo's military strength rested in a poorly trained and armed militia, which was supposed to block a disciplined, well-equipped American army. As the Americans drew near, Armijo made a decision that would forever cloud his reputation: to disband his forces and abandon Santa Fe to the foreign invaders. Without a shot having been fired in Santa Fe, New Mexico was declared a part of the United States.

The Americanization of Santa Fe has been a long process, occurring at political, economic, and social levels. Regular stagecoach and mail service from the East began in the 1850s, and by the following decade, thousands of wagons from Missouri had pulled up around the old plaza. Fort Marcy (p. 245) grew as a military administrative center near the plaza. After the Civil War, lawyers and businessmen arrived, some with entrepreneurial schemes that exploited native New Mexicans. The arrival of the railroad in 1880 accelerated change. The city's exotic character, which had long intrigued soldiers and travelers, began to draw artists and tourists, and the nearby pueblos intrigued anthropologists, who came to interview Indians and to probe ruins.

After World War II, Anglo-American preservationists spearheaded a move to "save" Santa Fe's historical character through an architectural-styles ordinance. To a certain extent their efforts succeeded, although the quaint Spanish Pueblo style they promoted is a much modified and modernized version of Santa Fe's original house styles. By the mid-1980s, Santa Fe had developed into a destination resort and tourist mecca and a major market for Native American and Hispanic craft arts. Remarkably, however, the city has succeeded in retaining many elements of its Hispanic heritage. Today, its impressive complex of museums emphasizes the region's multicultural heritage. Following is a selection of historic sites that you may wish to see while here.

THE PLAZA. In the heart of downtown Santa Fe, the plaza dates to the early 1600s and was the city's social, political, and economic core throughout most of its history. Bordered by the Palace of the Governors, private residences, other government offices, and La Castrense military chapel, it was once twice its present size, extending east to St. Francis Cathedral. The cathedral was built in 1869 by Bishop Jean B. Lamy around an earlier *parroquia* (parish church), using the earlier church as a scaffold. After completion of the cathedral, the old adobe church was demolished brick by brick and taken out the front door!

At various times, the plaza has been used to graze farm animals, grow corn, conduct bullfights, and stage military campaigns. For more than fifty years, trade caravans from Missouri pulled up here after weeks on the trail, some continuing on to Chihuahua. On August 18, 1846, General Stephen Watts Kearny stood here and proclaimed New Mexicans to be citizens of the United States. Today, numerous organized social, cultural, and political events are held in the plaza, but mostly it is used as a casual gathering place of tourists.

THE PALACE OF THE GOVERNORS. Now a museum, it functioned as the governing center of New Mexico from 1610 to 1900. After the Pueblo revolt of 1680, Tano Indians converted it into a pueblo and lived here until defeated in 1693 by Governor Diego de Vargas. Interestingly, between 1878 and 1881, Governor Lew Wallace wrote a large part of his popular novel *Ben Hur* in one of its rooms.

SAN MIGUEL CHURCH. At the corner of East De Vargas Street and Old Santa Fe Trail, this structure dates to 1710, although an older mission had existed on the same site. Its original facade was several times remodeled, and buttresses were added to support its venerable adobe walls; still, the church remains a fine example of eighteenth-century New Mexican ecclesiastical architecture.

EL BARRIO DE ANALCO. Located around East De Vargas Street and San Miguel Church, it was first a neighborhood of Mexican Indians and later of *genízaros,* Hispanicized nomadic Indians. East De Vargas Street still has numerous old residences, including the home of the late renowned anthropologist and historian Adolph F. Bandelier, at number 352.

EL SANTUARIO DE GUADALUPE. At the corner of Guadalupe and Agua Fria Street, this church was built of adobe after 1795 to honor Our Lady of Guadalupe. The Santuario has undergone extensive remodelings, including the addition of gothic windows and a peaked roof in the 1880s and California mission-style elements in 1922. Some beams from the older La Castrense, a military chapel on the south side of the

San Miguel Church and East De Vargas Street. (Photo by David Grant Noble.)

plaza, were incorporated into its construction. Today, the Guadalupe Historic Foundation operates this landmark as an exhibit and performance space.

CANYON ROAD. Although Canyon Road is not historically significant like the plaza, it reputedly follows the route of an ancient Indian trail that led up the Santa Fe Canyon and on to Pecos Pueblo. If you walk up Canyon Road, you will pass many older houses, including El Zaguan (no. 545) and the Borrego House (no. 724). Today, this street is a center for small shops, art galleries, and restaurants.

SENA PLAZA. Located on East Palace Avenue, just east of the plaza, this serene plaza was enclosed by the house of José D. Sena, a leading citizen of Santa Fe and a veteran of the Civil War. Its thirty-three rooms once included the residence of Don José's large family, as well as a coach house, chicken house, storerooms, and servants' quarters. Second-story additions to the north and east sides of the house were made in 1927, but the rest of the buildings are original. Today, the plaza is a lovely garden and the old Sena home contains shops and a restaurant.

Entrance to Sena Plaza. (Photo by David Grant Noble.)

EL CAMINO REAL. The Camino Real (p. 293) led southwest out of Santa Fe to Santo Domingo Pueblo, then down the Rio Grande Valley to Chihuahua and on to Mexico City. For centuries it was New Mexico's lifeline to the heart of Spain's empire in the New World. From downtown Santa Fe, the Camino Real followed what is now Agua Fria Street, along the south side of the Santa Fe River.

Santa Fe can serve as an effective base for numerous historical sidetrips. Highly recommended are Pecos National Historical Park (p. 42) and the Hispanic villages of Chimayo (p. 147), Truchas (p. 218), and Las Trampas (p. 157), along the High Road to Taos (p. 208). The Indian pueblos between Santo Domingo and San Juan also are but a short drive, and may be holding public dances during your visit. In addition, the ruins at Bandelier National Monument offer much insight into the region's Pueblo prehistory.

SUGGESTED READING:

Santa Fe: History of an Ancient City, edited by David Grant Noble (Santa Fe: School of American Research Press, 1989).

Santa Fe Today, preface by John Gaw Meem (Santa Fe: Historic Santa Fe Foundation, 1991).

SILVER CITY
AND THE SANTA RITA MINE

Silver City is located on U.S. 180, fifty-three miles northwest of Deming in southwestern New Mexico.

Ghost towns and abandoned mining camps are ubiquitous across the New Mexico landscape. These boom-and-bust settlements typically enjoyed spectacular, if brief, existences, often leaving little more to remember them by than a private fortune or two and a few broken timbers scattered across the desert. Silver City was an exception.

Silver City was founded in 1870, in an area where Native Americans had lived for thousands of years. The prehistoric Mogollon Indians began farming and hunting in the well-watered valleys and forested hills of southwestern New Mexico at least several centuries B.C., and between around A.D. 1000 and 1250, a branch of these prehistoric Indians, the Mimbres, inhabited numerous villages in the Silver City area. By the mid-1400s, the Mogollon had disappeared, but they were followed within two centuries by other Indians—nomadic Apachean tribes, who migrated here from the plains to the north and east.

When Europeans first entered the Silver City region, they found themselves in the heart of the Warm Springs and Mimbreño Apache country. In 1800, the Indians showed Colonel José Manuel Carrasco copper outcroppings in the Santa Rita Basin (twelve miles east of Silver

Early street scene, Silver City. (Courtesy Rio Grande Historical Collections.)

City), and in the following year he began mining. In 1804, Carrasco sold his claim to a wealthy Chihuahua businessman by the name of Don Francisco Manuel de Elguea. Elguea and his associates began mining immediately; it was one of the first mining operations by Europeans in the Southwest. They realized quick profits, thanks, in part, to their use of convicts to perform the backbreaking and dangerous labor involved in extracting the ore from a network of deep, dark, and claustrophobic tunnels. Much later, when Santa Rita developed into an open-pit excavation, ancient collapsed tunnels were unearthed with their entombed laborers.

After Elguea's death, his heirs leased the operation to other entrepreneurs who, by 1807, were reportedly producing some twenty thousand mule loads of ore annually, most of which was transported to Chihuahua, thence to the Royal Mint in Mexico City, to be made into copper coinage.

By the mid-1820s, intensified harassments of Mexicans by local Apaches had much inhibited mining activity. Santa Rita's owner jumped at an opportunity to lease the mine to an American beaver trapper, James O. Pattie, who achieved a temporary truce with the Indians. Pattie did well and even hoped to buy the mine until one of his employees absconded with thirty thousand dollars of company funds.

In 1831, for security against Indian attack, the mine operators built a triangular adobe fort with massive walls and a defensive tower at each corner. Several years later, local Apaches again threatened the security of the Santa Rita community, and mining activity was curtailed. By

1846, the mine lay abandoned, and in 1852, when the Gadsden Purchase was being negotiated with Mexico, the U.S. Army briefly established a post, Fort Webster, at the site of the old Santa Rita fort. The Santa Rita Mine operated sporadically under various owners for many years, with its ownership claims also undergoing intense scrutiny by the commissioner of the General Land Office. Eventually, it was acquired by the Kennecott Copper Corporation, which developed it into the largest open-pit copper mine in the world.

By the Treaty of Guadalupe Hidalgo (1848) and the Gadsden Purchase (1853), all of New Mexico officially became part of the United States, and military forts began to appear at strategic points across the frontier. This security allowed the Santa Rita mine to restart and prospectors to scour the hills. When gold was discovered at Pinos Altos in 1860, fortune seekers poured in.

The Apaches, understandably, were offended that the United States had negotiated with Mexico rather than with them over possession of their land, and they increased their raids on miners, settlers, herders, and travelers. Two of their principal leaders were the legendary Mangas Coloradas and Cochise, whose followers were effective guerrilla fighters familiar with every corner of their mountainous territory. Even their appearance impressed their American adversaries, one of whom described them as "all differently dressed, and some in the most fantastical style. The Mexican dress and saddles predominated, showing where they had chiefly made up their wardrobe. . . . Several wore beautiful helmets, decked with black feathers, which, with the short skirt, waist belt, bare legs and buckskins, gave them the look of pictures of antique Grecian warriors."

When the Civil War broke out and federal troops were transferred to the East, the balance of power in the Southwest quickly shifted to the Indians, and Pinos Altos mining activity slowed down. Following the war, however, a second gold strike at Pinos Altos brought a fresh influx of miners and troops. In 1870, when John Bullard found silver a few miles to the south, Silver City was born. Now the boom was on, with clusters of tents springing up on hillsides and would-be millionaires roaming the countryside in search of ore. Another major strike by Lorenzo Carrasco at Chloride Flat, two miles west of town, added to the frenzy of activity, and Silver City took on a typical mining-town atmosphere. On the heels of prospectors and miners came merchants, speculators, laborers, teamsters, soldiers, and cowboys; and before long, saloon keepers, gamblers, and prostitutes developed a vibrant red-light district in town.

Working the Santa Rita Mine, 1911. (Courtesy Museum of New Mexico, neg. 47636.)

The Apaches remained such a problem to the Americans that a new post, Fort Bayard (p. 228), was established specifically to protect the Pinos Altos mining operations. Even so, in 1871, Apaches raided Silver City and in the aftermath killed John Bullard. Recognizing the growing threat to their land and way of life, the Indians raided isolated ranches, drove off herds, and attacked stagecoaches and freight wagons. In 1883, the McComas family was attacked on the road to Lordsburg. The parents were killed and their young red-haired son, Charles, taken captive. For many years, reported sightings of the fair-skinned captive trickled in, but despite extensive searches, the boy was never found.

Silver City lays claim to being the locale where, in 1875, Billy the Kid began his career of crime. Known then as Henry Antrim, the fifteen-year-old lad robbed clothes from a Chinese laundry, was caught and jailed. However, in setting the pattern of later escapades, the budding criminal squirmed up a jailhouse chimney and escaped.

Silver City's silver mines eventually played out, but new mineral discoveries in the region revived the town's faltering economy, and the arrival of the railroad in 1883 helped it become a regional shipping and supply center. The Santa Rita Mine continues to operate, though at a diminished level. Other industries, such as ranching and freighting, also flourished; in addition, the air and climate drew health seekers from around the country. When Fort Bayard closed after the Apache wars, its buildings were converted for use as a sanitarium for tuberculosis patients. In addition, in the mid-1890s, a Normal school was founded that evolved into Western New Mexico University.

July 21, 1895, was a date to remember for Silver City residents. It was on this evening that heavy rains began to deluge the hillsides around town, which were denuded from woodcutting and overgrazing. At 9:30 P.M., the river was on the rise, and by midnight a twelve-foot wall of water swept downstream, eroding banks, tearing out trees, destroying houses and buildings, and tearing a twenty-five-foot deep gully along Main Street. The night's devastation was awesome, and it only worsened when subsequent storms brought down two more torrents. You can still see the channel cut through town by these floods, though it has since been quite effectively landscaped.

During its heyday, many of Silver City's commercial buildings were built of brick, good fire clay being readily available. As a building material, brick had particular appeal to the many eastern newcomers who disdained the native adobe style. Today, you will see numerous 1880s-era buildings along Bullard Street in the historic district. You may wish to pick up a copy of *Four Historic Scenic Tours,* at the Chamber of Commerce or at other tourist centers, to guide you to a variety of sites in and around town and in Pinos Altos. Some sites, like the H. B. Ailman House (now the Silver City Museum), are actual restored buildings, while others, such as the jail where Billy the Kid was held, have been replaced by modern structures.

TIPS FOR THE TRAVELER:

Other nearby historic sites include the old gold-mining town of Pinos Altos; the awesome open-pit copper mine at Santa Rita; and old Fort Bayard, which currently functions as a hospital. Forty-four miles north of town is Gila Cliff Dwellings National Monument, where you will be able to explore a series of prehistoric cliff houses along the Gila River.

There is also a wealth of recreation opportunities near Silver City, including scenic driving tours, hiking, camping, fishing, hunting, and horseback riding. For eating and lodging, you should plan to make Silver City your base.

SUGGESTED READING:

Built to Last: An Architectural History of Silver City, by Susan Berry and Sharmon Apt Russell (Santa Fe: New Mexico Historic Preservation Division, 1986).

Pioneering in Territorial Silver City: H. B. Ailman's Recollections of Silver City and the Southwest, 1871–1892, edited by Helen J. Lundwall (Albuquerque: University of New Mexico Press, 1983).

SOCORRO

*Socorro is located along Interstate 25, 78 miles south of Albuquerque and
145 miles north of Las Cruces.*

It was the summer of 1598, and Spain's first colonists to New Mexico
had already spent many grueling months on the trail north from Mexico. When they stopped to camp and rest along the Rio Grande, near
the site of present-day Socorro, Piro Indians from the village of Pilabo
offered them food. Later, in gratitude, the Spaniards gave their own
name to the town, *Nuestra Señora de Socorro de Pilabó* (Our Lady of
Succor of Pilabo); it has since been shortened to simply Socorro. At the
same time, they assigned friars here to try to draw the natives into the
Christian fold.

The Piros, like their Tiwa and Keres neighbors to the north, farmed
the fertile floodplains of the Rio Grande and its tributaries. Linguisti-
cally, however, they were related to the people of the Salinas Valley to
the east, whose villages included Abo, Quarai, and Gran Quivira (see
p. 55). Archaeologists trace Piro culture to around A.D. 1300, and the
oldest dwellings the Spanish saw at Pilabo Pueblo likely were built at
this time. During the fourteenth and fifteenth centuries, Piro population
increased substantially, and at the time the Spanish arrived these Indians
were living in a dozen or more villages like Pilabo. Fifty years later,
however, the toll of disease, famine, and warfare had drastically reduced
their numbers.

The Pilabos raised corn, beans, squash, and cotton, and ranged afar
to hunt game and to collect wild plant foods. A sister village, Teypana,
sat across the Rio Grande; such pairing of pueblos on either side of the
river was a typical method used by the Indians for the convenience of
irrigation and cultivation along both banks. Unfortunately, no detailed
descriptions of Pilabo itself exist; however, we can assume that like
most other contemporaneous communities, it consisted of single- and
multiple-storied apartment blocks built of puddled adobe and arranged
around a central plaza or several plazas. In 1641, its inhabitants numbered four hundred, a figure that had swelled to six hundred by the time
of the Pueblo revolt in 1680.

The Franciscans completed their Socorro mission in about 1626,
and while they found the natives reluctant to receive Christ, they apparently were able to maintain harmonious relations with the Indians. In
1680, the Piros, whose population was now concentrated in four pueblos, played no part in the Pueblo rebellion. Perhaps worried about bad

Early photograph of San Miguel Church in Socorro. (Photo by Bass, courtesy Museum of New Mexico, neg. 151682.)

relations with the triumphant northern rebels, they accompanied the retreating colonists to El Paso del Norte, where they established two centers, Socorro del Sur and Senecu del Sur. These communities have long since merged with the general El Paso–Juárez population. Soon after being abandoned, Pilabo and the Socorro mission were pillaged and burned by Apaches, who had migrated into the region from the southern plains. Pilabo never was reclaimed by the Piros, and settlement of the fertile Socorro area by the Spanish was precluded for more than a century by Apache hostilities.

Throughout the eighteenth century, immigration from Mexico greatly swelled New Mexico's population. As the colony expanded, interest was born in establishing a Socorro settlement. In 1815 or 1816, a contingent of colonists returned to Socorro, hoping to stave off the Apache threat and cultivate fields between the river and the mountains. The new settlers arranged for a land grant from the crown and set about rebuilding the church, which lay in ruins. The story is told that one day an Apache raiding party approached Socorro, but upon seeing a winged angel hovering over the church, aborted their attack. When the Spanish learned of this, they named their church after the archangel San Miguel.

The new Socorro colony took hold, and its members soon could look over vineyards and fields of wheat and corn. In 1836, they successfully repulsed an Apache attack, but were ambushed as they pursued the Indians and suffered forty-eight deaths. Normally, however, the town itself was relatively safe, although lands beyond remained the domain of the Apaches. In August of 1846, a United States army invaded New Mexico, and later the same year, hundreds of American troops marched down Socorro's dusty street, to the astonishment of its citizens. In the 1850s, the Americans established Fort Craig (p. 235) nearby, and brought a permanent sense of security to the region.

Since the early colonial period, the mountains west of Socorro were known to contain minerals. In the 1840s, Socorro resident Estanislao Montoya began mining and smelting ores, but he was soon put out of business by the Apaches. In these years, the town consisted of a series of informal plazas surrounded by low adobe houses and connected by a nameless dirt street with a few stores. A ditch ran through town, bringing water to its inhabitants and to some grist mills and irrigating fields. In 1863, Socorro was invaded by a plague of insects, which decimated the year's crops. Fortunately, the army was able to aid its citizens by importing flour and other provisions.

In the 1860s, lead was discovered in the Magdalena Mountains west of Socorro, and soon after, Socorro Peak was the location of a silver strike. With the arrival of the railroad and an infusion of American capital in the early 1880s, the pace of mining and smelting activity accelerated, giving birth to the towns of Kelly and Magdalena. Almost overnight, Socorro was transformed from a quiet farming community to a boomtown replete with stores, hotels, gambling halls, and saloons. In 1881, miners filed three thousand claims in a six-month period. Some people made quick fortunes; others went broke. Inevitably, differences between the longtime Hispanic residents and the business-minded or

The Juan José Baca House from the portal of the Juan Nepomoceno Garcia House in Socorro's Old Town. (Photo by David Grant Noble.)

rowdy newcomers led to tensions. Once, a riot broke out when the Kelly Mine hired a Chinese cook. The economic boom, skyrocketing population, and the crime rate overwhelmed the community's government and peace officers. In response to the murder of one of Socorro's leading citizens, Anthony M. Conklin, on Christmas Eve 1880, a vigilante-style citizen group, presided over by mine owner E. W. Eaton, took matters into its own hands. They ran down three suspects, all brothers in the Baca family, and then continued to hold power in town for several more years. Suspects of other crimes were apprehended and sometimes hanged from convenient tree limbs and gate posts.

The Socorro mines produced respectable quantities of lead, silver, and zinc, as well as some gold, copper, iron, and manganese. Peak production lasted through the 1880s, after which their output began to decline. By the mid-nineties, the fortune seekers who had brought on the good times began to seek opportunities elsewhere. With their departure, Socorro began to return to its former tranquillity as a farming and ranching center. It has been estimated that a quarter-century of mining in the area had produced nine million dollars in lead and silver ores. This figure was considerably enhanced by revenues from smelting, shipping, and supply operations. One significant mining-related activity did continue, however, in the form of the New Mexico School of Mines, and in 1989 this nationally known school—now called the New Mexico Institute of Mining and Technology—marked its centennial. It remains a major factor in Socorro's economy.

Most travelers see little more of Socorro than its modern commercial strip. But the town embraces an interesting historic district, centered around the old plaza and Kittrel Park. This district contains numerous buildings and houses that date back to the boomtown years and the turn-of-the-century era. There are even a few from the Spanish colonial and Mexican periods. When you visit Socorro, you will want to obtain a copy of the city's *Tour Brochure,* a handy guide with street-map locations to more than two dozen sites in the historic district. This free brochure, which is available at the Chamber of Commerce and at other tourist centers, will lead you to such sites as San Miguel Church, built between 1819 and 1821; the Juan Nepomoceno García House, an outstanding Spanish-Mexican period landmark adjacent to the plaza; the historic García Opera House, built by the same family in 1886; and the World War I–era Val Verde Hotel.

TIPS FOR THE TRAVELER:
You may wish to visit the nearby ruins of Fort Craig and, if you are headed toward Las Cruces, you should stop at Fort Selden State Monument (p. 249). Salinas Pueblo Missions National Monument (p. 55) is located near Mountainair, sixty-one miles northeast via U.S. 60. Also of interest is the Bosque del Apache National Wildlife Refuge, a waterfowl wintering ground located outside nearby San Antonio. This small village, incidently, was the birthplace of Conrad Hilton, whose family ran a small hotel near the railroad station.

SUGGESTED READING:
Socorro: A Historic Survey, by John P. Conron (Albuquerque: University of New Mexico Press, 1980).
The Territorial History of Socorro, New Mexico, by Bruce Ashcroft (El Paso: Texas Western Press, 1988).

TAOS

Taos is located along U.S. 64, forty-seven miles north of Española and seventy miles north of Santa Fe.

Taos is a quaint, though commercialized, town nestled in the western shadow of the Sangre de Cristo Mountains. Although the growth of tourism has much changed its character in recent years, its name (pronounced like "house") still evokes the mystique of New Mexico's Hispanic and Indian culture and of the art colony that thrived here several generations ago.

Although Europeans have been living in Taos for more than three centuries, they are newcomers compared to the Taos Indians, whose adjacent pueblo is more than five hundred years old. Unlike many other villages in the region that thrived for briefer periods, Taos has been an active population and cultural center throughout the long sweep of New Mexico history.

The Taos Valley was scouted by members of the Coronado expedition in 1541, but it was not until the seventeenth century that Spaniards actually settled here and began farming the valley. For protection, they lived close to the pueblo. Here, as everywhere on New Spain's northern frontier, colonists depended on the indigenous peoples for food and clothing supplies and sometimes for defense, as well. Much later, as the territory became more secure, they moved several miles south to establish their own village, San Fernando de Taos.

Due to the destruction of Spanish documents in New Mexico during the Pueblo revolt, little is known about the small Taos settlement prior to 1680. The revolt was organized in the kivas of Taos Pueblo; after it erupted, surviving members of the colony fled toward Santa Fe. When Spaniards returned here after 1693, their attitude toward the Indians had changed, becoming more cooperative than exploitive.

In the 1700s, attacks by nomadic tribes, especially by Utes and Comanches, grew so serious that everyone living in the Taos Valley worked together to defend themselves. Taos Pueblo was a veritable fortress within whose walls Spanish farmers frequently found safety, sometimes for extended periods. In 1760, a large Comanche war party stormed the Taos hacienda of Pablo de Villalpando, killed many of its occupants, and abducted sixty-four women and children. The following summer, Comanche traders had the audacity to offer seven of the captives for

La Hacienda de Don Antonio Severino Martinez, dating to c. 1804, in Taos. (Photo by David Grant Noble.)

ransom in Taos. During these dangerous times, the residents of Fernando de Taos bolstered the defenses of the plaza district by controlling access and making the outside walls of the surrounding houses contiguous.

All tribal and national groups recognized a truce during the annual Taos Fair. This annual week-long event, held at the pueblo after harvest, probably had its origins in pre-Columbian times, but it grew in importance after the Spanish colony reestablished itself in the 1700s. Attended by Pueblos, Utes, Apaches, Navajos, Comanches, and Spaniards, it became the biggest commercial and social event in the province and eventually was moved to the village. Those who attended the Taos fairs could trade, exchange news, conduct politics, and socialize in an atmosphere both fun and fraught with tension. In addition to trading buckskins, buffalo hides, and booty, the Plains tribes brought captives, mostly Indian women and children, to sell or ransom. Often the Spaniards did the same, to exchange for members of their community being held by the Indians. When the colonists acquired Indian captives, they brought them home to be trained as household servants and to indoctrinate them into the Catholic faith. Upon attaining adulthood, most of these Hispanicized Plains Indians, called *genízaros*, were released to live on their own.

After the Louisiana Purchase in 1803, the border of the United States drew to within 150 miles of Taos, and some Americans began to turn their attention toward New Mexico. Lieutenant Zebulon Montgomery Pike explored nearby in 1807, and soon after, adventuresome fur trappers began roaming the southern Rockies. These mountain men, who were trespassers under Spanish law, came to know the Sangre de Cristos and frequented Taos.

After Mexican Independence in 1821, Taos became the epicenter of a burgeoning trade in beaver pelts. The names of many mountain men associated with the town during this era—Ewing Young, William Wolfskill, Bill Williams, Milton Sublette, the Robidoux brothers, Pegleg Smith, Cerán St. Vrain, Kit Carson, and others—have found an enduring place in western folklore. It was they who first penetrated the mountain fastness and excited the imagination of later, official explorers. Although some actually settled in Taos, most only visited to sell their skins; to resupply; to partake of the town's infamous *aguardiente,* or "Taos Lightning"; and to enjoy some female company after months in the wilderness.

The trappers were an independent, fortune-seeking lot who disregarded regulations and avoided authorities. One later reminisced, "These [pelts] we sold in [Taos] at $4 per pound, or an average of $10 per skin. In those days although there was a heavy duty on all beaver skins brought into New Mexico, no one ever thought of paying it and, as in our case, they would be smuggled into town in the night." The mountain men rarely obtained permits, and nearly all of them invented subterfuges for avoiding taxation. Since New Mexicans seldom entered the lucrative trapping business, the trade was carried on at the expense of both the beaver population and the New Mexico economy.

Although that market collapsed in the early 1830s, the growing commerce with Missouri—a branch of the Santa Fe Trail reached Taos—kept the town's economy vigorous and assured prosperity, at least for a few.

Two Americans who prospered in Taos were the partners Cerán St. Vrain and Charles Bent, whose trading empire was based at Bent's Fort, along the eastern edge of the Rockies. Another well-known person here was Kit Carson, whose résumé could have listed him as mountain man, hunter, guide, rancher, and soldier. Still another was Charles Beaubien, a merchant, rancher, and justice of the peace. But although Carson called Taos home and was married to a local girl, he spent most of his time "on the road."

Among Hispanos, Taos's most illustrious citizen in this period was its priest Antonio José Martínez. Padre Martínez had his detractors, including Charles Bent, Bishop Lamy, and, later, Willa Cather; however, he was a dedicated educator and powerful advocate of his people. He established a school for the sons and daughters of prominent Taos families and printed New Mexico's first newspaper. Born in Abiquiu in 1793, Martínez moved to Taos in 1826, where his brilliance and ambition combined to place him for many years at the vortex of ecclesiastical and political activity and controversy.

Some people of Hispanic and Indian background in Taos resented New Mexico's occupation by the United States, and on January 19, 1847, they rose up in rebellion. Unlike the Pueblo revolt against the Spanish in 1680, theirs was disorganized and ineffective. In the night, a mob stormed the home of Charles Bent, who was now territorial governor. They scalped and assassinated Bent and slayed five other prominent citizens, then rushed on to Turley's Mill in Arroyo Hondo (where Taos Lightning was made) and killed seven more Americans. Led by Tomás Ortiz and Diego Archuleta, the uprising spread to Santa Cruz (p. 184) and Mora (p. 174) before it was quashed by U.S. troops at Taos Pueblo (p. 89) on February 4. In the aftermath, fifteen leaders of the revolt were sentenced to death and hanged in the Taos plaza.

With the arrival of the railroad in New Mexico, wagon trains no longer rumbled around the old Taos plaza and an era drew to a close, bringing with it a more relaxed and self-contained life-style. But the community was soon to begin its more modern career as an art colony. This really began with painter Joseph Sharp, from Cincinatti, who painted here in 1893 and returned in 1902 and 1908. Sharp was followed by Ernest Blumenschein, Bert Phillips, Oscar Berninghaus, Victor Higgins, and others. The migration, in fact, has continued to the present

Ernest L. Blumenschein's home in Taos. (Photo by David Grant Noble.)

day, though the Taos school has given way to different styles with the changing markets. The town's artistic life was further energized in the 1920s by the presence of colorful Mabel Dodge Lujan, whose hospitality attracted a parade of artistic and literary luminaries, including the English writer D. H. Lawrence and photographer Paul Strand.

In recent decades, the romance of Taos's past has collaborated with its scenic beauty and ski resort to create a thriving tourist industry. For the history buff, there is much here to see. The town plaza, though modernized with shops, galleries, and restaurants, still evokes a past in which one can imagine muddy streets, braying mules, and shouting wagoneers. According to legend, at the outbreak of the Civil War, Kit Carson hoisted the Stars and Stripes up the plaza flagpole and sat beneath it for an entire night, rifle by his side, challenging any Southern sympathizer to pull it down. Carson's home, now a museum, is only two blocks away.

Two other historic homes that you may visit are La Hacienda de Don Antonio Severino Martínez and the Governor Bent Museum. In the latter, the hole in the adobe wall through which members of the Bent and Carson family purportedly escaped on January 19, 1847, still may be viewed. You can get an appreciation of the Taos art colony by visiting the Ernest Blumenschein Memorial Home and Art Museum, the Harwood Foundation, the Nicolai Fechin Institute, and the D. H. Lawrence

Ranch and Shrine. The Morada de Don Fernando de Taos, the restored meeting place of the Taos Penitente Brotherhood, is a place where one can gain some insight into this historic religious society, and the Millicent Rogers Museum has excellent exhibits relating to the region's Hispanic and Indian cultural heritage. Perhaps the two most famous historic sites in the vicinity are the ancient and monumental Taos Pueblo, three miles north of town, and the beautiful San Francisco de Assiz Church in Ranchos de Taos, five miles to the south along New Mexico 68.

TIPS FOR THE TRAVELER:
From Taos, you can take U.S. 64 east to Eagle Nest and Cimarron (p. 151), passing through scenic mountainous country with excellent hiking, fishing, and hunting. If you are traveling to or from Santa Fe, the so-called High Road through the Santa Cruz Valley (p. 184) and villages of Truchas (p. 218) and Las Trampas (p. 157) is recommended; however, New Mexico 68, which follows the Rio Grande part way, is also a lovely drive.

SUGGESTED READING:
When Old Trails Were New: The Story of Taos by Blanche C. Grant (reprinted; Taos: Kit Carson Historic Museums, 1991).
The Taos Trappers: The Fur Trade in the Far Southwest, 1540–1846, by David J. Weber (Norman: University of Oklahoma Press, 1971).

TIERRA AMARILLA

Tierra Amarilla is located along U.S. 64/84 in northern New Mexico's Chama Valley, twelve miles south of Chama.

Santa Fe (see p. 189) was founded in 1610, Santa Cruz (p. 184) in 1695, and Abiquiu (p. 137) in 1754, but it was not until 1860 that Hispanic farmers put down their roots in the Tierra Amarilla region, at a place called Las Nutritas. Why did settlement of the fertile upper Chama Valley progress so slowly? This was the home country of Ute and Navajo Indians (see p. 125), who had been in conflict with New Mexicans since the early 1700s.

Tierra Amarilla's pioneers were pastoral folk, who tilled the land, herded sheep, and hunted deer and elk in the surrounding hills. Given

Main Street, Tierra Amarilla, c. 1890. (Courtesy Museum of New Mexico, neg. 142682.)

the community's distance from the capital, one would hardly expect it to be a center of political or social fomentation; yet, that is what it became.

The original group of settlers, led by Manuel Martínez, were issued their land grant by the Mexican government in 1832, after which they seasonally grazed their flocks in the valley for about twenty years. But due to the Indian presence, they did not begin settling here on a year-round basis until 1860, by which time New Mexico was a part of the United States. Under the 1848 Treaty of Guadalupe Hidalgo, the United States had pledged to honor Spanish and Mexican land grants and set up a lengthy system to adjudicate claims. Congress confirmed the Tierra Amarilla grant in 1860, but classified it as a private rather than community grant. This classification, which scholars now agree was in error, allowed the *ejidos*, or commons, to be sold.

Commons consisted of pastures, woods, and streams—the major part of a grant's acreage—which members of the community used as a shared resource for grazing and watering stock, irrigating fields and pastures, gathering wood, hunting, and other activities. The *ejidos* sustained a community's economy and, by law, could not be sold. Private grants, on the other hand, were issued to individuals, rather than to groups, and could later be sold by the grantee or his heirs. By classifying the Tierra Amarilla grant as private, the courts, in effect, had opened the door for the descendants of the Tierra Amarilla settlers to lose the major part of their land. Soon parcels of the grant came into the hands of land speculators, who sold them at healthy profits to real estate developers, ranchers, logging companies, and the railroad.

In the early 1860s, when settlers were moving into the upper Chama Valley, some built their homes in Las Nutritas, now Tierra Amarilla, while others founded Los Ojos and Brazos (along U.S. 64/84 north of Tierra Amarilla), Ensenada (2 miles north along New Mexico 573), and La Puente (2.5 miles west along New Mexico 531). These hamlets lay within the Tierra Amarilla grant and partook equally of its commons. In the late 1860s, their residents were protected from Indian attacks by U.S. troops stationed at Fort Lowell, a small post built of logs three miles northwest of Tierra Amarilla. After the fort's closing in 1869, its logs were quickly salvaged by area residents for use in new construction.

Had the Tierra Amarilla grant remained intact, the Chama Valley's old way of life would certainly have been extended in some ways, but probably not long preserved. The railroad, more than anything else, brought change, making the region's forests accessible to commercial interests, opening new markets to sheep and cattle ranchers, and providing transportation to young men attracted to wage jobs in the Colorado mines. Although commercial railroading in the Rockies declined in the twentieth century, the Denver and Rio Grande's line through Chama remained viable until 1967, after which a segment of it was restored as the Cumbres & Toltec Scenic Railroad (p. 300).

Most Hispanic residents of Tierra Amarilla and surrounding hamlets feel lingering regret and sadness over historical land losses, but have accepted the situation philosophically. For others, however, knowledge of such past injustices caused bitterness and still rankles deeply. In June of 1967, the *Alianza Federal de Mercedes,* an organization to reclaim lost land, conducted a raid on the Rio Arriba County Courthouse in Tierra Amarilla that briefly captivated national attention. Led by the charismatic Reies Lopez Tijerina, his band of two dozen armed men stormed the courthouse—"They burst out of a past that died with Pancho Villa," wrote *Newsweek*—intending to make a citizens' arrest of the district attorney, who happened to be absent at the time. The incident lasted less than half an hour, during which band members wounded two lawmen and terrified county employees as they sprayed bullets around the building. Finally, they left with two hostages. In the aftermath, 350 National Guardsmen, reinforced by helicopters and tanks, led a massive manhunt for the fugitives, who were eventually arrested.

While the courthouse raid failed in its narrow purpose, it succeeded in highlighting regional land-grant issues and bringing public attention

Norma Martinez weaving at Tierra Wools in Los Ojos. (Photo by David Grant Noble.)

to the depressed social and economic conditions in northern Rio Arriba County. In the aftermath, members of the community sympathetic with the cause founded La Clinica del Pueblo, a health clinic in Tierra Amarilla. Later still, Ganados del Valle, a sheep ranching and weaving cooperative based in Los Ojos, was founded. Twenty years after the raid, a private citizen, Amador Flores, claimed ownership of a parcel of land south of Tierra Amarilla that was being quiet-titled by an Arizona development company. Flores, with a small contingent of armed backers and considerable public support, ignored court orders to leave the property and even constructed a bunker with Vietnam-style defenses. Like the earlier courthouse raid, Flores's stand forced public awareness of historical and ongoing grievances. In the end, it also resulted in a tangible triumph for the land advocates; in the summer of 1989, Flores's attorneys negotiated a settlement with the Arizona firm, in which he gained legal ownership of two hundred acres of the disputed land.

The Tierra Amarilla area will offer you a glimpse into cultural aspects of northern New Mexico that you will not find in more developed, tourist-oriented centers like Santa Fe and Taos. Tierra Amarilla is the Rio Arriba County seat and the old courthouse, scene of Tijerina's raid, remains a prominent building in town.

A highlight of your experience in these parts will be a visit to Tierra Wools, the weaving workshop and showroom in Los Ojos, established by Ganados del Valle in an 1880s building on Main Street. Textiles here are woven from the wool of the rare *churro* sheep, a breed that had nearly disappeared and is now being revived. Los Ojos had the largest contingent of original settlers and was the area's commercial center until 1880, when the county seat was moved to Tierra Amarilla. If you have time, you will also enjoy touring the villages of Los Brazos, La Puente, and Ensenada. They have many older buildings and houses, whose architecture reflects a variety of northern New Mexico folk styles. The book *La Tierra Amarilla* (see below) describes five architectural tours through these villages.

TIPS FOR THE TRAVELER:
The Cumbres & Toltec Scenic Railroad, an historic narrow-gauge line, operates daily from June 16 to October 14, between Chama and Antonito, Colorado. The trip offers a unique way to view the mountains of northern New Mexico and southern Colorado, and to experience how it was to travel by rail a century ago.

Driving south on U.S. 84, you will pass Echo Amphitheater, a scenic and fun state park. In 1966, Tijerina's followers appropriated the park, declared it an independent country, and issued their own visas to enter. Just south of the amphitheater is the Ghost Ranch Living Museum, a roadside zoo with a collection of animals native to the area. Farther south still is Abiquiu, from where Tierra Amarilla's original settlers came, and home of the late painter Georgia O'Keeffe. The *Casa de Martínez* (call 505-588-7858), in Los Brazos, is a bed-and-breakfast inn located in a historic adobe house. Chama has a selection of motels, restaurants, and other travel services.

SUGGESTED READING:
La Tierra Amarilla: Its History, Architecture, and Cultural Landscape, by Chris Wilson and David Kammer (Santa Fe: Museum of New Mexico Press, 1992).

TRUCHAS

Truchas is located along New Mexico 76, seventeen miles northeast of Española.

In the high country above the Santa Cruz Valley sets a New Mexican village that often reminds modern travelers of the old hill towns of Spain. Descriptively called Las Truchas for "the trout" that abounded in nearby mountain creeks, it stretches along the crest of a ridge in the shadow of the highest peaks of the Sangre de Cristo Mountains. Just above the village lie fields and pastures watered by a long *acequia,* or ditch, that the original settlers dug with handmade tools. At the edge of the town, the land falls away precipitously into drainages that wind their way down through the hills to the Rio Grande.

The settlement of Truchas, whose full name was *Nuestra Señora del Rosario, San Fernando y Santiago del Río de las Truchas,* was founded in 1754 by settlers in the Santa Cruz Valley (Santa Cruz, Chimayo, Cordova) after they received a land grant from Governor Tomás Vélez Cachupín. Led by Juan de Dios, they had already built an *acequia* from a dammed-up stream above the village site and raised crops for two summers; these efforts demonstrated their commitment to founding the new hamlet. The grant was divided into three types of parcels: a fortified plaza, allotments for farming, and commons (*ejidos*) consisting of woods and pastures that belonged to everyone.

When he became governor in 1749, Cachupín revived the policy of expanding New Mexico's northern settlements beyond the environs of Santa Fe (p. 89) and Santa Cruz (p. 84). Due to constant depredations by Comanches and other nomadic tribes, the fertile Santa Cruz Valley had not reached its economic potential. Indian raiders crossed over mountain passes from the east to strike their farms with impunity, plunder the fruits of their harvests, and steal livestock. The governor managed to make an ephemeral truce with the Comanches and encouraged the valley farmers to expand their settlements into the high country. By establishing defensive hamlets near the access routes of the Comanches, he hoped to increase security in the valley. He ordered the Truchas pioneers to build houses

> which shall be united and adjoining, forming a square townsite, closed and with only one entrance, only large enough for the passage of one *carreta* [cart], in a manner that the inhabitants and families may be able to defend themselves from invasions and assaults of the barbarous enemies that may try to destroy it . . .

Cross along Highway 76 in Truchas. (Photo by David Grant Noble.)

Although the governor's directive probably fostered little optimism on the part of the apprehensive settlers, it realistically reflected the territory's desperate situation in the mid-eighteenth century. Isolated settlers lived in terror of the Comanche onslaughts. Often armed with only bows and arrows and spears (guns were a rarity), they were usually less than a match for the mobile Plains nomads, who excelled in warfare, knew the terrain, and carried the latest rifles, acquired through trade with the French to the east.

The first generation of Truchas colonists relied on their resources alone to survive. More than just toiling on the land, this meant having

Truchas today. (Photo by David Grant Noble.)

an effective plan for defense against the invaders. Their pleas to authorities in Santa Fe for troop assistance and guns went unheeded, and even a request for Pueblo auxiliaries to scout the mountain passes was denied. It wasn't that such demands were unwarranted; Santa Fe's small garrison simply was not equipped to respond to the needs of New Mexico's outposts.

The Comanche danger reached a peak after the founding of Truchas and Las Trampas (p. 157) and did not abate until after 1779, when Governor Juan Bautista de Anza defeated the principal chieftain Cuerno Verde (named after a green-painted horn on his war bonnet) and created a long-lasting truce with these former foes.

The Trucheros did work hard: they raised wheat and vegetables, for the growing season was too brief for corn; irrigated pastures; tended their cattle and sheep; hauled fuel and building wood from the surrounding mountains; built their houses and farm buildings; and even sent their conscripted men to join campaigns against the Indians. The last activity was done grudgingly, for the men often expected, when they returned, to find their own homes in ruins. Despite the problems, Truchas thrived; by 1800 its population had grown to 150, and by 1822, to nearly 300.

Life in Truchas, like the seasons, was cyclical. Memorable events for families consisted of births, baptisms, and deaths; for the community, they were droughts, floods, epidemics, and Indian raids. All were repeated throughout a person's life span. On the other hand, major developments of the day—Mexican independence and conquest by the

United States, for example—could occur with slight impact on the daily routine of Truchas residents. Even the Great Depression, it is said, passed by villages like Truchas with minimal trauma.

Until World War II, Truchas was fairly immune to the progressive, modernizing trends of mainstream America. Life here was based on small-scale farming and barter and an adherence to long-held cultural traditions and religious beliefs. Inevitably, however, the complexities of modern times have brought changes to New Mexico's mountain villages. Many of the youth have departed to partake of the culture promoted by television; but more than that, one no longer can survive solely by the type of farming long practiced in the narrow valleys of the Sangre de Cristo foothills.

Today, Truchas remains an active community whose members still irrigate some of their pastures and retain a good measure of their traditional values. Weaving shops in town show that, to some extent, old ways can be adapted to a modern economy. In addition, many villagers work in mainstream twentieth-century-type jobs both here and in nearby population centers. Truchas, then, is a mix of the past and present. Its lingering charm was recognized a few years ago by Robert Redford, who chose the townsite for the setting of his film *The Milagro Beanfield War.*

One true delight of a visit to Truchas is to view the village against its backdrop of mountains on which the snow lies deep six months of the year. This is the Pecos Wilderness, a popular place to hike, camp, fish, hunt, and photograph. Whereas, in a former day, this country was a place of insecurity and danger, today it is a precious resource in a vanishing natural world.

TIPS FOR THE TRAVELER:
Other villages in the area such as Santa Cruz, Chimayo, Cundiyo, Cordova, Las Trampas, El Valle, Mora (p. 175), and Taos (p. 208) also will give you a sense of northern New Mexico's Hispanic heritage. To learn more on this subject visits to the Museum of International Folk Art and the Palace of the Governors Museum in Santa Fe, and to the Martínez Hacienda and Millicent Rogers Museum in Taos, are recommended. In addition, a tour of Rancho de las Golondrinas (p. 325) in La Cienega is most worthwhile. You will find a wide selection of tourist facilities in Santa Fe and Taos and travel services in Española.

SUGGESTED READING:
Mountain Villages, by Alice Bullock (Santa Fe: Sunstone Press, 1973).

WARFARE IN
NEW MEXICO

New Mexico has experienced more than its share of warfare over the centuries. The first recorded battle, at the Zuñi pueblo of Hawikuh (see p. 103), happened almost as soon as Coronado's army arrived in the land of the Pueblos in 1540. Here, natives in a walled town defended themselves against soldiers on horseback with a new technology of war.

In prehistoric times, the Anasazi certainly knew fighting. Although evidence is scant of actual battles, pueblos such as Atsinna (p. 323) and Acoma (p. 9) were built so defensively that one must assume warfare threatened them. Others, like Pecos (p. 42) and Taos (p. 89) pueblos, had perimeter walls to help block attackers. Archaeologists speculate that if the Pueblos fought battles before 1540, it was probably among themselves—rival communities attacking each other in periods of food shortages.

The Pueblo-Spanish conflicts only began at Hawikuh. The Spaniards attacked several Southern Tiwa pueblos (p. 5) in 1541, and after Juan de Oñate brought colonists to New Mexico, they fought the Pueblos at Acoma and Quarai (p. 55). The Pueblo revolt came in 1680; now the Pueblos took the offensive against their colonial rulers, murdered priests, killed settlers, laid waste to churches, and drove all the survivors into exile.

A new picture of conflicts and alliances became apparent in the 1700s, when the Rio Grande pueblos and villages were surrounded by new foes: Navajos to the west; Utes to the north; Apaches to the south; and worst of all, Comanches, whose war parties swept over mountain passes from the eastern plains. These were hard times in New Mexico. Like their Anasazi ancestors, the Pueblos built fortresslike villages, and the Spaniards did likewise. What food supplies New Mexico's inhabitants did not lose to the usual threats—droughts, floods, hail—were frequently stolen by the invaders, who also took horses and sheep. The threats from the nomads, however, drew the Spaniards and Pueblos together into a defense alliance. Spanish presidial troops were far too few to defend the territory and counted on Pueblo auxiliaries and citizen militias to make up the bulk of fighting forces. Most offensive campaigns came to naught, but in 1779, Governor Juan Bautista de Anza led a relentless and successful drive against the Comanches, forcing a truce with this tribe that was formalized several years later.

U.S. soldiers at leisure, Fort Stanton, c. 1885. (Photo by Charles Harvey, courtesy Museum of New Mexico, neg. 11654.)

In 1846, an army from the United States marched eight hundred miles over the plains and, with little opposition, occupied Santa Fe (p. 89) and the rest of New Mexico. The Americans were not entirely unwelcome; indeed, many New Mexicans, weary of being ignored by the government in Mexico, already were profiting from the lucrative trade with Missouri. Others, however, especially in rural communities such as Taos (p. 208) and Mora (p. 175), rebelled against American rule.

One does not associate New Mexico with the Civil War; yet, in 1862, Confederate troops from Texas marched up the Rio Grande Valley from El Paso and set up headquarters in Mesilla (p. 170). Then they continued north. Forts Fillmore (p. 173), Stanton (p. 254), and Craig

(p. 235) were unable to stop their advance, and Albuquerque (p. 142) and Santa Fe were occupied. Finally, the Rebels were stopped at Glorieta Pass (p. 271).

No sooner had the Confederates withdrawn than a column of Union troops arrived in New Mexico from California. Since the Civil War here was over, the Californians, together with New Mexican volunteer units, turned their attention to subduing the "wild" Indians, or *indios bárbaros,* of the territory. Kit Carson took charge of these operations against the Apaches (p. 120) and Navajos (p. 125), and by the end of 1864 these tribes had been forced into an internment camp at the Bosque Redondo on the eastern plains. The only unpacified natives left in the Southwest were the Chiricahuas, but another two decades would pass before Gerónimo's surrender closed completely the period of independence experienced by the Southwest's indigenous peoples.

One final battle, however, remained for history to record, although only as a footnote; it remains the only occasion in which the continental United States has been attacked by foreign forces. It happened in the early morning hours of March 9, 1916, when Pancho Villa and the remnants of his once-illustrious army raided Columbus (p. 275), on the Mexican border.

Some years ago, a man digging footings for his house in Glorieta unearthed a mass burial. When archaeologists excavated the site, they discovered it to be the grave of thirty-two Confederates killed in the Battle of Glorieta Pass. After studying the skeletons and identifying many of the dead, attempts were made to notify their descendants. The majority of the deceased were eventually reinterred in the national cemetery in Santa Fe in the spring of 1993.

New Mexico's military history contains a full measure of sadness, along with traditions of glory and heroism. Today, many of the actual sites where people fought are lost or totally transformed by modern development. Even whole forts are gone, their adobe walls melted back into the earth from which they were originally taken. But other places, like the battleground at Glorieta, have been set aside to remind us of our past.

SUGGESTED READING:

Pueblo Warriors and Spanish Conquest, by Oakah L. Jones, Jr. (Norman: University of Oklahoma Press, 1966).

Turmoil in New Mexico: 1846–1868, by William A. Keleher (reprinted; Albuquerque: University of New Mexico Press, 1982).

First house built at Fort Bayard, 1862. (Courtesy Museum of New Mexico, neg. 111667.)

FORT BAYARD

Old Fort Bayard was converted to the Fort Bayard Medical Center near Silver City. From Silver City, follow U.S. 180 east for ten miles; the turnoff is well marked.

By the mid-nineteenth century, the United States' territorial control spanned the continent, and many people realized that the West's vast natural resources held inestimable potential wealth for the nation. New Mexico's population was growing, and caravans rolled across the prairies and deserts to the newly discovered gold fields of California. Expansion, settlement, and economic development were matters of national policy, backed up by the military and resisted only by disunified Native American tribes with declining populations. Beginning in 1861, various bands of southern Apaches, who made their homes in the mountainous fastnesses of southwestern New Mexico and southeastern Arizona, began to hinder Euro-American expansionist ambitions. Today, the Gila Wilderness lies in the heart of this country.

Fort Bayard was established in 1866, only ten miles from the burgeoning gold mines of Pinos Altos and even closer to the older copper mines at Santa Rita del Cobre. In the words of the secretary of war, "This post, with Fort Cummings [see p. 241] at Cook Spring, Fort Selden [p. 249] on the Rio Grande, Fort Stanton [p. 254] on the Bonito River, between the Rio Grande and the Pecos, form a line of posts covering the southern frontier of New Mexico from the Apache Indians." Fort Bayard's immediate function was to protect miners, freighters, travelers, and ranchers from attacks, especially by the Warm Springs Apaches, and troops went on regular patrols for this purpose. The fort's placement turned out to be fortuitous, for gold was soon discovered adjacent to it and within a short time some six hundred claims were being worked by a thousand or more miners.

The first troops stationed here were Company B of the 125th Colored Infantry, and it was they who constructed the post's first rough structures of adobe, logs, and fieldstones. Afterward, they were transferred to Fort Craig (p. 235), and Bayard received a full complement of three companies, two infantry and one cavalry. Whatever drawbacks duty at Fort Bayard may have entailed—crude quarters and strenuous field expeditions, for example—troops stationed here were exposed to one of the most scenic regions of the territory. One early observer, the post's first female resident, wrote in 1870 that

as far as the eye could reach, even the highest mountains were covered
with grass, scrub-oaks and cedars; while in the valley, and on the hills,
there was one bright carpet of grass and wild flowers. The white tents in
the valley, with the flagstaff in the centre, and the flag just moving in the
morning breeze, the dark-green trees shading the tents, the stream of
water . . . running around the camp—all this looked so refreshing, so
beautiful, after those long day's marches among the sand-hills of the Rio
Grande, and the weary tramps over the burning deserts we had lately left
behind us, that my enthusiasm rose to the highest pitch.

By 1879, Bayard's living quarters had been much improved to accommodate the needs of its 17 officers, 325 enlisted men, 14 laundresses, 14 civilians, and 25 Navajo scouts. In addition, there were more than 400 horses and mules. Much of the men's efforts went into obtaining hay and fuel wood, with the latter alone amounting to well over a thousand cords, which was hauled to the fort by ox-drawn wagons.

To some degree, Fort Bayard soldiers accomplished their security mission by their presence alone. Normal military operations included scouting expeditions in the field and pursuits of Indian raiding parties. The Apaches, who were often indiscriminately shot at by whites, retaliated with hit-and-run raids. Military patrols seldom even caught sight of their adversaries. Not so fortunate were local citizens who sometimes were killed by the Indians at their ranches, or as they traveled alone, or in small groups. The settlers and miners often lived in considerable fear of the elusive Apache warriors, whose leaders included such legendary names as Mangas Coloradas, Nana, Victorio, and Gerónimo. These figures, revered today as native patriots, were hated in their day by the whites and often treated as criminals when they were captured or came in from the hills to negotiate peace. The raids scored by their small, ill-equipped bands stimulated widespread complaints from an outraged citizenry. In addition, an unsympathetic press sometimes ridiculed the army for its inability to end the violence.

The U.S.–Apache conflict was irreconcilable. During the wars, most whites regarded the natives as treacherous savages, whose persistent resistance to settlement blocked legitimate progress. The military establishment aimed to rid the land of these nomads and to achieve this goal the Apaches were doggedly hunted down, killed, or captured and sent into exile.

The Indians, on the other hand, regarded the whites as avaricious and destructive usurpers who were not to be trusted. But the success of many raids did little to stay the flow of immigrants. What was more, their arms and ammunition were limited, and each year their population shrank. The strength and effectiveness of troops at Fort Bayard and other posts, on the other hand, only increased with time. In 1880, the death of Victorio intensified conflicts, but it was clear that an eventual U.S. victory was inevitable. By 1884, only Gerónimo and his dwindling followers held out, ever on the move and in hiding. Two years later, they too surrendered, thus ending the Apache war and bringing to a conclusion the primary mission of Fort Bayard.

Troops continued to garrison Fort Bayard through the 1890s. By this time, the fort was well appointed, and an assignment here, especially for an officer, promised a comfortable life. By 1899, however, no convincing argument could any longer be made to justify expending funds on a military presence here, and the fort was converted to a general hospital and sanitarium for tuberculosis patients. Initially, patients came here from the U.S. Soldiers' Home in Washington, D.C., but later, the hospital expanded to include active troops. Fort Bayard eventually developed into one of the country's leading medical centers for the treatment of tuberculosis.

Sixth U.S. Cavalry training at Fort Bayard. (Courtesy Arizona Historical Society.)

In those days, fresh air was the main ingredient recommended to cure this disease, and patients lived day and night on their screened porches, wearing knitted woolen helmets and heavy sheepskin coats in cold weather. During World War I, the hospital held as many as seventeen hundred patients. Today, many citizens of the Silver City area are the descendants of former Fort Bayard patients. The Fort Bayard Medical Center is now a long-term geriatic-care facility and a treatment center for alcoholics.

When you enter the grounds of Fort Bayard Medical Center, drive past the hospital and you will come to an open grassy meadow on the right. This is the parade ground of the old fort. The road encircling it passes by a row of handsome, tree-shaded houses fronted by verandas—the officers' quarters, later occupied by tuberculosis patients. The gentility of old Fort Bayard, in contrast to the rustic and remote character of posts like Fort Cummings, can still be felt in the ambience of the hospital campus. We are fortunate that after Fort Bayard outlived its military usefulness, it was revived with a humanitarian mission.

TIPS FOR THE TRAVELER:
In Silver City (p. 198), you will enjoy seeing the historical and archaeological collections at the Western New Mexico University Museum. Pinos Altos, the early gold-mining camp, is also worth a visit, as are the Mogollon Indian cave dwellings at Gila Cliff Dwellings National Monu-

ment. You should also stop to view the enormous Santa Rita Open Pit Copper Mine along U.S. 180. Mining here began about 1800. The nearby Gila Wilderness is an ideal backcountry area for hiking, fishing, hunting, or going on pack trips. Many motels, restaurants, and other travel services are located in and around Silver City.

SUGGESTED READING:

In the Days of Victorio: Recollections of a Warm Springs Apache, by Eve Ball (Tucson: University of Arizona Press, 1970).

Soldiers and Settlers: Military Supply in the Southwest, by Darlis A. Miller (Albuquerque: University of New Mexico Press, 1989).

FORT BURGWIN RESEARCH CENTER

The Fort Burgwin Research Center, the site of Cantonment Burgwin, is located fifteen miles south of Taos. From Taos, take New Mexico 64 south to Ranchos de Taos, then turn left on New Mexico 518 and proceed five and one-half miles to the Center.

> Snow beats against the windows. . . . The mountain which overhangs us and towers almost to the skies is clothed in its garb of white snow and dark evergreen foliage. The drooping branches of these trees cast a sombre hue upon the rocky clefts upon which the trees are rooted. The long dismal howl of wolves is heard.
>
> Private James A. Bennett
> Cantonment Burgwin, January 1, 1853

The beauty of Cantonment Burgwin's natural environment, in a narrow valley above the historic village of Ranchos de Taos, has hardly diminished in the years that have elapsed since the post was abandoned. The deep mountain snows that inspired the journal notations of a common soldier in 1853 remain a treasure to cross-country skiers and winter enthusiasts. In the spring, meadow grasses that once fattened army horses still blanket the valley of the *Rito de la Olla* (Pot Creek). Still, a century and a half ago, nature's beauty hardly compensated for the dreary tedium that characterized a trooper's life at this remote outpost.

Cantonment Burgwin (a cantonment is a category between camp and fort) was established in the summer of 1852, when its first commander, Lieutenant Robert Ransom, Jr., had only recently graduated

Fort Burgwin Research Center. (Photo by David Grant Noble.)

from West Point. The inexperienced but enthusiastic young officer had the post built in short order and proved to be the ablest among the series of officers who commanded Burgwin during its brief history.

The post's name memorialized Captain John H. K. Burgwin, who had been killed at nearby Taos Pueblo (see p. 89) five years earlier. At this time, many residents of the pueblo and village had risen in revolt against the U.S. troops who had invaded New Mexico. After the 1847 revolt, the U.S. military presence in Taos had been represented by Missouri Volunteers, notorious for their rowdy social behavior and disrespect for native New Mexicans. The deteriorated relations between the Missourians and locals contributed to the decision from headquarters to establish a cantonment outside town and garrisoned by regular troops.

Cantonment Burgwin was placed along the main road between Taos and Santa Fe in order to be able to protect travelers from potential attacks by Jicarilla Apaches (p. 115) or their allies, the Utes. Although patrols went out regularly to demonstrate their authority, they seldom even sighted the Indians, who knew better than take on the better-armed soldiers. Sometimes, however, the troops did engage the elusive Indians and, on one occasion, suffered a humiliating defeat.

It happened in March of 1854. Lieutenant John W. Davidson set out with sixty men in pursuit of a band of Jicarillas. On the morning of March 30, Davidson found the Indian camp along Cieneguilla Creek east of Taos, and attacked. When the fight ended, twenty-two soldiers lay dead, twenty-three more were wounded, and forty-five horses had been lost. Following the Cieneguilla battle, an expedition of about two hundred men, led by Colonel Philip St. George Cooke and guided by Kit Carson, pursued and defeated the Indians near Agua Caliente, on the west side of the Rio Grande. During the conflict, seventeen Jicarilla women and children became separated from their compatriots and are thought to have perished later in the cold weather.

Taos saw no further insurrections, and by 1855 the Indian threat was gone, too. But Cantonment Burgwin lived on. What did the troops do? Military records suggest that they did not do enough. Boredom and low morale increased, exacerbated by the ineptitude of a new commander, Major George A. H. Blake, who brought his discontented troops here after they rioted at Fort Massachusetts, Colorado. Symptoms of the deteriorating situation are reflected in accounts of drunkenness and alcoholism, venereal disease, desertion, professional irresponsibility, and even behavior bordering on mutiny. Symbolically, even the buildings, constructed of upright pine posts, began to collapse. As Burgwin had been planned as only a temporary post, the army refused to allocate rebuilding funds, and repairs only prolonged the discomfort of its occupants. By 1860, Burgwin clearly had no reason to be, and in May the army closed its gates. But Burgwin was to live again.

In the mid-1950s, Cantonment Burgwin was unofficially promoted to "Fort" Burgwin by parties interested in the archaeological potential of Pot Creek Pueblo, a large seven-hundred-year old Indian ruin near the old military post thought to be ancestral to the Tiwa-speaking Taos and Picuris Indians. They were successful, for several years later Southern Methodist University began conducting archaeological research at both the pueblo and cantonment through summer field-school programs. Between May 1 and October 1, you may walk around the campus, view restorations of many of the old cantonment buildings rebuilt on their original foundations, and attend lectures, musical and theatrical programs, and art shows. For further information, please call (505) 758-8322 in summer, or (214) 768-3657 during the rest of the year.

TIPS FOR THE TRAVELER:
Other nearby historic sites include Taos, Taos Pueblo, and Picuris Pueblo (p. 48). In Ranchos de Taos, only three miles away, you will

enjoy a stop at the famous San Francisco de Assiz Church. The Jicarilla Apaches, who once lived in the mountains around Fort Burgwin, now reside on a reservation in northwestern New Mexico; the Utes reside across the border in Colorado.

SUGGESTED READING:
"Cantonment Burgwin, 1852–1860," by Lawrence R. Murphy, *Arizona and the West,* vol. 15, no. 1 (1973).

FORT CRAIG NATIONAL HISTORIC SITE AND THE BATTLE OF VALVERDE

The ruins of Fort Craig, now a National Historic Site, are located thirty-two miles south of Socorro. From Socorro, take Interstate 25 to San Marcial (Exit 124); drive east one mile to an intersection with a paved road; turn right (south) and continue six and one-half miles to the Fort Craig turnoff on the left; continue four and one-half miles to the monument's entrance on the left.

Fort Craig was one of the more important military installations on New Mexico's frontier. While many posts were short-lived—its nearby predecessor, Fort Conrad, for example, only lasted three years—Fort Craig was in use for more than three decades and briefly held nearly four thousand troops.

Construction on the fort began in late 1853, and early the following year, troops from Fort Conrad moved here. Their principal mission was to protect travelers along the Jornada del Muerto ("journey of the dead man"), a treacherous segment of the Camino Real leading south to Fort Selden (see p. 249). Caravans and herders using this trail would raise a cloud of dust easily spotted by hostile Apaches and Navajos, to whom the travelers were easy prey. Fort Craig troops routinely patrolled the road as well as the region on the west side of the river, which was equally dangerous.

Regardless of its many Indian campaigns, Fort Craig is best remembered for its brief role in the Civil War. In 1861, Confederate volunteers, recruited in west Texas, assembled at Fort Bliss in El Paso, then marched north into New Mexico and set up a headquarters in Mesilla (p. 170), a town of Southern sympathies. Here, they awaited the arrival of the main Confederate force under the command of the colorful, heavy drinking

Ruins of Fort Craig today. (Photo by David Grant Noble.)

General Henry Hopkins Sibley. Sibley arrived on January 11, 1862, and three weeks later headed for Fort Craig with about twenty-six hundred men. After crossing the Jornada, the Rebels arrived in sight of Fort Craig on February 16, but dust storms kept them in camp for two days.

In January 1862, about a thousand federal troops were stationed at Craig under the command of Colonel Edward R. S. Canby, but these were soon augmented by enough militia to bring the force to thirty-eight hundred. In record time, the men built a massive defensive earthen wall around the fort that was ten feet high in places. Much of the wall material was excavated along its outside perimeter, thereby creating a dry moat approximately four-foot deep. With gun bastions at the corners, Fort Craig presented a formidable obstacle that the Confederates could only have captured at great human cost.

From his camp, Sibley reconnoitered the fort, skirmished with patrols, but wisely decided against a direct assault. Instead, his plan was to bypass it on the east side of the Rio Grande, recross the river a few miles upstream at Valverde, and continue north unimpeded to take Albuquerque and Santa Fe. This tactic would save his strength for the anticipated conflict at Fort Union. The Confederates began to move upriver on the nineteenth, and the following day made their way past

Fort Craig, using a convenient swale to cover their maneuver. They were led by Colonel Thomas Green, Sibley having taken ill. Union scouts, however, discovered the ploy and Canby made his own plans.

According to an oft-repeated but undocumented story, the night before the battle, Captain "Paddy" Graydon and his Union scouting party devised a scheme that led to one of the more comical episodes of the war. Hoping to create some havoc in the Rebel encampment, they loaded a dozen twenty-four-pound howitzer shells into wooden boxes that they lashed to two geriatric mules. They then stealthily crossed the river and drew close to the enemy camp. Their plan was to light the fuses, shoo the mules toward the Confederates, then sit back and enjoy the turmoil. Everything began according to plan. The loaded animals trotted toward the Rebel camp. The pranksters withdrew. But suddenly the mules, demonstrating atypical devotion to their masters, turned about and retraced their steps. Graydon and his men, now realizing their own imminent peril, took to their heels. Moments later, havoc was wreaked on both sides! The same night, several hundred of Sibley's mules, famished for water—the Rebels had made a dry camp—stampeded and were rounded up by the Federals. As a result of the loss, the Confederates had to abandon thirty supply wagons.

Early on the twentieth, Canby dispatched the majority of Fort Craig's troops to meet the enemy at the Valverde crossing. He himself stayed behind. Sibley resumed command of his forces late that morning, but soon withdrew to his ambulance, again leaving Green in charge. The battle began around nine o'clock, by which time, in the confusion of preparations, some New Mexico volunteers had already crossed and recrossed the chilling river four times. The fight initially favored the Federals, and in the afternoon Canby left for the field, leaving a small contingent at the fort.

But by midafternoon, the Rebels had won the initiative and launched a daring frontal attack upon Captain Alexander McRae's battery. In their first charge, McRae was wounded. He exhorted his support units—regulars and New Mexico volunteers commanded by Kit Carson—for help, but to no avail and his battery collapsed in two more Rebel onslaughts. Reportedly, Confederate officers, who had been McRae's classmates at West Point, called to him ineffectively to surrender. McRae was killed—a fort would later be named in his honor—and within minutes his undamaged howitzers were turned upon the routed Federals. Although Fort Craig itself remained in Union hands, Canby had lost the battle. It was left to troops from Fort Union to stop the Confederate advance, which they did on March 28.

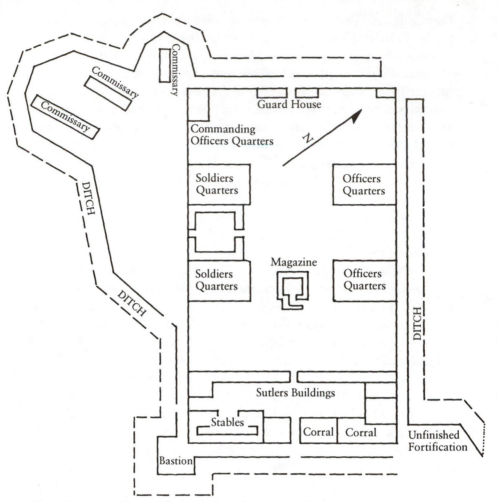

Commissary

Commissary

Commissary

Guard House

Commanding
Officers Quarters

N

Soldiers
Quarters

Officers
Quarters

DITCH

DITCH

Soldiers
Quarters

Magazine

Officers
Quarters

DITCH

Sutlers Buildings

Stables

Corral

Corral

Unfinished
Fortification

Bastion

Plan of Fort Craig. (Courtesy Bureau of Land Management.)

After Valverde, Fort Craig resumed its primary mission of defense against hostile Indians. General James H. Carleton, who replaced Canby, held New Mexico under martial law and forced men in Hispanic villages near Fort Craig to work without pay to strengthen its fortifications. Patrols regularly went on scouts, but seldom made contact with the elusive Indians.

In the postwar period, life at Fort Craig, as on so many southwestern posts, was monotonous. Trivial personal breaches of discipline probably accounted for most of the daily excitement. Post orders at Fort

Craig reveal interesting insights into daily problems and concerns: control of dogs, sheep, and goats; soldiers straying off designated pathways; drunkenness; firing of pistols at unauthorized targets; galloping horses to and from grazing fields; and thievery by visiting civilians.

Units garrisoned at Fort Craig included the regiment of Mounted Rifles, which had fought gallantly at Vera Cruz in the Mexican War, but whose reputation subsequently had become sullied by internal quarreling, poor discipline, and a high desertion rate. Also stationed here was the 125th United States Colored Troops, an infantry outfit. The fort experienced fifty-six commanders between 1854 and 1879.

Fort Craig, which was designed to hold two companies, was built mostly of adobe, though two buildings were constructed of stone and some enlisted quarters were of *jacal*—upright wooden posts chinked with mud. Residential quarters were fronted by porticos supported by whitewashed columns. Three commissary storehouses were excavated in the ground to a depth of up to ten feet and had buttressed walls extending five feet above ground level. With roofs of layered dirt, gravel, and plaster, these structures served as effective root cellars to help preserve perishable foodstuffs such as bacon.

Like so many frontier forts, Craig had required constant maintenance and began to crumble soon after abandonment. Lydia Spencer Lane, an officer's wife whose memoirs, *I Married a Soldier* (UNM Press, 1987), make fascinating reading, described her dismal arrival at Fort Craig. A young eastern woman with a new baby, she had been traveling for weeks over rough trails in bad weather. No doubt, she anticipated a few on-post luxuries.

> All we wanted was a dry, comfortable room for the baby. What was my dismay when I heard that the dirt roofs of the adobe quarters were leaking all over! Mrs. Porter was quite ill, and the water was pouring into the room where she was in bed under a tent fly, with an umbrella over her head! Colonel Crittenden's quarters were in the same building, and the rain streamed through the ceiling like a shower-bath.

In 1878, with the Indian threat seemingly subsided, Fort Craig was abandoned save for a small caretaker contingent. However, it was reactivated in 1880, when the Apache chieftain Victorio went on the warpath, and it stayed in service another five years. After 1885, Captain Jack Crawford, who had served as scout, postmaster, and sutler at the fort and was renowned for his poetic presentations, stayed on as custodian for several years. In 1894, the post was sold at auction and

Interior of Captain Jack Crawford's quarters, c. 1885. (Courtesy Museum of New Mexico, neg. 14513.)

remained in private ownership until 1981, when the Archaeological Conservancy acquired the site and donated it to the Bureau of Land Management. This agency is systematically stabilizing the ruins and developing an interpretive program for the public.

Inevitably, over the decades, erosion has taken a heavy toll on the adobe structures at Fort Craig, and treasure hunters have even toppled some walls in futile quests for buried treasure. Still, much is known about the site from historical records, and some parts of the site, which have evaded the relic hunter's shovel, may still reveal interesting archaeological data.

From the Fort Craig parking area, you can follow a formal trail through the extensive ruins, which take about an hour to see thoroughly. Most apparent are the high-standing stone walls of the commanding officer's house and the remains of the guard house, which was built of basalt rock. The semisubterranean commissaries also are visible, as are the fort's earthen ramparts. The remains of other buildings, such as officer and enlisted quarters, shops, stables, and hospitals, can be identified with the aid of a site map. From the wall bastions, you can see miles of surrounding countryside, which will help you visualize the maneuvers of the Confederate army in 1862. The Valverde battlefield itself is difficult to reach and buried under layers of silt from river flooding. However, a monument in honor of the Confederates stands along the road to San Marcial, at its intersection with old New Mexico 85.

TIPS FOR THE TRAVELER:
You will find travel facilities at San Antonio and Socorro, to the north, and Truth or Consequences, to the south. Nearby places of historical interest include Socorro (p. 203), a town dating to the Spanish colonial period, and Fort Selden State Monument (p. 249). You also may be interested in visiting the nearby Bosque del Apache Wildlife Refuge, which is a wintering ground for tens of thousands of migratory waterfowl.

SUGGESTED READING:
Life and Death of a Frontier Fort, Fort Craig, New Mexico, 1854–1885, by Marion C. Grinstead (Socorro: Socorro County Historical Society, 1973).
Louis Felsenthal, Citizen-Soldier of Territorial New Mexico, by Jacqueline Dorgan Meketa (Albuquerque: University of New Mexico Press, 1982).

FORT CUMMINGS

The ruins of Fort Cummings are located northwest of New Mexico 26, between Deming and Hatch. At the tiny settlement of Florida, seventeen miles east of Deming, take the unpaved road (across from the railroad water tank) and proceed for one mile to a cattle guard. Immediately after crossing the cattle guard, turn left and continue four and one-half miles to the fort ruins.

No stretch of John Butterfield's stagecoach road from Missouri to California was more perilous than the four-mile defile through Cooke's Canyon in southern New Mexico. Many a traveler lost his life here, in the bosom of Apache country. When General James H. Carleton took command of New Mexico in 1862, he determined to increase security in this desolate region.

Carleton had marched to New Mexico in July with his California Column to fight Confederates. However, he arrived too late, with the Rebels having already withdrawn to Texas after their defeat at Glorieta

Pass (p. 271). Carleton, with a restless army on his hands, soon turned his attention to the Indians.

Fort Cummings was built by the Californians in 1863, three hundred yards from Cooke's Spring at the southern end of Cooke's Canyon. Lieutenant Philip St. George Cooke, for whom these places were named, had explored the region in 1846. The canyon was a key point for security, with its spring being the sole watering hole for forty miles around, used by travelers and Indians alike.

No fort on the frontier was more precariously located than Cummings. Far from any towns or military posts, surrounded by miles of desert, it was constantly threatened by the Mimbreño and Chiricahua Apaches. So dangerous was the vicinity that individuals were forbidden to wander about alone, and small groups going for firewood or water required armed escorts. One Fort Cummings resident recorded that the Indians often could be viewed outside in the daytime and that occasionally, at night, they would pull themselves over the fort's walls with horsehair ropes and leave their footprints in the dust of the parade ground for the soldiers to see in the morning.

The ten-foot adobe wall surrounding Fort Cummings made living here feel almost like an incarceration. The installation had a standard complex of military buildings: barracks, officers' quarters, quartermaster depot, commissary, stables, hospital, and offices. This was a fortified oasis, and assignment here amounted to a type of exile.

Between 1866 and 1900, some thirty-five hundred black infantrymen and cavalrymen served at various army posts on the New Mexico frontier. Members of the 125th and 38th regiments of U.S. Colored Infantry, including Civil War veterans from the north and freed Southern slaves, were stationed at Fort Cummings. Their main mission was to defend communication and travel routes from Indian depredations, and to this end they spent untold hours patrolling the dusty desert. The Indians dubbed these troops "buffalo soldiers" because their hair resembled that of bison and they demonstrated the fighting spirit of these revered animals. The duties of Fort Cummings' troops, however, were usually more routine than fighting Indians. One ongoing task involved raising and repairing the post's adobe buildings. Another was cutting and hauling fuel wood, sometimes from as far away as twenty-five miles. They also provided escort service for east-west travelers, government supply trains, and even herds of cattle.

Having experienced an arduous march across the western prairies and lost men to an epidemic of cholera, the black troops at Fort Cummings suffered from morale problems that reportedly were exacerbated

Fort Cummings ruins. (Photo by David Grant Noble.)

by some of their disciplinarian white officers. In December 1867, internal discontent boiled over and a series of minor incidents resulted in seven soldiers being court-martialed on various charges, including mutiny. Their defense counsel was Thomas Benton Catron, later to become a powerful entrepreneur in the territory and a controversial figure in New Mexico economic and political circles. At the end of the trials, only one man had been convicted of the mutiny charge, though some others were found guilty of lesser offenses.

The near-mutinous incidents at Fort Cummings give some insight into the stress that soldiers often experienced on the frontier. This condition grew out of a life of confinement, isolation, monotony, loneliness, and occasional danger. In addition, African-American soldiers often had to endure racist attitudes on the part of white officers. At Cummings, other problems contributed to low spirits and quick tempers: supplies frequently were depleted (soldiers reportedly even contrived makeshift clothing out of burlap gunny sacks); food was of poor quality and rations sometimes short; and occasionally even ammunition stocks ran alarmingly low. In their quarters, soldiers placed the legs of their beds in cans of water to fend off red ants, and they hung sheets overhead to intercept centipedes and scorpions that dropped from the ceiling. To economize and help stave off scurvy, the troops started a vegetable garden, but the desert conditions proved too extreme for its survival.

In 1873, Fort Cummings was closed only to be reactivated in 1880, in response to renewed Apache uprisings. For several years, troops from the fort fought against Gerónimo, Chato, Loco, Nachite (son of Cochise), and Nana, who staged a legendary raid through New Mexico in 1881 and then escaped to Mexico. Photographs of the fort at this time show the troops quartered in tents outside the perimeter walls, suggesting that the barracks may already have become too decrepit to use. When the Apache wars finally ended in 1886, Fort Cummings became obsolete and was closed. For several years, a local rancher leased the site to corral livestock; range cattle still wander through the brush and up and down the arroyos. Today, forty acres of the site are privately owned and the remainder is administered by the Bureau of Land Management.

Fort Cummings' adobe buildings have weathered poorly over the hundred years since its abandonment. Most are totally collapsed, their wall alignments being only faintly visible on the ground. But a few walls still stand and, against the scenic backdrop of Cooke's Peak, are a poignant reminder of military life on the southwestern frontier. Sporadic interest in reconstructing the fort as a frontier military monument never materialized, and only in recent years have federal resources become available to protect and interpret the ruins. The site is well off the beaten track and overgrown by mesquite, creosote, and desert grasses.

You may explore Fort Cummings' remains at will, but do not climb on walls or remove artifacts. A short walk south of the ruins will bring you to Cooke's Springs, now covered by a circular stone pump house. If you should witness any vandalism or looting, please report it (with relevant license numbers, if possible) to the Bureau of Land Management, 1800 Marquess Street, Las Cruces, New Mexico 88005; call (505) 525-8228.

TIPS FOR THE TRAVELER:
If you are interested in New Mexico's old forts, you will wish to include in your itinerary Fort Bayard (p. 228), near Silver City; Fort Selden (p. 249), north of Las Cruces; and Fort Craig (p. 235), near Socorro. Other nearby historical sites are the town of Mesilla (p. 170) and Pancho Villa State Park (p. 275). You will find travel services in Deming and Hatch.

SUGGESTED READING:
"Mutiny at Fort Cummings," by Lee Myers, *New Mexico Historical Review*, vol. 46, no. 4 (1971).

Engraving of Fort Marcy parade ground, 1885. (Courtesy School of American Research collections in the Museum of New Mexico.)

FORT MARCY

The ruins of Old Fort Marcy are in Santa Fe, less than a half-mile east of the plaza. To visit the site, follow Kearny Avenue east from Sunset Street, or Prince Avenue south from Artist Road. This will bring you to the L. Bradford Prince Memorial Park, which borders the ruins.

Old Fort Marcy, located on a promontory overlooking downtown Santa Fe, has been called "the forgotten fort," and, indeed, the grassy mounds that cover its once massive ramparts have never been the focus of much interest among local citizens. Named in 1846 after Secretary of War William L. Marcy, it was the first United States military post in the Southwest and became a tangible symbol of the United States' quickly developing success in the Mexican War.

Diplomatic relations between the United States and Mexico were severed in March 1845, and war was declared in May of the following year. In June, the sixteen-hundred-man Army of the West, under the command of Colonel Stephen Watts Kearny, began its arduous march from Missouri to New Mexico. The actual outbreak of hostilities had come as no surprise; indeed, Kearny had been planning his campaign for at least six months and was well prepared to lead his troops across the plains from Fort Leavenworth to Bent's Fort on the Arkansas River and, after resting, to Santa Fe. The 856-mile journey stands as one of the great marches in military history. The army rested at Bent's Fort in Colorado, where it let its size be known to New Mexican scouts. At Glorieta Pass, east of Santa Fe, Governor Manuel Armijo assembled the New Mexico militia to block the Americans, but disbanded it before they came in sight. On August 18, 1846, the troops arrived in Santa Fe, where, after negotiations, they easily took possession of the city.

In Las Vegas (see p. 161) and other villages along the route, Kearny, by now promoted to general, had repeatedly assured New Mexicans of the United States' benevolent intentions and that American rule would benefit everyone. He also viewed his mission as one of liberation and protection—to free the citizenry from what was perceived as an uncaring, corrupt, and unpopular Mexican regime, and to defend it from the unchecked depredations of nomadic Indian tribes.

Still, beneath expressions of goodwill clearly lay nationalistic motives; the general headed an imperial army with expansionist objectives. As Kearny declared in the city's historic plaza, "We have come among you to take possession of New Mexico, which we do in the name of the government of the United States." To underscore his authority, he immediately ordered plans for a fort, construction of which began several days later.

In an intensive effort, teams of soldiers and local brick masons erected massive nine-foot-high adobe walls surrounded by a deep ditch. The fort became operational by early November. From its high vantage point, the fort commanded a wide-angle view of the town and surrounding countryside, and was an effective, even intimidating, symbol of American authority over the inhabitants of New Mexico's ancient capital.

The fort's rapid construction soon allowed Kearny to carry forward his country's ambitious goals. Only five weeks after occupying Santa Fe, he struck out for California with his First Dragoons, and shortly thereafter, Colonel Sterling Price arrived in town with his Second Missouri Volunteers and Mormon Battalion. Price relieved Colonel Alexander Doniphan, who headed south to Mexico. Meanwhile, from its parapets, Fort Marcy's six-pound guns gazed down upon the city, with the capability of razing any house at a single command. But no cannon shot was ever heard—Fort Marcy was a peacemaker.

Originally planned as a garrison for 280 men, Fort Marcy could have accommodated more than three times as many troops in an emergency. However, from the beginning, its commanding officer lived in the Palace of the Governors, while his troops were quartered in the old

Banquet, Headquarters Building, Fort Marcy, c. 1880. (Courtesy Museum of New Mexico, neg. 1706.)

Mexican barracks downtown. Fort Marcy's unusual tri-decagon plan was a modification of the defensively effective star-fort design, later to be employed at Fort Union (see p. 264). Its perimeter walls, constructed of 24-by-20-by-6-inch adobe bricks, were erected on massive earthen embankments that were surrounded by a ditch. The 17-foot vertical ascent from ditch bottom to parapet rim would have impeded the progress of any potential aggressor. An arsenal was completed in the spring of 1847, and just outside the fort's entrance the construction of a blockhouse was begun, but perhaps not finished.

Many Santa Feans, especially members of the business community, had welcomed the Americans. In retrospect, the building of Fort Marcy would seem to have been a superfluous exercise. But resentment over Americanization did fester in other places, notably in Taos (p. 208), eighty miles to the north, and in Mora (p. 175), nestled deep in the Sangre de Cristo Mountains. In January 1847, a group of Taos inhabitants, including some from Taos Pueblo (p. 89), assassinated Charles Bent, the newly appointed governor, and advanced upon the capital. Had this Taos rebellion been better organized and found wider popular support, Old Fort Marcy might well have seen action. As it was, the Taos rebels were confronted by Price and his Missourians well north of town, and were repulsed.

By the time the Confederates briefly occupied Santa Fe in 1862, military functions were being carried out in leased quarters downtown, and the old fort on the hill had long since fallen vacant. The downtown Fort Marcy, briefly called the Post of Santa Fe, was an administrative center for the military department. Its headquarters building was located at the corner of Palace and Lincoln avenues, where the Museum of Fine Arts now stands. Two other Fort Marcy buildings, both former officers' quarters, are still in service in the downtown area. Hewett House, at 116 Lincoln Avenue, is used for offices of the Museum of New Mexico, and the A. M. Bergere House, at 135 Grant Avenue, is an office building. The facade of Hewett House, having been built of brick, was later remodeled in the Spanish Pueblo style, and both buildings have been modernized.

As for the old adobe fort on the hill, it has been reduced to soft grassy mounds. In 1887, the reported discovery of a cache of old Spanish coins under one of its walls precipitated a rush of local looters whose shovels must have greatly accelerated the fort's natural decay. You will find little historical interpretation at the site, but using a ground plan, you can easily trace the walls and locate the blockhouse outside the east gate. There is irony in the fact that Santa Fe, a city that promotes its historical character, has ignored these ruins. Perhaps the site is a reminder of an era that would as soon be left buried.

TIPS FOR THE TRAVELER:
Santa Fe (p. 189) is one of the oldest cities in North America, and has many interesting buildings and districts. From the Spanish period, most notably, are the Palace of the Governors (now a history museum), San Miguel Church, and the plaza. There are collections of Indian arts at the Museum of Indian Arts and Culture, School of American Research, and American Indian Arts Institute. Guided walking and bus tours around town are available. Pecos National Historical Park (p. 42) and Bandelier National Monument also make fascinating side trips. Santa Fe has a wide selection of fine hotels and restaurants and many shops and art galleries.

SUGGESTED READING:
"The American Occupation of Santa Fe: 'My Government Will Correct All This,' " by John P. Wilson in *Santa Fe: History of an Ancient City,* edited by David Grant Noble (Santa Fe: School of American Research Press, 1989).

FORT SELDEN STATE MONUMENT

Fort Selden State Monument lies just east of New Mexico 185, between Las Cruces and Hatch. From Interstate 25, take the Radium Springs exit and continue one mile to the monument's entrance.

During Fort Selden's twenty-five-year life span, the territory of New Mexico was being transformed from a rustic, insecure frontier to a land where Anglo-American settlers, merchants, miners, and entrepreneurs increasingly could find opportunities. For many years, new people, goods, and ideas had come over the Santa Fe Trail (see p. 309), but after 1880, they came via the railroad. In 1881, the Atchison, Topeka, and Santa Fe linked up with the Southern Pacific at Deming to form the country's second transcontinental line; a branch of the AT&SF crossed the Fort Selden Military Reservation.

Fort Selden was built in 1865 at the southern end of the treacherous Jornada del Muerto ("dead man's journey"), an eighty-mile expanse of desert on the route between Santa Fe and El Paso. For more than two centuries, travelers on this stretch of the Camino Real (see p. 293) had to contend not only with thirst, but also with raiding Apaches. Troops from the fort provided protective escort to wagon trains crossing the Jornada and going into the mining country around Silver City and Pinos Altos. They also protected settlers in the fertile Mesilla Valley.

The fort was ideally positioned on high-level ground close to the Rio Grande. The river provided ample, if muddy, drinking water, and along its banks were cottonwood groves and riparian habitats for wildlife. Hunters from the fort often were able to supplement their normally bleak soldiers' fare with fresh venison and waterfowl. The fort was surrounded by good grazing and farm lands (a necessity for most New Mexico posts), and contracts were let to locals for the provision of hay, grain, and fuel wood. The fort also was strategically situated near the Robledo campground. In 1598, Juan de Oñate and his colonists had camped across the river, as had Governor Otermín, when he led his weary followers into exile in 1680. Texas Confederates established a temporary camp at Robledo in 1861, and recruited locals here to join their attempted conquest of the territory.

Fort Selden's sally port led into a rectangular parade ground surrounded by single-story adobe buildings. At the north end were the officers' quarters and opposite them the sometimes overcrowded soldiers' barracks. In between were a small hospital, shops, corrals, guardhouse, and administrative building. East of the fort quadrangle were corrals and, to the north, the trader's store. The commander's house was located west of the officers' quarters; however, this structure collapsed sometime after 1878, when the fort was temporarily abandoned, and was never restored. Normally, a company of infantry and one of cavalry were stationed at Fort Selden, totaling between 125 and 185 men. But between frequent scouting and escort patrols, the compound was often at minimal strength.

One of the Fort Selden museum displays represents the typical daily routine of a soldier posted on the frontier and offers a clue to why desertion rates were high.

Reveille	Sunrise
Stable Call	immediately after
Sick Call	7:15 A.M.
Breakfast Call	7:20 A.M.
Fatigue Call	7:50 A.M.
Grazing Call	8:30 A.M.
Guard Mount	8:45 A.M.
Water Mount	9:30 A.M.
Drill Mount	10:30 A.M.
Recall from Drill	11:30 A.M.
Recall from Fatigue, Dinner	12:00 noon
Sergeant's Call	12:00 noon
Fatigue Call	12:45 P.M.
Drill Call	1:00 P.M.
Recall from Drill	2:00 P.M.
Water Call	3:00 P.M.
Stable Call	4:30 P.M.
Recall from Fatigue	5:10 P.M.
Dress Parade and Retreat	5:45 P.M.
Tattoo	8:00 P.M.
Taps	8:30 P.M.

It is little wonder that troops looked forward to "scouts" and other field expeditions that freed them from such monotonous chores. While in the field, however, the men rarely saw combat and, for that matter, seldom even saw Indians, for the latter were too adept in guerrilla tactics to engage regular troops.

Still, post life had some moments of excitement. In 1867, for example, Apaches twice attempted to run off stock grazing close to the

Fort Selden, 1880s. (Photo by J. R. Riddle, courtesy Museum of New Mexico, neg. 14523.)

fort, and the following year the Indians captured a herd of mules. In 1869, the fort established two picket posts to enhance security in particularly dangerous places: to the north at Aleman Station, a travelers' haven midway across the perilous Jornada; and to the east near San Augustine Springs, another hotspot of Indian attacks. In the 1870s, troops from Selden staged a grueling summer campaign to try to interdict an illicit arms trade between Mexico and hostile tribes on the southern plains, and on one occasion, soldiers rushed to the town of Mesilla (p. 170) to quell a violent political riot.

Two names stand out in Fort Selden's history, the first one that of Henry Raymond Selden, for whom it was named. Colonel Selden was born in Vermont in 1820, attended West Point, and fought gallantly at the Battle of Valverde (p. 235), where he waded under fire across the icy Rio Grande with his men to charge the Confederates with fixed bayonets. He also saw action at Glorieta Pass (p. 271), where Union forces finally succeeded in halting the Confederate army. Selden died in 1865, while serving as commander of Fort Union (p. 264).

Fort Selden's second celebrity, though later in time, was Douglas MacArthur, who arrived in 1884 at the age of four. His father, Captain Arthur MacArthur, had marched his infantry company here from Fort Wingate (p. 267). Douglas, who would eventually wear five stars, later told about his boyhood rides from the fort to the river in the

Fort Selden ruins. (Photo by David Grant Noble.)

water wagon. He also remembered once seeing a feral camel that, to everyone's astonishment, appeared near the post from its perambulations on the Jornada. The beast, it seems, was a descendant of the camel herd used thirty years before as part of an experiment in desert transportation.

When the railroad came through Fort Selden, General William T. Sherman and other members of the military establishment favored the enlargement of the fort and its conversion to a major regional military center that would consolidate the functions of a half-dozen frontier posts. In forceful opposition to this idea, however, were the citizens of El Paso, Texas, who lobbied for Fort Bliss to play this role. The state of Texas had more political clout than New Mexico territory, and it soon became clear that Fort Selden's days were numbered. However, before closing, the fort did play a minor role in the U.S. Army's campaigns against the the Chiricahua Apaches in the mid-1880s. At this time, soldiers from Selden staffed one of General Nelson Miles's heliograph stations, set up on Mount Robledo across the Rio Grande. From this station, signals could be flashed to a network of other stations by using the sun's reflection on a mirror. This communication method was highly effective (on sunny days) and helped federal troops monitor the whereabouts of the elusive Apaches.

Today, the Museum of New Mexico administers the ruins of Fort Selden. At the monument, you will find a visitor center with interesting exhibits of military equipment from the period, including uniforms and period clothes, saddles, cannons, and excavated artifacts such as bottles, shoes, tobacco pipes, and toilet articles. A child's boot dug up at the site is thought perhaps to have been MacArthur's. There also are photo murals taken when the fort was in service. A self-guiding interpretive trail leads through the fort site.

TIPS FOR THE TRAVELER:
While in the area, consider visiting the old town of Mesilla and the Pueblo Indian community of Tortugas, both on the south side of Las Cruces. Other fort sites in the region include Fort Craig (p. 235) and Fort Cummings (p. 241). You will find many travel and tourist services in the Las Cruces area.

SUGGESTED READING:
Fort Selden, New Mexico, by Timothy Cohrs and Thomas J. Caperton, (Santa Fe: Monuments Division of the Museum of New Mexico, 1974).

FORT STANTON

Fort Stanton is located just south of U.S. 380, between Capitán and Lincoln. From Lincoln, drive west on 380 for eight miles to the Fort Stanton turnoff, then continue another two miles to the old fort complex, which today is the Fort Stanton Hospital and Training School.

Of the scores of frontier forts and posts that were once strung along communication lines and travel routes across New Mexico's rugged frontier, all eventually outlived their original function and were abandoned by the army. Over the years, as summer thunderstorms and winter freezes eroded their adobe walls and local settlers salvaged useable roof timbers, the old forts melted back into the earth from which many originally had been built. Not so Fort Stanton. By good fortune, this post, which once protected settlers in the Rio Bonito and Rio Hondo valleys from hostile Indians, survived and is now the Fort Stanton Hospital and Training School, a medical and educational facility for the mentally handicapped.

In the early 1850s, it became clear that the proximity of Apaches to newly arrived Hispanic and Anglo-American settlers called for a strengthened military presence in southeastern New Mexico. In 1855, therefore, the army established Fort Stanton along the Rio Bonito, nine miles from the hamlet of Placitas, later to be renamed Lincoln (see p. 166). The new post, which commemorated Captain Henry W. Stanton, a Mexican War veteran recently killed by the Mescaleros (p. 120), was located in a scenic area noted for its rarified air, temperate climate, and many sunny days. The surrounding hills and mountains provided excellent wild turkey and deer hunting, and local streams were well stocked with trout. Fort Stanton's troops experienced their share of danger while on patrol, but enjoyed relative comfort for a frontier assignment.

In her 1858 journal, later published as the book *I Married a Soldier*, the cultivated Lydia Spencer Lane commented that Fort Stanton was "a beautiful post, with the best quarters in the army at that time, but it was like being buried alive to stay there." She bemoaned the solitude of the place and noted how fervently everyone anticipated the monthly mail service. One special joy for her was having a piano to play, a rare treat for a frontier soldier's wife. When she was there, the Mescaleros were encamped nearby and frequented the post, which was minimally fortified. Having been raised in a relatively sophisticated environment in Pennsylvania, Mrs. Lane was astonished at the customs of the Apaches,

U. S. troops on dress parade at Fort Stanton, 1885. (Courtesy Museum of New Mexico, neg. 77640.)

some of whom would walk uninvited into her living room to watch what she was doing. The Indians, apparently, were no less fascinated by the strange habits of the white intruders, whose activities they unabashedly enjoyed observing.

The Civil War, which flared briefly in New Mexico, did not leave Fort Stanton unscathed. When Confederate forces occupied Mesilla in July of 1861, the entire five-hundred-man garrison of nearby Fort Fillmore retreated across the Jornada del Muerto desert toward Fort Stanton. By midday, the march and heat had so exhausted and dehydrated the troops (some of whom had filled their canteens with whiskey prior to evacuating Fort Fillmore) that their Confederate pursuers easily took them captive. The humiliating incident, and especially the behavior of the Union commander, created a brief national scandal.

The Fort Fillmore fiasco left weakly defended Fort Stanton vulnerable, and it was decided to pull out its two companies and destroy its buildings and supplies rather than let them fall into the enemy's hands. Even this act, however, proved difficult to accomplish; not long after the troops set fire to the post and left for Albuquerque, a rainstorm quenched the flames and local people looted the smouldering ruins.

While the whites warred among themselves, the Apaches had intensified their raids, causing mounting anxiety and resentment among the

Hispanic and Anglo-American population. After the Confederates were driven from New Mexico, Fort Stanton—or what remained of it—was reoccupied by Kit Carson's troops while campaigning against the Mescalero Apaches. Most of the Mescaleros surrendered to Carson and spent three years in captivity at Fort Sumner (p. 258). In 1865, they fled back to their homeland in the mountains in the Sierra Blanca, and once again Fort Stanton troops were busy.

After the "pacification" of the Mescaleros, life at Fort Stanton became truly monotonous. As an escape, soldiers went hunting and fishing, prospected for gold in the surrounding hills, or got passes to nearby Lincoln. As the Lincoln County War (p. 166) heated up and citizens and lawmen were gunned down in the town's streets, Fort Stanton's commander resisted involving the army in what he regarded as a purely civil affair. However, during Lincoln's notorious five-day shoot-out in July of 1878, the Murphy-Dolan faction (Murphy and Dolan were ex-soldiers who had been sutlers at Fort Stanton) persuaded him to dispatch troops to town to protect the citizenry and to regain order.

There was one celebrity who stayed briefly at the fort—Billy the Kid, who was quartered in the guardhouse while awaiting execution. He escaped. In the 1880s, a fresh young West Point graduate by the name of John J. Pershing was stationed here. Years later, "Black Jack" Pershing would chase Pancho Villa across the deserts of Chihuahua (p. 275) and would eventually achieve renown as the World War I commander of the American Expeditionary Forces in France.

Fort Stanton was decommissioned by the army in 1896. However, many recognized that it could become an ideal center to treat patients suffering from tuberculosis, which was then a national and worldwide epidemic. As one medical journal reported of the climate, "The warm, sunny days of winter, no less than the cool, shady days of summer, invite the invalid and the robust to the outdoor life." Thus, in 1899, this old frontier station became the Fort Stanton Marine Hospital, the first federal hospital in the country dedicated to the treatment of tuberculosis. To qualify for admittance, one had to have served for at least three months on a merchant vessel flying the American flag; consequently, many patients were ex-seamen from foreign countries.

Sailors were not the only foreigners to live at Fort Stanton in its post-Indian fighting days; in 1939, it became the country's first internment camp of World War II. It was in December of that year that Captain Wilhelm Daehne scuttled his German luxury liner, Columbas, off the coast of Cuba to avoid capture by British warships. The captain and crew were picked up by American vessels and eventually moved to San

Former officers quarters on the Fort Stanton campus today. (Photo by David Grant Noble.)

Francisco, from where about 200 managed to repatriate themselves via Japan. The resourceful Captain Daehne then arranged for his 410 remaining charges to wait out the war at Fort Stanton. Their quarters, of course, were a far cry from the "floating palace" they had enjoyed aboard the Columbas, but they managed. Expertly led and organized, the Germans, most of whom spoke fluent English, fixed up their dusty barracks, painted the walls, planted gardens, landscaped the grounds, and even built a tennis court. While their compatriots suffered the ordeals of war across the Atlantic, they enjoyed gourmet meals prepared by the Columbas's renowned chefs.

In 1953, the state of New Mexico took over Fort Stanton and continued to operate it as a sanitarium for fourteen more years. By that time, tuberculosis had all but disappeared in the United States—regrettably, this disease has since made a comeback—and the hospital was converted to care for the mentally handicapped. Its historic buildings, surrounding a well-groomed grassy quadrangle, create a tranquil campus atmosphere that seems ideal for its present residents and their caretakers. Although the Fort Stanton Hospital and Training Center does not offer public tours, you may stroll at your leisure around the campus.

The Bureau of Land Management is developing interpretive trails around Fort Stanton for use by hikers, horseback riders, bicyclers, and spelunkers interested in exploring Fort Stanton Cave. For further information, call (505) 622-9042. You will enjoy visiting nearby Lincoln State Monument, especially in the summer months when the Wortly Hotel and all the exhibits are open. Nearby White Oaks was once a thriving gold mining and commercial center and a haunt of Billy the Kid. For a glimpse into the area's prehistory, plan a detour to the Three Rivers Petroglyph Site, located five miles east of Three Rivers along U.S. 54. The Ruidoso area and Mescalero Indian reservation area offer a variety of recreational activities, including skiing at Ski Apache. An abundance of tourist and travel services also are available here, as well as along Highway 380.

SUGGESTED READING:

I Married a Soldier: Or, Old Days in the Old Army, by Lydia Spencer
   Lane (reprinted; Albuquerque: University of New Mexico Press,
   1987).

FORT SUMNER STATE MONUMENT

Fort Sumner State Monument is located near the town of Fort Sumner in east-central New Mexico. From town, drive approximately three miles east on U.S. 60/84, then turn south on Billy the Kid Road and continue three and one-half miles to the monument entrance. The monument is open Thursday through Sunday.

Fort Sumner and Bosque Redondo: these two names recall one of the most painful chapters in the history of relations between Native Americans and the United States.

The Bosque Redondo (Round Grove) was an oxbow lake along the middle stretch of the Pecos River in eastern New Mexico. Surrounded by cottonwood trees, the spot had long served as a gathering place for nomadic Plains Indians and probably was known to hunter-gatherers thousands of years earlier. In historic times, the Bosque was a trail stop between the Rio Grande and the Great Plains, where New Mexico *ciboleros* (buffalo hunters) and *comancheros* (traders to the Comanches) would rest and water their animals. In the nineteenth century, shepherds from farther up the Pecos Valley would bring their flocks here to graze. Against the seemingly boundless and arid plains of eastern New Mexico, the Bosque Redondo was a true oasis.

In late 1862, the Bosque's history took a new turn, for it was here that the U.S. government established a fort and Indian reservation to serve as an internment camp for more than 9,000 Navajos and Apaches. Fort Sumner began as a mere cluster of army tents, but within weeks about 450 Mescalero Apaches (see p. 120) had been brought here from their homeland to the south and put to work in constructing adobe buildings. By the end of 1864, they were joined by approximately 8,600 Navajos (p. 125).

For at least two hundred years prior to the internment of the Apaches and Navajos, there had been conflicts between the Indian nomads and European colonists. Recent grievances on the part of the Indians included encroachments on their land and the enslavement of thousands of their children. The whites, on the other hand, viewed the region's sparsely occupied and seemingly unused lands as public domain. They also resented their losses of livestock to Indian raiders. By the mid-1800s, the better-armed New Mexicans had gained a distinct advantage in their war with the Indians, and their campaigns against these indigenous tribes began to take on a genocidal character.

In October 1862, Brigadier General James H. Carleton took command of the Department of New Mexico. Frustrated in his desire to fight Confederates, who had already been driven back to Texas, Carleton set his sights on breaking the independent spirit of the Apaches and Navajos. His strategy was to overwhelm the defiant tribes by military force and place them on a reservation, where they would receive a Christian education and instruction in farming. To execute his plans, Carleton chose Kit Carson, the already famous mountain man, scout, and soldier. Carson, who was unwell, accepted the job with reluctance and sent troops first against the Mescaleros, who lived in the Sacramento Mountains near present-day Ruidoso.

Then, in the late summer of 1863, Carson turned his attention to the approximately fifteen thousand Navajos whose bands were widely dispersed in western New Mexico and eastern Arizona. Carleton's attitude was simple: Bosque Redondo or extinction. The campaign was slow but nonetheless effective, and by January 1864 the first groups began their "Long Walk" eastward from the main gathering point at Fort Wingate (p. 267). Within a year, more than eight thousand Navajos had surrendered or had been captured, while an estimated fifteen hundred had perished from starvation, exposure, and the hardships of the four-hundred-mile trek to the Bosque. Around twenty-five hundred Navajos had kept their freedom by taking refuge in remote canyons in Arizona.

Carleton's Bosque Redondo experiment encountered problems at nearly every turn. Ill-conceived plans compounded by poor management resulted in much suffering for the destitute survivors of the walk. In addition, old hostilities between the Navajos and Mescaleros grew so intense that the latter finally fled the reservation and returned to their homeland. Food rations, which were meted out to the Indians every other day, often ran short. Supplies of tools, clothing, medicine, building materials, and fuel were painfully inadequate. In addition, problems ranging from poor seed to insect infestations contributed to a series of crop failures. As a result of their mistreatment, many of the captives succumbed to starvation and disease.

The faltering programs and the tragic human conditions at Bosque Redondo became the subject of fierce public controversy and were condemned by a committee from Congress. What galled New Mexicans most was the continuation of raids upon Pecos Valley settlers by Navajo warriors who allegedly used the Bosque Redondo reservation as a staging area and haven. Despite the criticism, Carleton, who had placed New Mexico under martial law, refused to shut down the Fort Sumner program, which was costing taxpayers more than a million dollars a year to maintain. By the time he resigned, another fifteen hundred Navajo lives had been sacrificed.

The fiasco at Fort Sumner and the Bosque Redondo was finally ended in 1868, when General U.S. Grant sent a peace commission there, headed by General William Tecumseh Sherman. Following the Civil War, the army was being "downsized" and all unnecessary military expenditures questioned; Fort Sumner was a prime target for closure. Sherman and his deputy, Colonel Samuel F. Tappan, recognized the Bosque Redondo failure and sat down to negotiate a new treaty with a delegation of Navajo headmen. Their spokesman was Hastiin Dagha, known as Barboncito. Barboncito resisted Sherman's initial desire to send his people to the Oklahoma Indian Territory and pushed strongly for their return to their home country. Sherman finally agreed to set aside a reservation for the tribe astride the New Mexico–Arizona border. The Navajos began their journey home on June 18, this time aided by wagons to carry persons without the strength to walk. Having arrived at Bosque Redondo four years earlier as a collection of loosely allied bands, they now returned home as one people on the verge of a new era in their history. They had become the Navajo Nation.

Navajos under military guard at Fort Sumner. (Courtesy U. S. Army Signal Corps collections in the Museum of New Mexico, neg. 28534.)

After its evacuation, Fort Sumner was sold to Lucien B. Maxwell for five thousand dollars. An old friend of Kit Carson who had created a business and real estate empire based in Cimarron (p. 151), Maxwell moved his headquarters here and began ranching. With him came a large entourage of family, friends, and employees who lived in and around the fort, forming the community of Fort Sumner. Maxwell converted one building along officers' row into a two-story mansion for his own family. When he died in 1875, his son, Pete, took over the operation and continued to live here until he went bust in the early 1880s. Although times had grown hard for ranchers in New Mexico, the old fort continued to be used until it was damaged by a flooding Pecos River in 1904. Salvaging what they could from the collapsing adobe structures, its residents moved to a site five miles upriver along the new railroad—the present town of Fort Sumner.

The Fort Sumner story cannot be told without mention of its most notorious visitor, Billy the Kid. William Bonney had come to the fort as early as August 1878, when he and other members of his gang—known as "The Regulators"—accompanied one of John Chisum's cattle caravans here, and Billy, then eighteen, paid court to the legendary cattleman's niece, Sally. He enjoyed living in the small Hispanic community that had grown up in and around the old fort, and he felt safe here. He was fluent in Spanish and made friends easily, and he was accepted into this frontier society despite his lawless reputation. Pete Maxwell's sister, Paulita, later described Fort Sumner as "a gay little place" that held a

Billy the Kid. (Courtesy Lincoln County Heritage Trust, Upham Collection.)

weekly dance that attracted girls from towns and ranches as much as fifty miles away. "Billy cut quite a gallant figure at these affairs," she recalled. "He was always smiling and good-natured and very polite and danced remarkably well, and the little Mexican beauties made eyes at him from behind their fans and used their coquetries to capture him and were very vain of his attentions." Separated by a day's ride from the nearest law officer, Fort Sumner also drew an assortment of low-life characters and wanted men with whom Billy no doubt consorted.

After his escape from the Lincoln jail (p. 169) on April 28, 1881, Billy ignored friends' advice to flee to Mexico. Instead, he headed for Fort Sumner, where he kept a low profile, sheltered by friends and cohorts. Still, word of his presence slipped out, and on the night of July 14, Sheriff Pat Garrett made a stealthy appearance at the Maxwell residence to question Pete about the Kid's whereabouts. During the conversation, Billy happened to enter the room, was recognized by the sheriff, and was shot dead.

When Fort Sumner State Monument was created in 1868, little remained above ground to testify to the site's extraordinary history. Using modern blocks, the Museum of New Mexico reconstructed the walls of one building complex to a height of about three feet, and developed a short interpretive trail across part of the old fort grounds. A small visitor center also was erected, which includes several exhibit cases displaying artifacts from the site, examples of historic arms and uniforms, and photographs of the Indians and soldiers taken between 1862 and 1868. A memorial to the Navajos and Mescaleros is being planned.

TIPS FOR THE TRAVELER:
While visiting Fort Sumner, you may enjoy stops at two local private museums. The Billy the Kid Museum, in town along U.S. 60/84, includes an extensive collection of antiques and artifacts as well as Fort Sumner and Billy the Kid relics. Another museum, located just outside the monument, emphasizes Billy the Kid memorabilia and features the outlaw's grave.

The Goodnight and Loving Trail (p. 303) passed through Fort Sumner, and it was here that Oliver Loving died in 1867 of wounds inflicted by Apache warriors. Another related site is the historic town of Lincoln (p. 166), the site of the Kid's most daring jailbreak.

SUGGESTED READING:
The Army and the Navajo: The Bosque Redondo Reservation Experiment, 1863–1868, by Gerald Thompson (Tucson: University of Arizona Press, 1976).

FORT UNION

Fort Union National Monument is located off Interstate 25, between Las Vegas and Wagon Mound. From Las Vegas, follow the interstate highway eighteen miles north to the Fort Union exit (New Mexico 477) and continue eight miles farther to the monument.

When a United States army marched into New Mexico in 1846, its commander, General Stephen Watts Kearny spoke to the citizens of Las Vegas (see p. 161) from a rootop on the plaza, not many miles west of the future site of Fort Union. In his declaration, Kearny said,

> From the Mexican government, you have never received protection. The Apaches and the Navajos come down from the mountains and carry off your sheep, and even your women, whenever they please. My government will correct all this.

Five years later, under orders of New Mexico's new commander, Colonel Edwin V. Sumner, construction began on Fort Union. The site Sumner selected was at the western end of the Santa Fe Trail, in Jicarilla Apache country (p. 115) and a region also frequented by Utes and Comanches. Kearny's promise had not nearly been realized and among Sumner's highest priorities was the effort to increase the safety of travelers, traders, and mail coaches arriving over the Santa Fe Trail.

Sumner garrisoned the new fort with troops from Santa Fe, which he viewed as a "sink of vice and extravagance." One can imagine how the soldiers felt upon learning they had to abandon the many entertainments of the exotic capital in favor of months on the drab and lonely prairie. Their first task was to construct the new post, which they did hastily, using raw pine logs laid directly on the ground. By 1854, the leaky pest-infested buildings had already deteriorated enough to consider relocating the fort.

In fact, construction on a new fort did not begin until the summer of 1861, when Texas Confederates were planning an invasion of New Mexico, with Fort Union providing their principal target. Their commander, Brigadier General Henry Hopkins Sibley, knew his objective well, having served only a year before at the fort. The second Fort Union was a massive, earthen, and star-shaped structure, designed to fend off an onslaught that never happened.

This fort, too, offered the most rustic living conditions, and after General James H. Carleton assumed command of New Mexico in 1862,

Fort Union, c. 1870. (Courtesy U. S. Army Signal Corps collections in the Museum of New Mexico, neg. 1835.)

he supervised the constuction of an elaborate territorial-style complex built of brick masonry. Carleton's interest was to wage war on the Apaches and Navajos, who were accused of attacking New Mexicans and stealing their livestock. To subdue the Indians, he envisioned a string of frontier posts, with Fort Union serving as their main supply depot. This third fort, therefore, included the Fort Union Quartermaster Depot, with warehouses, shops, sheds, offices, and facilities for mechanics, carpenters, wheelwrights, and blacksmiths. The depot quickly outgrew the military post.

Fort Union's extensive complex of buildings and its large number of personnel became by itself a costly enterprise. In 1869, General Philip H. Sheridan commented that it had "grown into proportions which never at any time were warranted by the want of the public service." He called it an "unnecessary waste of public money."

Life at Fort Union, though certainly more comfortable than at smaller posts on the frontier, was tedious, especially for the enlisted soldier. Unless some expedition were in the offing, the repetitive routine of daily tasks stretched out over weeks and months, with little to alleviate the monotony. For the troops, principal diversions consisted of drinking, fighting, and gambling in the notorious off-post settlement of Loma Parda. Officers, who often were accompanied by their families, were more inclined to hunt, read, and play parlor games.

Protection from hostile Indians had been Kearny's first promise to New Mexicans, and this mission remained a concern of Fort Union commanders for many years. Campaigns against the Indian foes, while

Remains of Fort Union today showing same buildings as previous photograph. (Photo by David Grant Noble.)

stressful and potentially dangerous, offered troopers some excitement. In the mid-1850s, expeditions focused on the Utes and Jicarilla Apaches to the north, but in the following decade most campaign activity was directed against the Navajos to the west, the Mescalero Apaches to the south, and the elusive and much-feared bands of Comanches and Kiowas to the east. It was these latter tribes who harassed travelers along the Santa Fe Trail.

Fort Union's demise began with the arrival of the railroad in 1879. Thereafter, it served little purpose, and in its final years, troops here made only a token effort to maintain the deteriorating buildings. When Fort Union was abandoned in 1891, after a life span of forty years, it had creditably addressed all of its original goals: to help pacify the region; to guard the Santa Fe Trail; and to be a military supply center for the territory. In addition, its troops had stood fast against an attempt to bring New Mexico into the Confederacy.

Following the removal of the garrison and for several generations, the old fort site was ignored, and any deterioration not produced by the natural elements was accomplished by vandals and by local people salvaging materials. Eventually, some citizens began to recognize the historical significance of the fort ruins, and in the late 1930s, a popular movement arose to conserve the site. This ultimately resulted in the creation of Fort Union National Monument in 1959.

Operated by the National Park Service, the site today has a visitor center with a small museum and self-guiding trails through the ruins. The interpretive trail passes by the remains of the officers' and soldiers' quarters, the commander's house, the guardhouse, the quartermaster depot, the corrals, and the large hospital. Historical photographs are displayed to help you visualize the impressive appearance of the fort in its heyday. Depending on your level of interest, you can spend one to three hours here in exploring the ruins, the other fort sites, and even wagon-wheel ruts on the Mountain Branch of the Santa Fe Trail. There is a picnic area here, but no nearby restaurant or lodgings.

TIPS FOR THE TRAVELER:
Two nearby towns you may enjoy including in your travels are Las Vegas and Cimarron (p. 151). Mora (p. 175), too, has several points of historical interest, and east of Springer you can visit, by appointment (call 505-375-2222), the old Dorsey Mansion (p. 317), built by Senator Stephen W. Dorsey in 1880. Remember, too, that the two branches of the Santa Fe Trail (p. 309) joined at Watrous and ran approximately parallel to Interstate 25.

SUGGESTED READING:
Fort Union and the Winning of the Southwest, by Chris Emmett (Norman: University of Oklahoma Press, 1965).

FORT WINGATE

The historic remains of old Fort Wingate are located off Interstate 40, between Grants and Gallup. From Gallup, take the interstate highway east for twelve miles, then follow New Mexico 400 south for four and one-half miles, through the town of Fort Wingate to the entrance to the former fort, which is now an Indian school.

Fort Wingate has been a fort of many names. Established in 1860 at Ojo del Oso (Bear Spring), its first designation was Fort Fauntleroy, named after Colonel Thomas T. Fauntleroy, commander of the First United States Dragoons. However, when the colonel joined the Confederacy, the army renamed it Fort Lyon, after Nathaniel Lyon, a Union general who had recently fallen in the Battle of Wilson's Creek. General Lyon's

A parade at Fort Wingate, 1919. (Courtesy Museum of New Mexico, neg. 112252.)

name stuck with the fort until 1868, when the Navajos, who had been interned at Fort Sumner (see p. 258), stayed here before returning to their former homes. At that time, Fort Wingate, located just south of present-day Grants, was closed and its troops were transferred here, bringing with them the name of their abandoned post. Captain Benjamin Wingate, incidently, also was a Civil War casualty, having been killed at Valverde (p. 235).

The Ojo del Oso site had long been a Navajo meeting place known as *Shushbito;* it was here, in 1846, that a group of their headmen had signed a treaty with the United States. Like other treaties of the period, it was not ratified by Congress and was ignored by both sides. In 1860 and 1861, Navajos came here every month, according to treaty, to receive their rations. On September 22, 1861, an event occurred that was a tragedy to the Navajos and seriously undermined the Indians' tenuous relationship with the United States. On that day, as was customary, horse races were held following the rations distribution. This was a spirited contest, in which both money and honor were at stake. After the Navajos lost the main-event race, they discovered that the bridle of their pride racehorse had been severed prior to the start. Much upset, they demanded a rematch, which was denied by the army's referees. In the ensuing confusion, U.S. troops shot at Navajos indiscriminately; then, on orders from the commander, they fired cannons at the Navajos as they fled with their families. When it was over, twelve Navajos had been killed and many more were wounded.

In 1863 and 1864, General James H. Carleton waged a final war against the Navajos (p. 125), which ended in the tribe's defeat and internment at Fort Sumner and Bosque Redondo, on New Mexico's eastern plains. Here, the Navajos languished until 1868, when the government faced up to the failure of the Fort Sumner experiment and negotiated a new treaty with the Indians. General William T. Sherman, who spoke for the U.S. government, favored sending the Navajos to the Oklahoma Indian Territory, but the Indians' eloquent spokesman, Barboncito, insisted above all else that the People be allowed to return to their homeland. Finally, it was agreed, and on June 18, 1868, 7,111 Navajos, led by Barboncito, began their walk home from Fort Sumner and arrived back in their beloved home country three weeks later.

Fort Lyon (Fauntleroy), which had been vacant during the Civil War, was situated at the edge of the Navajos' newly delineated reservation, and seemed the most convenient place to oversee Navajo affairs; the army, therefore, reopened this post and shut down old Fort Wingate. Because the Navajos were destitute and it was too late to plant, they stayed at Fort Wingate through most of the winter. Living on inadequate government rations, they looked forward to the next stage of their repatriation, when they would return to their homes.

In the latter decades of the nineteenth century and the early years of the present century, Fort Wingate's troops usually had little of consequence to do beyond routine police duties in the region. Occasionally, however, other assignments did arise; for example, once they captured a small party of Mescalero "renegades," and in 1891, four companies of troops marched to Oraibi on the Hopi reservation to enforce an order that Hopi children attend a U.S. government school. When Hopi leaders resisted the action, nine were taken to the fort and jailed for eighteen months.

Interestingly, two army officers stationed at Fort Wingate later achieved considerable distinction: Lieutenant John J. "Blackjack" Pershing would become commander of American Expeditionary Forces in World War I; and Captain Arthur MacArthur would raise a son who would become an American military legend. Incidently, Pershing, while at Fort Wingate, had occasion to rescue three white men from an angry group of Zuñi Indians, who had accused the whites of stealing horses.

In 1914–15, Fort Wingate had an unusual function: to host four thousand Mexican refugees, remnants of the Mexican Federal Army

An original Fort Wingate building. (Photo by David Grant Noble.)

that had fled into United States territory with their families during the Pancho Villa (p. 275) uprising. After the return of the Mexicans, the post was shut down, only to be reactivated after World War I as a storage facility for large quantities of bulk powder and surplus ammunition. The munitions-storage "igloos," however, were located several miles away from the old cavalry post. In 1925, part of Fort Wingate was turned over to the Department of the Interior for use as a trade school for Navajos, as many of the fort buildings were well suited for this purpose. Navajo students received instruction here in such vocations as dairy farming, surveying, and making traditional crafts.

Up until the razing of many of the old fort buildings in the 1960s, Fort Wingate was the best-preserved frontier post in New Mexico. Today, a Bureau of Indian Affairs elementary school for Navajo children uses the campus. One of the original fort buildings, in fact, houses its administrative offices and classrooms, and another has been preserved.

While the Fort Wingate campus retains some historical ambience, no public interpretive program is offered. Still, you will easily recognize the original fort buildings on the north and west sides of the quadrangle. When classes are in recess, young Navajo boys and girls play on the quadrangle lawn; as you watch them, you may find it moving to reflect on the history of the ground beneath their feet.

Other places of historical interest near Fort Wingate include the pueblos of Zuñi (p. 103) and Acoma (p. 9) and El Morro National Monument (p. 321) with its famed Inscription Rock. You may also enjoy hiking the old Zuñi-Acoma Indian trail across the lava flows at El Malpais National Monument in Grants. Travel services can be found in the town of Fort Wingate as well as in Gallup and Grants and along Interstate 25.

SUGGESTED READING:
Navajo Stories of the Long Walk Period (Tsaile: Navajo Community College Press, 1973).

GLORIETA PASS BATTLEFIELD

Glorieta Battlefield is located fifteen miles east of Santa Fe along New Mexico 50, one mile east of its junction with Interstate 25. A small pitched-roof adobe building on the north side of the road marks part of the battlefield. For current information on visiting this site, contact the Pecos National Historical Park.

Before a United States army marched into Santa Fe in 1846, New Mexico belonged to other nations—Indian, Spanish, and Mexican. In 1861–62, Confederate soldiers came here, too, and hoisted their emblem up flagpoles around the territory. People are often surprised to learn that the Civil War was fought in New Mexico. To be sure, the battles were small in scale and hardly decisive to the war's outcome; still, armies clashed here, soldiers were killed, and many citizens passed a year of insecurity and fear.

The Civil War came to New Mexico in the summer of 1861 and gathered momentum in January of the following year, when General Henry H. Sibley led a brigade of Texas Confederates up the Rio Grande Valley. It ended abruptly on March 28, when the Rebels met a coalition of Colorado volunteers and Fort Union regulars at Glorieta Pass. Here, they were defeated.

The Battle of Glorieta Pass may not have been "the Gettysburg of the West," as some have romantically dubbed it, but it was a significant military engagement that terminated Confederate aspirations to extend its control deep into the American West. Their defeat was something of

Brigadier General Henry H. Sibley.
(Courtesy Museum of New Mexico, neg. 50541.)

a fluke; had they won the day instead, the Confederacy's fortunes quite literally may have risen, at least for the short term.

General Sibley envisioned the conquest of the Southwest as a key to winning the war for the South. After resigning his U.S. Army commission—he was the commander of Fort Union (see p. 264)—he returned to his home state of Texas, recruited an army, and launched his campaign. In July, before he even set foot in New Mexico, Fort Fillmore, near Mesilla, fell to an advance unit. Six months later, with Sibley now in command (though allegedly bedridden from intoxication), the Confederates detoured Fort Craig (p. 235) and thumped its Union defenders at Valverde. Socorro (p. 203), Belen, and Albuquerque (p. 142) fell in rapid succession, and on March 10, the Texans entered Santa Fe. Governor Henry Connelly had already left for the safety of a hotel in Las Vegas. As the post's former commanding officer, Sibley was confident that he could drive back its weak forces, then continue unopposed to the Colorado gold fields, whose wealth, he figured, would bolster the depleted Confederate treasury. Then it would be on to California, to establish a Southern port on the Pacific. It was an ambitious plan.

Fort Union awaited the advancing Rebels with no little trepidation. Its strength was low. Many officers, like Sibley, had joined the Confed-

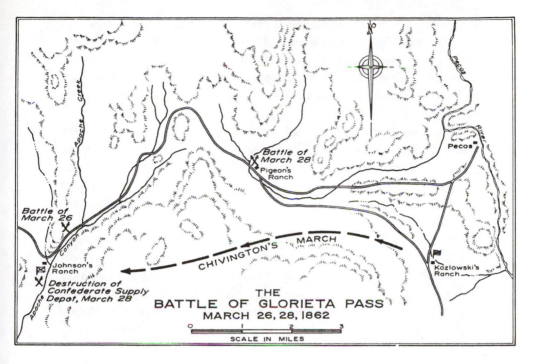

THE BATTLE OF GLORIETA PASS
MARCH 26, 28, 1862

SCALE IN MILES

eracy, and some troops had been transferred to the east, where the real war was being fought. But as the Texans drew near, a new factor entered the equation: the arrival of the First Regiment of Colorado Volunteers. The Coloradoans, under Colonel John P. Slough, had staged a heroic forced march from Denver, covering an average of forty miles per day through the worst kind of weather.

The Confederate troops in Santa Fe, who numbered about two hundred, set off for Fort Union on March 26, led by Major Charles L. Pyron. Unexpectedly, however, they encountered and skirmished with an advance unit of Union forces at Apache Canyon near Glorieta Pass, and had to retreat to camp at Johnson's Ranch in Cañoncito. Here, they were joined by the rest of the Confederate army, which had advanced by way of Galisteo. Interestingly, it was at this same pass, sixteen years earlier, that Governor Manuel Armijo had gathered his New Mexican militia to oppose General Stephen W. Kearny's Army of the West. Recognizing the insurmountable odds, Armijo had disbanded his troops and departed for Mexico.

On the morning of the twenty-eighth, the Federals advanced to Kozlowski's ranch, near Pecos, from whence Major John M. Chivington (later of Sand Creek Massacre notoriety) and four hundred troops were sent on a circuitous route through the hills to strike the Confederates from the rear. The latter, however, had moved with such dispatch up the canyon that Chivington missed them altogether. What he did stumble upon was their weakly defended supply train, including eighty wagons of food, clothing, equipment, medical supplies, and ammunition. He destroyed all, even the mules.

Meanwhile, the Federals had marched west from Pecos to meet the Rebels at Pigeon's Ranch in Glorieta Pass. For most of the day, the opposing forces fought each other, inconclusively, from the rocky hillsides. But by late afternoon, with both sides tiring, the Texans pressed hard and gained ground. Then, with the smell of victory at their nostrils, they received the stunning news of their losses to the rear. In a single, fateful stroke, Sibley's hopes for a western empire had been dashed. He made a truce, withdrew to Santa Fe, and retreated to Texas.

Today, all that remains of the original Pigeon's Ranch is a single adobe building on the north side of the highway. According to legend, until recent years you could see a cannonball embedded in a gnarled juniper tree opposite the building. Each year, usually on the anniversary of the battle at the end of March, a multitude of enthusiasts gather at El Rancho de las Golondrinas (p. 325) for a public reenactment of the battle, which took the lives of twenty-nine Union and approximately thirty-six Confederate soldiers.

For years, a mystery prevailed regarding the whereabouts of the graves of the fallen Confederates. Then, in 1987, a Glorieta resident accidently uncovered several skeletons while digging foundation trenches for a house. Archaeologists were summoned and when they had completed their work, they had excavated the remains of thirty-two dead soldiers. Six years later, in a full Confederate military funeral reenactment, their remains were reinterred in Santa Fe's national cemetery.

In 1990, federal legislation was passed designating Glorieta Battlefield as a national historic site to be protected by the National Park Service. Since much of the battlefield lies on private land, the full transition to a public monument will take some years. A parcel, however, already is being administered by Pecos National Historical Park, located only a few miles away, and the park's staff will provide information on access to the battleground.

TIPS FOR THE TRAVELER:
You should certainly visit nearby Pecos National Historical Park (p. 42), which has a fine museum as well as Pueblo and Spanish colonial ruins.

To the east, along I-25, are the old villages of San Miguel del Vado and San José (p. 179). Las Vegas (p. 161) is a few miles farther. Fort Union, whose troops fought at Glorieta, is a national monument northeast of Las Vegas. A few travel services are available in the village of Pecos and many more in Santa Fe.

SUGGESTED READING:

The Battle at Valley's Ranch, by Marc Simmons (San Pedro Press, 1987).

Rebels on the Rio Grande: The Civil War Journals of A. B. Peticolas, edited by Don E. Alberts (Albuquerque: University of New Mexico Press, 1984).

PANCHO VILLA STATE PARK

Pancho Villa State Park is located in Columbus, along the Mexican border in southwestern New Mexico. From Deming, on Interstate 10, take New Mexico 11 south for thirty-two miles.

Back in 1916, Columbus was a sleepy crossroads community of some four hundred people around which the desert seemed to stretch endlessly in all directions. Deming, to the north, and El Paso, seventy miles east by train, were the nearest towns of any size. Three miles south, at Palomas, was the Mexican border and the equally barren region of Chihuahua. Still, Columbus had places to eat, hotels, a general store, market, bank, telephone office, post office, and railroad station. And there was Camp Furlong, whose Thirteenth Cavalry made regular patrols along the border. Most of Columbus's residents lived in simple adobe houses that were located in or at the fringes of town. The soldiers, except for a few officers with families, were quartered in the camp on the south side of the railroad tracks.

In the predawn hours of March 9, Columbus's residents were awakened by gunfire and cries of "Viva Villa, Viva Mexico!" Then, for several hours, as they huddled in their homes or hid in the desert, their quiet, orderly world was shattered. The town and adjacent military post were being stormed by the forces of the Mexican renegade revolutionary Francisco "Pancho" Villa.

Pancho Villa, born in 1878 of humble family and orphaned while a child, had risen through Mexico's revolutionary ranks to become, by

Left to right: General Alvaro Obregon, General Pancho Villa, General John J. Pershing, Lieutenant George S. Patton at the El Paso-Juarez bridge, 1914. (Courtesy Museum of New Mexico, neg. 65501.)

1914, commander of the formidable *División del Norte*. With this army and enormous popular support, especially in Chihuahua, Villa had become a leading contender for the country's presidency. Two years later, however, beaten in battle by his former ally Venustiano Carranza, his fortunes were at a low ebb and his army mostly disbanded. Nevertheless, he still had about five hundred followers who, while remaining loyal, were frustrated, hungry, and short of supplies, arms, and munitions. Pancho Villa, who had met with U.S. representatives earlier, bitterly resented President Woodrow Wilson's recognition of Carranza and the aid given him in his struggle against Villa. By 1916, Villa's formerly proud revolutionaries had been reduced to a ragtag band of outlaws who survived by banditry, plunder, and extortion. Only two months before the Columbus raid, a group of Villistas—their leader was not among them—had forced sixteen Americans from a train at gunpoint at San Ysidro, robbed, and shot them.

Columbus's isolation made it an easy target for the Villistas. Its stores and armory alone were lure enough for the desperados, who were encamped on March 8 only a few miles southwest of town. In the hours after midnight, they crossed the border two and a half miles west of Palomas and stealthily advanced toward town. Success hung on surprise.

When the attack began, surprise was, indeed, total. The town was asleep, and Camp Furlong's troops were only awakened when a sentry exchanged gunfire with a group of the marauders outside regimental headquarters. The troops scrambled out of bed and tried to find their clothes and boots in the dark. Then they discovered that their arms were locked in the armory and few officers were present. Confusion reigned as soldiers stumbled about, trying to organize themselves, occasionally bumping into groups of guerrillas. Miraculously, few were killed, and eventually order was restored.

If confusion characterized Camp Furlong, Columbus was in a state of pandemonium as hundreds of Mexicans rode up and down the streets, yelling, shooting out windows, looting stores, and setting fire to buildings. One of these was the Commercial Hotel, some of whose guests were robbed or shot as they tried to flee. Soon the whole town was illuminated by blazing buildings. One resourceful man saved himself by writing personal checks to the guerrillas. Another, less fortunate, slumped over his car's steering wheel, dead from a bullet as he tried to escape. A terror-stricken family fled from its home to the mesquite bushes, where the father, in front of his wife and children, beat a Mexican attacker to death with the butt of his pistol. A mother, hiding with her baby, stuffed the corner of a pillow slip in the infant's mouth to silence it until danger passed.

By daylight, soldiers from Camp Furlong, now armed and organized, had advanced to town and counterattacked the Mexicans, who found themselves caught in a deadly crossfire. Slowly, the Villistas withdrew to the edge of town, then retreated southward into the desert, pursued by members of the Thirteenth Cavalry. The rebels had seized a considerable quantity of arms and supplies, but paid dearly; ninety of their comrades lay behind on the ground, and more died during the retreat. For them, it had been a bold attack, successfully begun but badly ended. The Americans had fewer losses—ten civilians and eight soldiers were killed. And a section of town lay in smoldering ruins.

The following day, the soldiers and citizens of Columbus respectfully prepared their dead for burial. As for the bodies of the Mexicans, they were unceremoniously stacked between layers of oak wood in two funeral pyres, soaked in coal oil, and cremated. A week later, General John J. "Blackjack" Pershing, soon to command the American expeditionary forces in France, arrived by train with ten thousand troops. This "punitive expedition" pursued Pancho Villa for nearly a year across the

Columbus in ruins after Pancho Villa's raid, 1916. (Courtesy Museum of New Mexico, neg. 13785.)

barren deserts of northern Mexico. The bandit's mobility, knowledge of the terrain, and local popularity, however, made him no match for the lumbering U.S. Army. Finally, in February 1917, Pershing's trail-weary troops marched back to Columbus, where they passed a reviewing stand and down a street filled with clapping citizens, who had spent a lucrative year at the expedition's busy supply hub.

Curiously, while Pershing's foray south of the border had accomplished little and aroused the ire of many Mexicans, it made the military record books. This was the last true cavalry action ever mounted by the U.S. Army, and the first military operation to use motorized vehicles; even its famous commander traded his mount for a staff car. What was more, for the first time, planes were used for military reconnaisance and courier duty, initiating a new era in warfare.

Pancho Villa's raid on Columbus created a brief national sensation. It represents the sole instance in which an armed foreign force has invaded the continental United States. Soon, however, Americans would be falling on more distant battlefields and the Columbus incident would seem trivial by comparison.

Today, the Camp Furlong site is Pancho Villa State Park, noted for its cactus gardens and the rock-wall ruins of the old military post. Among the latter is a grease rack to service army vehicles—the first of its kind. Adjacent to the park is the Old Customs House, which has an exhibit of photographs relating to the infamous raid. Across the tracks, in the former railroad depot, is the Columbus Historical Museum, displaying many historical artifacts, pictures, and memorabilia. As for the town, it is again just a quiet crossroads community, where Villa and his raiders live only in story.

TIPS FOR THE TRAVELER:
Other historic sites in the region include Mesilla (see p. 170), Fort Selden (p. 249), and Fort Cummings (p. 241). You may also enjoy visiting the ancient ruins of Paquimé, in Casas Grandes, which are a two-hour drive south from Columbus on good highways. (You will need appropriate papers for entering a foreign country.) Columbus has a restaurant, service station, and motel; however, you will find better travel services in Deming.

SUGGESTED READING:

Pershing's Mission in Mexico, by Haldeen Braddy, (El Paso: Texas Western Press, 1966).

Revolution on the Border: The United States and Mexico, 1910–1920, by Linda B. Hall and Don M. Coerver (Albuquerque: University of New Mexico Press, 1988).

THE TRINITY SITE

The Trinity Site is located on the White Sands Missile Range west of Carrizozo. The Trinity Site is only open to the public on the first Saturdays of April and October; on these dates, the Stallion Gate is open from 8 A.M. to 2 P.M. A car caravan to the site leaves from the Alamogordo Fairgrounds parking lot at 8 A.M. From Carrizozo, follow U.S. 380 west for fifty-two miles to New Mexico 525, then turn south and continue four miles to the Stallion Gate of White Sands Missile Range. Register here, then continue seventeen miles farther to Ground Zero. From Interstate 25, take U.S. 380 east for twelve miles to the New Mexico 525 turnoff. For further information, call (505) 678-1134.

In south-central New Mexico, east of the Rio Grande, lies a bleak desert known as the Jornada del Muerto (Journey of the Dead Man). For centuries, travelers on the historic Camino Real (see p. 293) between Santa Fe (p. 189) and El Paso del Norte had to traverse this arid wasteland, with not a few perishing from thirst, exhaustion, or Apache arrows. It seems somehow fitting, then, that scientists chose this lonesome place for the world's first atomic-bomb explosion. The event reportedly inspired its mastermind, J. Robert Oppenheimer, to quote the ancient Hindu text, "I am become Death, the destroyer of worlds."

What happened at 5:29:45 A.M., July 16, 1945, changed the world

First atomic explosion, Trinity Site, 5:29:45 A.M., July 16, 1945. (Courtesy Los Alamos National Laboratory.)

and, in a fraction of an instant, put our civilization in the Nuclear Age. It was the culmination of the Manhattan Project, centered in Los Alamos, which had begun two years earlier by bringing together the nation's foremost physicists to design and build an atomic bomb. The project's immediate objective was to end World War II.

Scientists had already observed uranium fission and created a nuclear chain reaction. As early as 1939, Albert Einstein had advised President Roosevelt of the bomb-making potential of this research and warned that the Germans were moving in this direction. The remoteness of Los Alamos, on the Pajarito Plateau northwest of Santa Fe, made it an ideal place in which to conduct the project in secrecy. The illustrious team of scientists, led by Oppenheimer and including such names as Enrico Fermi and Edward Teller, gathered at Los Alamos in the spring of 1943 and worked under intense pressure on the experiment for just over two years. Backing up the researchers was a high-powered logistical operation, whose job it was to build a virtual city and complex of laboratories where only a ranch and boys' school had existed. At short notice, the support crew also had to keep the scientists supplied with a formidable list of hard-to-find items.

The team encountered difficulties on the implosion technique of achieving a nuclear explosion. By this altogether new and untried method, a charge of high explosives would compress a subcritical mass of plutonium to attain supercriticality. They could not risk a test, and possible failure, over enemy territory; furthermore, they wanted to test the explosion and its effects in many ways, which would have been impossible under combat conditions. The Jornada site, which Oppenheimer named Trinity, was selected over other suggested places because it was far from population centers and usually had good weather. In addition, it was close enough to Los Alamos to facilitate transportation and travel, yet far enough away to minimize the connection between the anticipated visible blast and the curious goings-on at the secret research hub.

May and June of 1945 were taken up by a frenzy of work to prepare the "gadget," as it was often called, and to ready the test site. Speed and secrecy were paramount, and procurement and transportation always a challenge. At the Trinity Site, troops constructed roads, buildings, and laboratories as well as an elaborate communications system. In addition, a vast store of equipment and supplies accumulated, including a 214-ton steel bomb container called "Jumbo," which, ultimately, was not used. It remains on the site.

A deserted ranch house, located two miles from Ground Zero,

was taken over by the scientific team as the place in which to assemble the core components of the bomb, which came to be called Fat Man. The house had been built in 1913 by homesteaders Franz and Esther Schmidt, who ran as many as twelve thousand sheep and one thousand cattle on the ranch.

The plutonium arrived from Los Alamos on July 11, and team members assembled the bomb's high explosive components in the ranch house on the following day. At 1 A.M. on the morning of the thirteenth, they carried the components to Trinity where, in a tent at the base of a hundred-foot-high steel tower, the final assembly of active materials and high explosives took place. As one team member later understatedly recalled, "We were given plenty of time for the assembly of active material. By then it was pretty much a routine operation. It was simply a matter of working very slowly and carefully, checking and re-checking everything as we went along." The only hitch occurred when the two major bomb elements would not fit together. The plutonium component, having expanded under the effects of its own generated heat, would not fit together with the other element, which was cold. The team placed the two parts together and the resulting heat exchange soon allowed them to slip together.

On the morning of the fourteenth, the bomb was raised to the top of the tower and a new team installed its detonators, a most delicate operation. On Sunday, the fifteenth, everyone waited until that night, when a small party of scientists climbed the tower for the last time to arm the bomb. Now all was readied except the weather, which was threatening. The scientists retreated to their wood and reinforced concrete observation shelters, protected by mounds of earth. Here, elaborate instrumentation panels would record implosion and explosion data, the release of nuclear energy, the extent of damage caused by blast pressure, and earth shock. In addition, they made spectographic and photographic recordings of the event, with some movie cameras recording the explosion at up to eight thousand frames per second.

That night, it rained intermittently but when a favorable weather report was issued at 4:45 A.M., project leaders agreed to proceed and set zero hour for 5:30 A.M. One observer later wrote that at the control point "most everyone present was praying. Oppenheimer grew tenser as the seconds ticked off. He scarcely breathed. He held on to a post to steady himself."

The cataclysm which occurred that morning had a profound effect upon every witness, from scientists watching from ten thousand yards away to a blind person over a hundred miles distant, who perceived

Trinity Site memorial. (Photo by David Grant Noble.)

the flash of light. The physical happening itself was awesome; as Fermi put it, "suddenly the countryside became brighter than in full daylight." The initial seconds seemed like an eternity to many observers. Fermi, who after the initial flash watched the developing explosion through protective lenses, described "a huge pillar of smoke with an expanded head like a gigantic mushroom that rose rapidly beyond the clouds . . ." Another official observer compared it to "the grand finale of a mighty symphony of the elements, fascinating and terrifying, uplifting and crushing, ominous, devastating, full of great promise and great foreboding."

On a strictly visual level, the Trinity Site today is unimpressive. The shallow crater formed by the blast has been filled in, and the glass shards, called trinitite, created by the heat have long since been collected, save for a few pieces preserved under a protective shed. The remnants of a concrete footing is all that remains of the observation tower. Next to it is a modest stone monument memorializing the site. Of course, in the spiritual and historical dimensions, the Trinity Site is still awesome. On the two occasions annually that it is opened to the public, a line of approaching cars stretches far across the desert. Visitors approaching Ground Zero walk slowly and speak in hushed tones as they explain to their children what happened here.

When you visit the site, unless you arrive early, expect a wait to be parked. Plan about half an hour to see the Trinity Site itself and another forty-five minutes for a tour of the McDonald Ranch, which was restored by the National Park Service in 1984. The ranch houses several displays, including a scale model of Fat Man. It is a good idea to bring water and picnic supplies with you as the nearest travel services are in San Antonio and Carrizozo.

TIPS FOR THE TRAVELER:
Other sites of historic interest in the region include the towns of Socorro and Lincoln (pp. 203 and 166, respectively), and Fort Craig (p. 235). For a glimpse into the region's prehistory, take a short detour from Three Rivers, along U.S. 54, to the Three Rivers Petroglyph Site. Sierra Blanca, to the east, is one of New Mexico's finest all-season recreational areas, located in the heart of Mescalero Apache country (p. 120).

SUGGESTED READING:
Los Alamos: Beginning of an Era, 1943–1945, (Los Alamos: Los Alamos Historical Society, 1986).
The Day the Sun Rose Twice: The Story of the Trinity Site Nuclear Explosion, July 16, 1945, by Ferenc Morton Szasz (Albuquerque: University of New Mexico Press, 1984).

HISTORIC TRAILS

THE BUTTERFIELD TRAIL

The Butterfield Trail was the route followed by the United States' first overland mail and passenger service between the Mississippi River and the Pacific Ocean. Entering New Mexico from El Paso, Texas, it followed the Rio Grande north to Mesilla, then headed westward across wilderness deserts to California. Specific points of interest along the New Mexico segment of the Trail are described below.

Following the Mexican War and the discovery of gold in California, popular pressure mounted on the federal government to improve public travel and transportation service between the nation's two oceans. In 1855, with their population burgeoning, New Mexicans made a formal appeal for better mail service, declaring, "Our geographical position, being in the centre of the American continent without navigable rivers or means of communication by rail-road, renders our situation as remote from the federal capital in communications through mail facilities as the Sandwich Islands." At the time, a citizen would consider himself fortunate to receive a reply to a letter to the East within three months. Californians were even more frustrated than New Mexicans by their geographical isolation and their dependence on a steamship monopoly. Rumors circulated that this rich new American territory might even move toward independence if nothing were done soon.

In 1857, in response to these pressures, Congress authorized the establishment of a mail service across the West, from St. Louis to San Francisco. The contract was won by John Butterfield and his partners in the Overland Mail Company. Butterfield was a successful, self-made entrepreneur from Utica, New York, and a friend of President Buchanan. Starting as a stagecoach driver, he had set himself up in the livery business and eventually acquired numerous mail and passenger coach lines in western New York State. As stagecoaches became obsolete, he moved into the steamer trade on Lake Ontario, invested in railways, and, in the mid-1800s, became a founding director of the American Express Company. He was considered a man of high integrity and expert managerial skills, who understood the business potential of rapid transport. Amazingly, he set up the 2,795-mile service between St. Louis and San Francisco in a single year. After surveying the route and finding appropriate station and watering sites, his crews had to grade roads and build

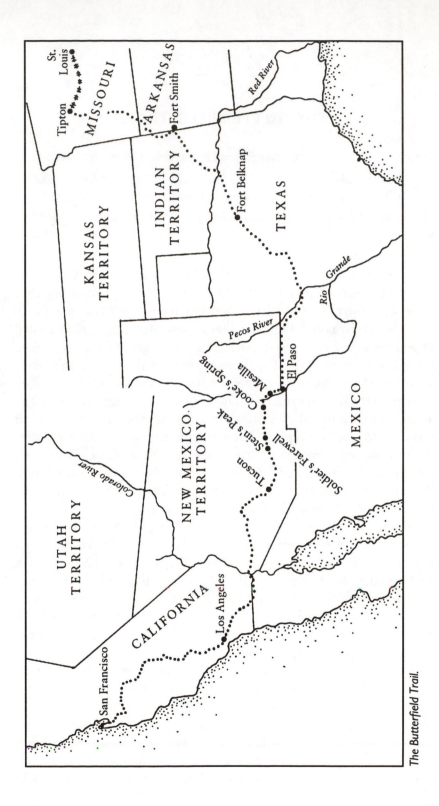

The Butterfield Trail.

bridges, transfer stations, passenger facilities, and corrals. A myriad of other arrangements had to be completed as well, including hiring 800 employees, acquiring and distributing over 1,500 horses and mules, stocking stations with hay and feed, and purchasing 250 coaches and mail wagons and other equipment. His drivers, mostly old hands from the eastern stage business, were trained to cope with emergencies and breakdowns; provide safety, security, comfort, and courtesy to passengers; and strictly maintain schedules. In the case of breakdowns or inclement weather, the mail was transferred to extra wagons that pressed on to the next station. "Remember boys," Butterfield said, "nothing in God's earth must stop the United States mail!"

When the first westbound mail left St. Louis in September 1858, Butterfield, aged fifty-six, accompanied it on the journey's first leg. With him was a reporter, William L. Ormsby, who described him as "the most energetic president I ever saw. He appears to know every foot of the ground and to be known to everybody. . . . Certainly, if the overland mail does not succeed, it will not be for lack of his arduous exertions."

After impassioned political controversy over the route to be followed, the Santa Fe Trail had been rejected in favor of a southern route with two eastern terminals, St. Louis and Memphis. The Trail ran south through the northwest corner of Arkansas, across Indian Territory, and sliced across Texas to El Paso, the midway point. Here, it turned up into New Mexico territory and ascended the Rio Grande Valley as far as Mesilla (see p. 170). Today, U.S. 80 parallels the old Trail's route through the present towns of Anthony, Berino, and Mesquite. Stage passengers probably passed over the site of the Brazito Battlefield, where Colonel Alexander W. Doniphan's forces had routed General Ponce de León's Mexican army on Christmas day 1846. Coaches dropped off mail at Fort Fillmore and continued another six miles north to busy Mesilla, already a junction of the Santa Fe Mail, a north-south line, and the San Antonio–San Diego Mail. The historic station building now houses a restaurant on the south side of Mesilla's old plaza.

From Mesilla, travelers headed west to Cooke's Spring, fifty-two miles away; this was the longest station-to-station span of the entire journey. Their route crosses New Mexico 26 between Deming and Hatch 3.3 miles north of Florida. Initially, only a tent marked the Cooke's Spring Station; however, a building and corrals were later constructed a quarter-mile southeast of the site where Fort Cummings (p. 241) was later built. Cooke's Spring was named for Captain Philip St. George Cooke, who arrived here on November 16, 1846, while leading his Mormon Battalion from Santa Fe to San Diego. The spring,

Former Butterfield station, southeast corner of the Mesilla plaza. (Photo by David Grant Noble.)

which has since been walled and roofed, lay along an historic Indian and emigrant trail in the heart of Apache territory, and it was justifiably considered one of the most dangerous places on the journey. Its waters have quenched the thirst of Mangas Coloradas's warriors, transcontinental travelers, and frontier troops, and were even piped to Florida, five miles east, for use by the railroad.

From western movie traditions, we tend to envision stagecoaches being set upon by Indian hordes or bandits. It is interesting to note, however, that while stage drivers and station masters armed themselves to the teeth and passengers feared attack, neither of these threats posed a problem for the Butterfield line. During the period of its operation, the Mimbres and Chiricahua Apaches, who ruled much of southern New Mexico, honored an informal truce and allowed coaches to traverse their lands unscathed. As for road agents, they were little motivated to hold up stages that, by company policy, did not carry shipments of gold or silver. With the outbreak of the Civil War, however, the Apaches intensified their raiding, and anyone foolish enough to be caught traveling across their lands was at risk. In 1861, for example, seven Overland Mail employees in the El Paso office hurried west over the Butterfield Trail to escape invading Confederates, only to be killed by Mangas Coloradas's warriors at Cooke's Spring.

From Cooke's Spring, the Butterfield Trail led west through Cooke's Canyon and into the Mimbres Valley. A highway marker is placed approximately where the Trail crossed U.S. 180 north of Deming. The next station was Soldier's Farewell, at the south edge of the Burro Range. According to legend, at one time a disconsolate soldier, who was camping at this lonely site, ran out of his tent shouting goodbye to his friends, then shot himself. Continuing west, travelers' last stop in New Mexico was at Stein's Peak, eight miles north of where present-day Interstate 10 meets the New Mexico–Arizona border.

The Overland Mail Company's best vehicles were the sturdy, oval Concord coaches, whose excellent suspension allowed them to roll rather than bounce over bumpy roads. Also used, especially over rough or mountainous stretches of the Trail, were the more elongated, small-wheeled Celerity wagons. These three-thousand-pound vehicles could carry a four-thousand-pound load and had fold-down seats for easier sleeping, and windows and doors that passengers could roll up in fair weather. Through-trips on the Butterfield Trail cost passengers two hundred dollars and took just under three weeks. Postage for a letter was ten cents, and freight cost a dollar per one hundred pounds per one hundred miles. In addition to passenger fares, the company received a substantial federal subsidy to run the mail service. Travel was accomplished by day and night, with stops being made only to change horses, repair broken axles, and consume two daily meals, which cost extra. The latter often consisted of such delicacies as hardtack, beef jerky, and raw onions, washed down with black coffee. Way stations—small rough-hewn buildings with adjacent corrals and a well or water tank— were spaced at an average of twenty miles apart. Although the scenery often was memorable, the ride grew wearisome and passengers learned to nap on board as they rocked over rough trails. Still, everyone deemed the ordeal preferable to the steamship alternative.

The Overland Mail Company's service over the Butterfield Trail was an immediately recognized success and a personal triumph for its organizer. When the first eastbound mail delivery arrived at St. Louis on the morning of October 9, 1858, Butterfield received a cable from President Buchanan, which stated, "It is a glorious triumph for civilization and the Union. Settlements will soon follow the course of the road, and the East and West will be bound together by a chain of living Americans

"Celerity" stagecoach.

which can never be broken." One can surmise that had Mangas Coloradas, Cochise, or Gerónimo read this accolade, they might have rethought their permissive policy toward the use of the Trail. For Americans crossing the continent, however, the experience of traveling the Butterfield Trail, over such vast and wild expanses of prairie and desert, generated adventures and stories that have become part of western folklore.

In 1861, when the outbreak of the Civil War prohibited further use of the Trail, the line was operating at nearly full capacity. Understandably, John Butterfield felt profound disappointment at its demise. Still, the North had to maintain communications with California and did so by shifting mail and passenger service to a central route from Missouri to Salt Lake City and on to Sacramento.

TIPS FOR THE TRAVELER:
Be sure to walk around the Mesilla plaza and see the old Butterfield stage station (El Patio Restaurant). A visit to Fort Cummings, a minimally developed historic site between Deming and Hatch, may also be of interest. Beyond its crumbling ruins rises Cooke's Peak, a regional landmark. Most of the rest of the Butterfield Trail in New Mexico traverses rugged terrain on private ranches and is inaccessible to all but the most avid explorers. Other places of interest in the area include City of Rocks State Park, midway between Silver City and Deming, and Rock Hound State Park, southeast of Deming.

SUGGESTED READING:
The Butterfield Overland Mail: 1857–1869, by Roscoe P. Conkling and
   Margaret B. Conkling (Glendale: Arthur H. Clark Company, 1947).

EL CAMINO REAL

Opened in 1598, El Camino Real (the royal road) linked Mexico City to Santa Fe by way of Chihuahua City and El Paso del Norte. After 1821, it connected with the Santa Fe Trail leading to Independence, Missouri.

Much is said about New Mexico's isolation and self-dependence in colonial times, but this land, which Diego de Vargas called "remote beyond compare," had one life link to urban centers in Mexico: the Camino Real, or royal road. It began as a rough trail whose route shifted to accommodate the needs of explorers, colonizers, and traders. Much of its extent certainly had its origins in prehistory, for it was the indigenous peoples of the Americas who guided the Spaniards to places the latter sought to discover.

As a Spanish road, the Camino can most neatly be dated to 1598, the year Juan de Oñate led a multitude of prospective colonists and their entourage of Mexican Indian servants north from Zacatecas to the land of the Pueblos. The party, accompanied by a lumbering herd of domestic stock and a long string of carts and wagons pulled by oxen, set off in February and by mid-March had reached the Rio Chaviscar, near where Chihuahua City would be built. Then they boldly struck north across hundreds of miles of trackless Chihuahuan desert, striking the Rio Grande in April, just south of the future site of El Paso del Norte. Oñate followed the river north through the country of the Manso Indians and into that of the Piros. They camped and briefly rested near the present ruins of Fort Selden (p. 249), naming the place after Pedro Robledo, a member of the party who died here. This campsite would remain a favorite of travelers for another three hundred years.

From here, the river looped west, but Oñate led his followers due north across an eighty-mile stretch of desert later to be dubbed the *Jornada del Muerto,* or Journey of the Dead Man. Once again, they struck the Rio Grande, now south of the present ruins of Fort Craig and the Valverde ford, where, 264 years later, Union and Confederate armies would clash (p. 235). From here, it was easy traveling to the hospitable Piro pueblo of Teypana, near present-day Socorro (p. 203). After resting, they continued slowly upriver past La Joya, whence some members explored the Indian town of Abo (p. 55), then proceeded to a series of Tiwa villages in the vicinity of Isleta Pueblo (p. 25) and Albuquerque (p. 142). Still they pressed northward through the Province of Tiguex, where Coronado's army spent the winter of 1540–41, and on into the

El Camino Real.

country of the Keres. By this time, Oñate's weary followers had been on the trail for six months and urgently needed to find a place to settle. They chose the Tewa village of Ok'eh at the confluence of the Rio Grande and the Rio Chama; Oñate renamed it San Juan de los Caballeros (p. 72).

Oñate's route became, in effect, the Camino Real, although a dozen years would pass before the first supply caravan from Mexico City would rumble over its rough course. By this time, Oñate's struggling colonists had reestablished themselves in Santa Fe, which was the road's northern terminus. From then on, about once every three years, a thirty-two-wagon caravan would pull into New Spain's frontier capital, laden with provisions and supplies. Although the supply trains were subsidized by the crown and intended solely to support the missions, corrupt civil officials often would appropriate wagons to carry out their own private commercial ventures. Other people, especially official visitors, availed themselves of the protection offered by the caravans' military escorts to travel up and down the Camino.

In the 1700s, Chihuahua's population grew as this crossroads town developed into a major mining and commercial center and military headquarters. Since it was illegal to trade overland with the United States or France, New Mexicans had little choice but to do business with the Chihuahua merchants, who enjoyed a regional monopoly. The sums they paid for New Mexico goods transported down the Camino were too low; in contrast, the prices demanded for needed supplies, which were imported from the south, were inflated. Trade on the Camino Real, which had begun as a subsidized service to the missionaries, evolved into a privately managed commerce that kept New Mexicans impoverished, even though they produced substantial quantities of marketable goods. Without alternatives, they grudgingly accepted the situation, exporting sheep, wool, hides, piñon nuts, salt, and Indian blankets. Even captive Apaches were brought down in chains, with many fated to die as laborers in the mines of Parral.

Travelers along the Camino Real, especially south of Albuquerque, were frequently imperiled by Apache and Navajo raiding parties. Since the Indians were reluctant to attack large groups, however, the Spaniards usually consolidated their caravans and were accompanied by a detachment of troops, sometimes reinforced by local militia or by Pueblo auxiliaries. When herds of sheep were driven down the trail (fifteen thousand in 1807), hundreds of civilian herders came with them.

In addition to wagons, colonial New Mexicans utilized two forms of transportation that are closely associated with the Camino Real: the *atajo* (pack train) and the *carreta* (cart). Admired for its intelligence, strength, stamina, and sure-footedness, the mule was a basic beast of burden in New Mexico, carrying goods over the Camino for centuries. The animals were trained by muleteers, who were highly skilled in riding, roping, loading, and caring for their animals, as well as in managing the long trains over rough trails. With a pair of heavy packs secured over its back, a mule could cover more than a dozen miles a day for weeks on end. The animals were so much in demand in Missouri that when American traders arrived in Santa Fe or Chihuahua, they frequently sold their Conestoga wagons at a profit, bought mules to carry back their bullion and specie, and then resold them at home for another profit.

The *carreta* was a heavy, solidly built, two-wheeled cart that served as a basic mode of transport in Spain's New World colonies. It came

Mule-drawn wagon, c. 1890. (Photo by Saunders, courtesy Museum of New Mexico, neg. 14875.)

into use in Mexico as early as the 1530s, was part of Oñate's caravan to New Mexico in 1598, and well into the nineteenth century, it was a standard conveyance along the Camino Real, especially for local and short-distance transport, Technologically, the *carreta* was just a simple wooden box that rested directly upon a hand-hewn axle of cottonwood or pine. Its wheels were disks cut from the trunk of a large cottonwood tree. As the wheels rotated on their axle, the constant piercing screech that ensued was only slightly softened by the application of tallow.

After Mexico's independence was won in 1821, the road's traffic increased exponentially as long-frustrated commerce between that country and the United States was allowed to flourish. New Mexicans had a hunger for American goods, which were cheaper and of better quality than anything they heretofore had been able to buy. However, the limited New Mexico market could not satisfy the mounting quantities of goods soon being exported from Missouri; thus, the traders pressed on to El Paso and Chihuahua, where they made stunning profits.

Over the next twenty-five years, the economic and cultural impact of the trade on New and Old Mexico was tremendous. Cloth was a staple trade item, but other popular goods included jewelry, personal toilet articles, clocks and watches, pots and pans, axes and shovels, window glass, books, rifles, traps, and even champagne. When New Mexicans joined the commerce as middlemen, their previous trade imbalance with Chihuahua was reversed, and for the first time, hard currency began to flow northward.

Replica of a Spanish colonial era carreta at Rancho de las Golondrinas. (Photo by David Grant Noble.)

Apart from mules, exports to Missouri consisted mostly of silver coin and bullion, which were sorely needed by Missouri's banks. Mexican pesos, whose silver content was at a par with that of the American dollar, invigorated Missouri's unstable economy and soon became a common currency in that state's western counties.

In 1846, the Camino Real became the thoroughfare for an American army in its war with Mexico. After Kearny's bloodless seizure of Santa Fe, Colonel Alexander S. Doniphan led a column of troops down the Camino, followed by scores of traders' wagons, and routed a Mexican army at Brazito, below Mesilla (p. 170). Doniphan then pressed his campaign down the Camino to El Paso and all the way to the city of Chihuahua.

By the early 1850s, traffic on the Camino Real had begun to fall off as other shorter routes to the Mexican markets through Texas superseded the venerable royal road from Santa Fe. A segment of the Camino was used by a Confederate army in 1862, in its attempt to capture New Mexico. Twenty years later, however, when the Atchison, Topeka and Santa Fe Railroad linked Chicago to El Paso and connected with the Mexican Central Railroad to Mexico City, the Camino's days were over.

Lane in Agua Fria Village connecting Agua Fria Street to Lopez Lane believed to be a segment of the original Camino Real, 1993. (Photo by David Grant Noble.)

The Camino Real was never an improved road, and its specific route sometimes shifted as necessitated by local travel conditions. Over the more than a century since the road was last used by trade caravans, much of it has been replaced by modern highways. But traces of wagon ruts still remain across barren stretches such as the Jornada del Muerto and Chihuahuan desert. While these sections are relatively inaccessible or lie on private property, they are easily seen from the air. Following are some suggestions where you will find yourself close to, or actually traveling along the route of the Camino Real.

From downtown Santa Fe, follow Agua Fria Street west from Guadalupe Street to Airport Road, and continue to La Cieneguilla and Cienega, where Ranchos de las Golondrinas (p. 325) once served as a way station for Camino travelers. The Camino ran south on the east side of the Rio Grande, passed through Santo Domingo Pueblo (p. 85) and on to Algodones. In Algodones, you can pick up its approximate track on New Mexico 313. In Albuquerque's outskirts, turn onto New Mexico 47 and take this highway south to Isleta Pueblo, Peralta, Valencia, Tomé, and Belen. At Belen, bear right onto New Mexico 305 and continue to La Joya. From here, the route continued down the east side of the river, past Socorro (p. 203) and the Bosque del Apache National Wildlife Refuge. South of the Fort Craig ruins (p. 235), where the Rio Grande bends westward, the Camino cut across the Jornada del Muerto, passing through Engle, and striking the river again near Radium Springs and Fort Selden (p. 249). You can follow its track approximately from here south on Interstate 25 to Las Cruces, then on Interstate 10 to El Paso and Mexico 45 to Chihuahua City.

TIPS FOR THE TRAVELER:
You may enjoy visiting Salinas Pueblo Missions National Monument, around Mountainair, and Petroglyph National Monument, in Albuquerque. For information on the latter, call (505) 766-8375. Forts Craig and Selden guarded the northern and southern ends of the Jornada del Muerto segment of the Camino; both are now historical monuments. Mesilla, in south Las Cruces, is an interesting historic town and was a major stop along the Butterfield Trail (p. 287).

SUGGESTED READING:
New Mexico's Royal Road, by Max L. Moorhead (Norman: University of Oklahoma Press, 1958).
Over the Chihuahua and Santa Fe Trails, 1847–1848: George Rutledge Gibson's Journal, edited by Robert W. Frazer (Albuquerque: University of New Mexico Press, 1981).

THE CUMBRES & TOLTEC SCENIC RAILROAD

The Cumbres & Toltec Scenic Railroad runs daily from June 16 to October 14 between Chama, New Mexico, and Antonito, Colorado. Passengers can travel round trip from either Chama or Antonito to the midway lunch stop at Osier, or continue through and return by van along a scenic highway. Also available is an overnight package, which includes through-trip train rides in both directions, as well as lodging and meals. For reservations, contact the Cumbres & Toltec Scenic Railroad, Box 789, Chama, New Mexico 87520, or call (505) 756-2151.

For those of us who yearn for a time machine to transport us into the past, "living museums" are perhaps our best hope. The Cumbres & Toltec Scenic Railroad, a narrow-gauge line still operating through the mountains of northern New Mexico and southern Colorado, offers a chance to project ourselves, at least for a few hours, into a romantic bygone era of western history.

During the heyday of mining in the southern Rockies, railroads were needed to supply remote silver-mining camps, carry passengers, and haul lumber and cattle. In a span of only a few years, a network of track was laid that wound through broad valleys and deep canyons and snaked along precipitous slopes from Denver to Santa Fe, in the east, and westward to such Colorado towns as Leadville, Alamosa, Silverton, and Grand Junction.

This ambitious system included a tortuous stretch of the Denver and Rio Grande Western Railroad linking a string of mining camps and towns between Alamosa and Silverton. From its starting point in Alamosa, the track dropped south to Antonito, then snaked west to Chama, New Mexico, and finally pressed on to Durango and Silverton. Construction crews began work on this line in early 1880, reached Chama at the end of December, and attained Durango by July of the following year. A year after that, trains were hauling their loads up the steep grades to Silverton, the end of the line. The rails were laid only three feet apart (hence the term *narrow gauge*) rather than the standard four feet, eight-and-a-half inches. This specially adapted track facilitated construction across the mountainous terrain and allowed trains to negotiate sharper curves.

Passenger and freight business initially thrived for the D&RG; however, when Congress repealed the Silver Purchase Act only a decade after the completion of the line, the market for silver coinage collapsed.

Climbing Cumbres Pass. (Photo by David Grant Noble.)

The consequences were predictable—abandoned mines and diminishing railroad revenues. The San Juan Extension, as the Silverton line was called, was fortunate, for its other freight and passenger revenue sustained it, at least for seventy-five more years.

After World War II, Americans turned to the automobile to go places, and in 1951 the D&RG discontinued regular passenger service on its San Juan Extension. By 1967, when the railroad announced the termination of all service on the now historic line, preservationists and railroad buffs had already begun organizing. With narrow-gauge steam railroads having become a rarity in North America and the world, public enthusiasm to save this line soon saw tangible results. New Mexico and Colorado collaborated to purchase the scenic Antonito-to-Chama stretch of track—the price was 547,120 dollars—to create the Cumbres & Toltec Scenic Railroad, a living railroad museum to be operated for the benefit of the public and to preserve intact a romantic part of North America's western heritage. Also acquired were the railroad's locomotives, rolling stock, and maintenance equipment, as well as the train yard and depot in Chama. Operation of the line was then leased to Scenic Railways, Inc., a private company.

On the Cumbres & Toltec, you will ride on refurbished original cars with large windows that can be pulled up to facilitate photography. The train traverses high-spanning trestles; plunges through tunnels; winds around Tanglefoot, Whiplash, and Phantom curves; and snakes along the precipitous edge of Toltec Gorge. You will also catch a stunning view over the Chama Valley, on the west side of Cumbres Pass (elevation, 10,015 feet). A midway rest stop is made at Osier Station, where a hot buffet lunch is served (or you can bring your own sack lunch). It was here that passengers dined a century ago.

This railroad is especially interesting to serious train buffs, for almost every operating element—trestles, rolling stock, locomotives, steam rotary snow plows—is original. If you are interested in railroad engineering and technology, take the trip from west to east in order to have time to see the virtually intact nineteenth-century terminal at Chama. Its locomotive service facility includes a boiler house, round-house, machine shop, bunkhouse, passenger depot, and a variety of cars and locomotives. In addition, the tortuous route followed by the train, with up to four-percent grades and twenty-degree curves, exemplifies historic railroad surveying and engineering principles. When you ride the Cumbres & Toltec, bring warm clothing as the cars are unheated and can chill down in the mountains. Also, have a handkerchief handy in case engine smoke blows in your direction.

TIPS FOR THE TRAVELER:
One other segment in the D&RG's San Juan Extension—between Durango and Silverton, Colorado—has been revived as a scenic ride for tourists. The Chama Valley was settled by Hispanic people in the 1860s. The villages of Tierra Amarilla (p. 213), Los Ojos, Ensenada, La Puente, and Los Brazos retain an historical ambience and have many buildings dating to the turn of the century and earlier. Today, hunting, fishing, horseback riding, cross-country skiing, and rafting the Rio Chama from El Vado Dam to Abiquiu Reservoir have become popular recreational activities in this area. You will find restaurants, gas stations, and lodgings in Chama and Antonito.

SUGGESTED READING:
The Cumbres & Toltec Scenic Railroad by Spencer Wilson and Vernon J. Glover (Albuquerque: University of New Mexico Press, 1980).
New Mexico's Railroads: A Historical Survey, by David F. Myrick (revised edition; Albuquerque: University of New Mexico Press, 1990).

THE GOODNIGHT AND LOVING TRAIL

The Goodnight and Loving Trail began in north-central Texas and ran southwest, past present-day Abilene and San Angelo, to the Pecos River, where it turned northward through eastern New Mexico. The Trail passed through Fort Sumner and eventually continued to Las Vegas, Denver, and even into Wyoming. See below for details on where the old trail route crosses modern highways.

The passage of human beings over the land, be they immigrants, gold seekers, soldiers, or cattle drivers, gives an aura of romance to historic trails. The Goodnight and Loving Trail, with its poetic sounding name and tales of adventure, is no exception. This trail thrived during the heyday of the great southwestern cattle drives that followed on the heels of the Civil War. The men who blazed it—Charles Goodnight and Oliver Loving—overcame awesome challenges to become legends in their own time.

Goodnight, who was born in Illinois in 1836, came to Texas as a youth, and by the age of twenty he was working in the cattle business. In 1860, following raids on Texas frontier settlements by the Comanches and Kiowas, he was appointed scout for a military expedition into Indian country and continued to serve in this capacity with the Texas Rangers through the war years, chasing Indians instead of Yankees.

Early in the Civil War, Federal forces cut off the Confederate army from its sources of Texas beef, and with nearly all able-bodied Texas men off to war, cattle roamed wild over the Texas prairies, multiplying into the millions. After five years of war, the presence of so many unfenced, unbranded cattle created chaotic and lawless conditions in the Texas ranching industry. At the same time, vigorous markets for cattle were opening up to the north and west.

In 1866, Charles Goodnight learned of government contracts to purchase beef to feed more than eight thousand starving Navajo and Apache captives at Fort Sumner in eastern New Mexico, and he planned a cattle drive there by a new route. Heretofore, Texas cattle had only been driven directly north through the heartland of the fierce Comanches. Goodnight decided to try a southwestward route that while substantially longer, would be safer, at least in theory. Most cattlemen scoffed at the scheme, considering the eighty- to ninety-mile drive across the waterless Llano Estacado, between the upper Middle Concho and the Pecos rivers, to be an impassible barrier. But Oliver Loving, already a tough and experienced cattle driver, thought it worth a try and offered

Charles Goodnight in his later years. (Courtesy University of Oklahoma Press.)

to join Goodnight. Loving, who was in his mid-fifties, had been the first man to drive herds north on the traditional route and had firsthand knowledge of the dangers involved.

In June of 1866, with two thousand cows and steers and sixteen hands, the two entrepreneurs set off on an adventure that would immortalize their names. Initially, they followed the old abandoned route of the Overland Mail, known as the Butterfield Trail (p. 287). They passed in the vicinity of what would later become Abilene, crossed the North Concho above present-day San Angelo, and followed the Middle Concho into the Llano Estacado. At its headwaters, they grazed and watered the herd for several days before setting out across the formidable stretch of desert leading to the Pecos River. It took them three days to cross, and when they drew close to the Pecos they could barely control the cattle, so crazed were they from thirst. Finally, catching the scent of water, the herd stampeded toward the river, while the cowhands tried to steer it away from nearby poisonous alkaline pools. At the Pecos, the cattle poured over the banks, with the force of the herd pushing the forerunners clear across the river before they could drink. Their bodies temporarily dammed the river until it reached flood level, and in the mayhem many drowned or became inextricably bogged down in quicksand.

When Goodnight and Loving regained control of the herd, they headed upriver. As the drive continued, hundreds of cows gave birth to calves that were too young to keep the pace and had to be shot. When they arrived at Fort Sumner, Goodnight and Loving sold their steers at eight cents a pound on the hoof, a healthy profit over what they had paid for them in Texas.

Loving trailed the remaining stock cattle north for sale in Colorado, while Goodnight and some of the cowboys returned to Texas to fetch another herd. One stormy night on his return trip, the mule carrying his food provisions and all the proceeds from the cattle sale ran off into the darkness and rain. Goodnight pursued the beast and finally caught it, but not before every scrap of food save a single small slab of bacon had been scattered and lost. Fortunately, the well-packed money was saved, but the cattleman later commented, "Here you are with more gold than you ever had in your life, and it won't buy you a drink of water, and it won't get you food." Goodnight and his men were lucky, however, for they soon met another party of travelers who shared their provisions with them. According to legend, the runaway-mule incident stimulated Goodnight to invent a wagon designed just to carry and dispense provisions on the trail. This was the first chuck wagon and it eventually became a standard feature of cattle drives.

From Fort Sumner, Loving blazed the northern segment of the Goodnight and Loving Trail, traveling by way of Las Vegas (see p. 161), over Raton Pass into Colorado, and through Trinidad and Pueblo to Denver. He rejoined Goodnight when the latter was returning from Texas with the second herd, which they wintered at Bosque Grande, periodically driving small bunches of cattle to market in Santa Fe.

On Goodnight and Loving's third trip across the trail that now bore their name, the partners encountered a series of disasters that ended in tragedy. Storms spooked the herd into almost nightly stampedes, which made progress slow and exhausted the men. They lost many cattle to drownings and theft by Indians. Then, as they made their way north along the Pecos in late July 1867, Loving decided to go ahead in order not to miss the scheduled letting of beef contracts in early August. "One-Armed" Bill Wilson, a hardy veteran of the trail, accompanied him with warnings from Goodnight to travel only at night in order to avoid being

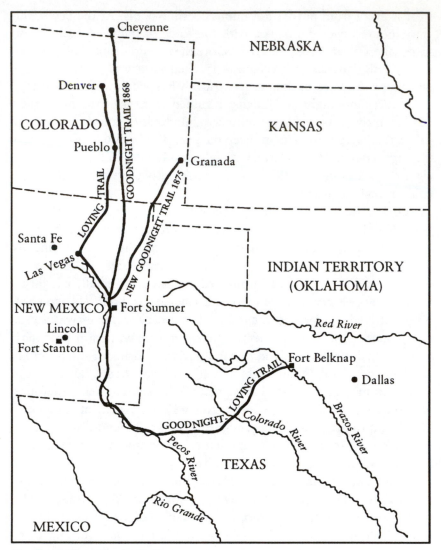

The Goodnight and Loving Trail.

spotted by Indians. Once on their way, however, the impatient Loving decided to ride in daylight, and as they traversed a stretch of high country on the west side of the river just over the New Mexico border, they were attacked by a large force of hostiles. The two men fled four miles back to the river, abandoned their mounts, and took refuge in a narrow gully. Here, they were surrounded by the warriors, who lobbed flights of arrows into their hiding place. Loving was finally shot by bullets in his side and wrist. Even so, under cover of darkness, the two men ultimately slipped away separately from their refuge and escaped. Half-naked and barefoot, Wilson made his way back to Goodnight's outfit, where he was revived from hunger and exposure. After walking a long way, Loving was picked up by a New Mexican family, who carried him in their wagon to Fort Sumner. Sadly, available medical services failed to cure his infected arm and he died in late September. Goodnight transported the body of his friend and partner back to Texas for burial.

Goodnight drove cattle for a decade, blazing new trails to Colorado and beyond. When "Uncle Dick" Wootten set up a toll road across Raton Pass and began charging ten cents a head for cattle, the ornery cattleman found an alternate way to the east over Trinchera Pass. By 1869, he had accumulated seventy-two thousand dollars in cattle-sale profits, and he soon married and settled down in southern Colorado. His wealth was ephemeral, however, for he subsequently lost most of it in the Panic of 1873. After the defeat of the Comanches in the mid-1870s, Goodnight bought ranchland in Palo Duro Canyon in the Texas Panhandle. This canyon, now a state park, had been the Indians' traditional winter camp. When Goodnight moved his cattle in, he routed some ten thousand buffalo out of the canyon. The days of the buffalo were nearly over, however, and in later years the rancher established a small remnant herd on the ranch, thereby helping to avoid the extinction of this species. After demonstrating his personal courage and integrity over a decade of moving cattle herds great distances, Goodnight became a highly respected cattle breeder. He survived to his nineties.

Many other men drove cattle over the Goodnight and Loving Trail. One of the first to follow was an individual whose name also became a legend in Western history, John S. Chisum. After Oliver Loving's death, Chisum and Goodnight worked together for several years in the cattle trade. Chisum established his ranching headquarters in eastern New Mexico, near present-day Roswell, and played an active part in the history of Lincoln County, New Mexico. In his prime, he ran the biggest cattle-ranching operation in the country.

As western cattle ranches developed their own herds and railroads

New Mexico plains over which the Goodnight and Loving Trail passed. (Photo by David Grant Noble.)

began crisscrossing the continent, the great cattle drives dwindled, and by 1880 the Goodnight and Loving Trail was little used. Today, it is better seen on historical maps than on the ground. Still, should you happen to cross sections of the two thousand miles of trail, even though they are unmarked, you may be able to imagine the dangers and ordeals encountered by the cowboys more than a century ago.

The town of Loving, along U.S. 285 south of Carlsbad, is situated near the place where Oliver Loving was wounded by Indians in 1867. The following highways cross the old Goodnight and Loving Trail: U.S 62/180, east of Carlsbad; U.S. 82, east of Artesia; N.M. 31, east of Hagerman; U.S. 380, east of Roswell; U.S. 70, west of Elkins; U.S. 60/84 at Fort Sumner; U.S. 84 approximately follows the trail between Fort Sumner and Las Vegas; and I-25 approximately follows the trail between Las Vegas and Raton. Goodnight's 1868 branch struck due north from Fort Sumner to the Colorado border. New Mexico 129, between I-40 and Conchas, lies close to the old trail; N.M. 65 and N.M. 120 both cross it east of the Canadian River; U.S. 56 crosses it near Gladstone; and U.S. 64/87 crosses it near Capulin.

Along or near the Goodnight and Loving Trail in eastern New Mexico are the towns of Lincoln (p. 166) and Las Vegas (p. 161), both with interesting frontier-era histories. Other sites you may wish to see are Fort Sumner State Monument (p. 258) and the Dorsey Mansion (p. 317). Not far from where the Goodnight and Loving Trail entered New Mexico are the famed Carlsbad Caverns—they were unknown to the cattlemen—and in Roswell, you will find the Roswell Museum and Art Center well worth a visit.

SUGGESTED READING:

Charles Goodnight: Cowman and Plainsman, by J. Evetts Haley (reprinted; Norman: University of Oklahoma Press, 1992).

Forgotten Frontier: The Story of Southeastern New Mexico, by Carole Larson (Albuquerque: University of New Mexico Press, 1993).

THE SANTA FE TRAIL

The Santa Fe Trail began in Independence, Missouri, and ran west into Kansas, where it divided into two routes: the safer but longer Mountain Branch into Colorado and over Raton Pass to New Mexico; and the shorter but waterless "Cimarron Cutoff," which angled southwest across the tip of the Oklahoma Panhandle and the eastern New Mexico plains. The two branches joined near Fort Union and continued to Santa Fe and a linkup with the Camino Real.

The Santa Fe Trail, like the Oregon Trail, has become a romantic symbol of the westward expansion of Anglo-American culture. Over its eight-hundred-mile route came traders, settlers, adventurers, and even a conquering army. Most people came with a practical objective, such as making money or joining a military unit; but whatever their purpose, all who traversed the oceanic prairies and deserts met Plains warriors, hunted buffalo, and had experiences they would not easily forget.

In 1806, Lieutenant Zebulon M. Pike led a small party of explorers into southern Colorado, on the northern edge of Spain's colonial empire. Pike and his cohorts, in fact, were trespassing on Spanish territory, and before long they were intercepted by a detachment of soldiers and escorted to Santa Fe as prisoners. It was strictly illegal for United States citizens to travel to or trade with New Mexico, and Pike saw why; the

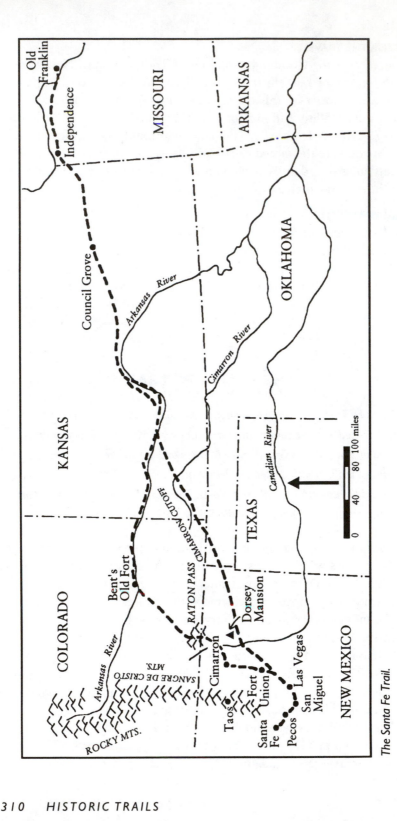

The Santa Fe Trail.

few goods available to the populace, imported from the south, were exorbitantly priced and often of inferior quality. He saw the enormous commercial potential that might one day be tapped. That day came in 1821, shortly after Mexico won its independence from Spain.

The so-called Father of the Santa Fe Trail was a merchant named William Becknell, who headed west from Missouri in 1821, apparently aware of Mexico's newly won independence from Spain. He encountered a troop of New Mexico soldiers near Las Vegas (see p. 161), who urged him to bring his goods to Santa Fe. He did, and sold his entire stock on the city plaza: the Santa Fe trade had begun.

New Mexico was the poor cousin of Spain's New World territories, most of whose colonial inhabitants were subsistence farmers. When they had surpluses, they would travel to the far-off markets of Chihuahua to sell them at deflated prices. On their return, they would bring home whatever imported necessities they could afford. As a result, most of what New Mexicans owned—food, clothing, tools and utensils, and house furnishings—were made at home. When the Missouri merchants arrived, with their high-quality metal tools, fine cotton fabrics, and astonishing inventory of items not even available from Mexico or Spain, they found a willing market.

Unlike emigrant routes such as the later Oregon and California trails, the Santa Fe Trail was basically a commercial road, and the economical freight costs—it was 850 miles to Santa Fe from Missouri versus 2,000 from the port of Vera Cruz—gave Missouri traders a distinct advantage. Five years after Becknell's unexpected bonanza, their caravans hauled 90,000 dollars worth of merchandise westward; in the 1830s, that figure rose to an average of 130,000 dollars per annum; and in 1846, when the United States invaded New Mexico, a million dollars worth of goods was pouring over the Trail.

From the outset, Santa Fe alone was unable to absorb the volume of incoming merchandise, and many fully laden Conestoga wagons hardly paused here before pushing on to El Paso and the city of Chihuahua. New Mexicans and Chihuahuans desired a wide variety of manufactured items. Sturdy cotton fabrics often accounted for half a given assortment of goods, but there was also a limited market for finer fabrics such as linen, silk, and cashmere. For New Mexican women, the traders brought jewelry, toiletries, sewing supplies, and pots and pans, and for the men, shovels, hoes, axes, knives, and rifles. Writing materials and books were valued, too, as were sherry and champagne.

Typically, trade caravans would leave Missouri in the spring, when the prairie grasses were greening, spend the summer selling in Santa Fe and points south, and return in the fall. They sold everything, often even their wagons, which were of greater value in Chihuahua than in Independence. Before winter snows threatened, they would load the proceeds from their sales—specie, silver bullion, and some gold dust—on a string of locally bought mules and head for home. Sometimes they returned with loads of raw goods such as hides and wool, but the meager profits these brought hardly paid their freight. The mules, on the other hand, found a ready market in Missouri, and the Mexican silver was a welcome boon to that state's sluggish economy.

Folklore concerning the Santa Fe Trail, which abounds in fiction and film, usually emphasizes battles with hostile Plains tribes; such tales, however, are much exaggerated. Comanche and Pawnee raiding parties did steal stock when they could, and occasionally their takings were impressive. But only rarely did they directly attack the large well-armed caravans, and relatively few travelers lost their lives on the journey, at least to Indian perils. Even so, after 1851, travelers probably looked forward to the possibility of meeting army patrols from Fort Union (p. 264), located east of Las Vegas.

Josiah Gregg, in his classic narrative *The Commerce of the Prairies,* describes encountering a group of two to three thousand Indians, including a thousand armed warriors, along the dry Cimarron Cutoff in 1831. The contact, though initially frightening to the outnumbered whites, turned out to be amicable. The native women and children gazed in amazement at the Americans' wagons, and the following day, two warriors returned one of their horses that had wandered off in the night.

The natural elements presented a greater threat to travelers than did the nomads. In heavy rains, oxen and wagons would bog down in mud and rivers would become too swollen to cross. If a caravan got started back to Independence too late in the season, it risked encountering an early winter storm, an event that could be fatal in the shelterless expanses of the Great Plains. Perhaps most feared, however, were prairie fires, which ignited unpredictably and swept over the landscape, engulfing every plant and animal in their path.

On the Plains, buffalo were usually close at hand, and their meat formed the main food staple of travelers on the Santa Fe Trail. Of buffalo consumption, one adventurer, Lewis Garrard, later wrote, "The men ate the liver raw, with a slight dash of gall by way of zest, which . . . was not very tempting to cloyed appetites; but to hungry men, not at all

Wagon ruts along the Santa Fe Trail near Fort Union, c. 1895. (Courtesy Museum of New Mexico, neg. 12845.)

squeamish, raw warm liver with raw marrow, was quite palatable." Another specialty favored by Garrard and his trail companions was *boudins,* buffalo intestines stuffed with partially digested grass roasted over hot coals.

If meat was readily available, water often was not and thirst presented more of a threat than hunger. This was especially true for travelers who elected to take the dry Cimarron Cutoff, or "water scrape," as it was dubbed. At the Arkansas River, wagons would fill their water barrels and strike out across a landscape in which not a single topographical feature was visible for days.

The Cimarron Cutoff route enters New Mexico northeast of present-day Clayton; crosses U.S. 64/87 between Mt. Dora and Grenville; crosses New Mexico 193 about six miles north of Farley; intersects U.S. 56 about eight miles east of Springer; and passes by Wagon Mound, a well-known landmark next to the present-day town of the same name. From here, its route approximately parallels I-25 all the way to Santa Fe.

Near Fort Union, the Cutoff merged with the Trail's original northern route, known as the Mountain Branch. This longer, safer trail followed the Arkansas River, looped through southeastern Colorado, climbed over Raton Pass, and continued south to Cimarron (p. 151) and Fort Union. Travelers usually stopped in Las Vegas and San Miguel del Vado (p. 179), which initially was the port of entry, and they sometimes camped at the ruins of Pecos Pueblo (p. 42).

Today, visible traces of the Trail consist mostly of faint wagon ruts in undisturbed sections of prairie. One set of ruts can be seen at Fort Union National Monument. The plazas of Las Vegas, San Miguel, and Santa Fe, where travel-weary teamsters would rein in their wagons amid great shouting and commotion, were important points along the Trail that one can still visit. Interestingly, there is a neighborhood just east of Santa Fe still known as La Barberia. It was so called because many a trail-weary drover or passenger stopped here for a shave and haircut before showing his face in town.

In the 1870s, the Santa Fe Trail grew incrementally shorter as railroad tracks crept westward along its route. By 1879, only the Raton to Santa Fe segment remained, and on February 9, 1880, when the first train arrived in Lamy, twenty-five miles from Santa Fe, a famous era in history was ended.

TIPS FOR THE TRAVELER:
Key places along the route of the Santa Fe Trail in New Mexico are Fort Union, Cimarron, San Miguel, Pecos National Historical Park, and Santa Fe. The best way to find many other locations is by using Marc Simmons's book *Following the Santa Fe Trail*. From Cimarron, a secondary branch of the Trail cut directly over the Sangre de Cristo Mountains to Taos. Today, the drive on U.S. 64 over this route is among the most scenic in New Mexico. The trip can even include an overnight stay at the historic St. James Hotel in Cimarron.

SUGGESTED READING:
The Santa Fe Trail, by Robert L. Duffus (reprinted; Albuquerque: University of New Mexico Press, 1979).
Following the Santa Fe Trail, by Marc Simmons (Santa Fe: Ancient City Press, 1986).

OTHER
HISTORIC PLACES

THE DORSEY MANSION

The Dorsey Mansion is located in the northeast corner of New Mexico. From Springer, along Interstate 25, drive twenty-five miles east on U.S. 56, then turn north and continue another twelve miles. The mansion is open only by appointment: call (505) 375-2222.

To build a mansion way out on New Mexico's plains, far from centers of society and culture, demanded the energy, imagination, and self-assurance of an extraordinary individual. This Stephen Wallace Dorsey was!

Born in Vermont in 1842, Dorsey was raised in Ohio and graduated from Oberlin College. In 1861, he enlisted as a Union officer in the Civil War and saw plenty of action while serving under General James A. Garfield. After the war, he returned to Ohio, where he married, entered business, and became active in Republican politics.

As a budding politician and entrepreneur, Dorsey was fascinated by the future of railroading. Not one to waste time, he soon became president of the new Arkansas Central line and began to accumulate wealth by selling railroad bonds. With his growing family, he moved to Arkansas, where his political involvements intensified and he won a seat in the U.S. Senate in 1873. He was only thirty-one.

Just how Senator Dorsey got interested in New Mexico is unclear, but it may have been through Stephen B. Elkins, who was the territory's delegate to Congress and a member of New Mexico's influential political cabal known as the "Santa Fe Ring." In the 1870s, New Mexico offered various opportunities to a well-connected and financed easterner. Not only were vast tracts of land (especially Spanish and Mexican land grants) up for grabs, but the railroad was coming, and it looked like fortunes might soon be made by selling cattle. In 1876, Dorsey purchased the heretofore-unknown Una de Gato (cat's claw) Land Grant, estimated (depending on the surveyor) at around 600,000 acres. He visited the place the following summer and began construction of a home on his new range. Probably, at this time, he learned that the grant was a fake—it apparently had been concocted by a local confidence man, who had forged official papers stolen from the surveyor general's office in

The Dorsey Mansion as it appeared in about 1880. (Drawing by Betsy James.)

Santa Fe. Quick to respond, Dorsey began acquiring 160-acre home-steads surrounding water holes within the "grant," which was public domain. This maneuver, too, was outside the law, but New Mexico's authorities were accustomed to looking the other way on such land dealings.

When completed in 1880, Dorsey's two-story, twenty-two-room log house contained just about every comfort and convenience that one would have expected to find in an antebellum southern mansion. The house and the Dorseys' parties soon were the talk of the territory. In addition to its living room, parlor, and bedrooms, Mountain Spring Ranch included a large billiard room and a "museum and sportsman's retreat" for the display of game trophies, guns, and, in later years, a collection of French paintings. The mansion's cellar was well stocked with imported wines and liquors, and its cherry, mahogany, and walnut woodwork and polished onyx fireplace mantles bore obvious testimony that no expense had been spared in interior decorating. The estate's lavish landscaping included flower gardens and a 180-foot free-form lily pond with islands, on one of which stood a gazebo. Behind the house were a barn, carriage house, bunkhouse, and other structures—including an eight-hole outhouse—required of a substantial ranching operation.

Dorsey's life was not a simple one. His career in national politics was meteoric, thanks especially to the election as president of his old regimental commander for whom he had campaigned vigorously in Illinois. After his senatorial term expired in 1879, Dorsey was appointed secretary of the Republican National Committee. Meanwhile, his business interests expanded, too. In addition to ranching in New Mexico, he invested in Colorado mining ventures and Star Route mail contracting. It was the latter that precipitated his downfall, when it was revealed that the Star Route business had been swindling the U.S. Postal Department. By 1881, when Dorsey and his cohorts were indicted for conspiracy to defraud the government, his former protector, President Garfield, lay in his grave from an assassin's bullet and could be of no help. To further darken the picture, the new president, Chester A. Arthur, was a Dorsey political foe.

It took two years, two trials, and untold sums of money before Dorsey was finally acquitted of the charges. Free but wounded, he retreated to his prairie estate, where at least his cattle business, the Palo Blanco Cattle Company, was thriving. In 1884, shipments of over ten thousand head of cattle infused about 400,000 dollars into Palo Blanco's accounts. At this time, Dorsey also began major renovations on his log home, replacing the east wing with an immense castlelike sandstone tower. This Gothic Revival addition had no aesthetic relationship with the connecting log structure; but the hundred or so guests at its opening party on November 14, 1886, found Dorsey's questionable taste easy to forgive as they refilled their glasses with imported champagne and danced until dawn.

Despite the appearance of affluence afforded by the Dorseys' legendary parties at the mansion, their fortunes declined alarmingly through the late 1880s. Senator Dorsey had been unable to revive his stalled political career and faced endless legal problems over his real estate holdings. As if that were not enough, fierce blizzards in the winter of 1886–87 devastated all ranches in northeastern New Mexico. Dorsey's debts mounted, lawsuits multiplied, and even friends became scarce. He also quarreled bitterly with his ranching partners. In 1893, after a failed attempt to convert the estate into a sanitarium for tuberculosis patients, he sold out and quit New Mexico to pursue more promising prospects elsewhere. He died in Los Angeles in 1916, still living in high style.

The new owners of Mountain Spring Ranch had their own difficulties, not the least of which were title disputes that encumbered their desire to ranch. In 1901, the place was sold at auction for 5,500 dollars to a creditor, who operated it for a few years as a health resort. Then it

The Dorsey Mansion today. (Photo by David Grant Noble.)

changed hands again, and again. By the time the state of New Mexico bought the property in 1973, Mountain Spring's mansion and outbuildings had been repeatedly looted and had fallen into disrepair. Recognizing its historic significance, the state invested 300,000 dollars to stabilize the collapsing mansion, planning for it to open to the public as a historic monument. In fact, it did open in 1977, but proved too costly to operate and was soon boarded up. In 1984, the Mountain Spring Ranch, now called the Dorsey Mansion, was once again put on the market. At the present time, it is privately owned and only open to the public by appointment.

TIPS FOR THE TRAVELER:

As you drive from New Mexico 56 to the mansion (about five miles south of the mansion), you will cross the Cimarron Cutoff of the Santa Fe Trail. Nearby Chico Springs was a travelers' camping spot. To experience more local history, you should stop and see the ruins of Fort

Union (p. 264) and plan a visits to Cimarron (p. 151) and Las Vegas (p. 161). You will find travel services at Springer and other towns along Interstate 25.

SUGGESTED READING:

Rogue! Being an Account of the Life and High Times of Stephen W. Dorsey, United States Senator and New Mexico Cattle Baron, by Thomas J. Caperton (Santa Fe: Museum of New Mexico Press, 1978).

INSCRIPTION ROCK

Inscription Rock, in El Morro National Monument, is along New Mexico 53, forty miles west of Grants.

Nearly four centuries ago, as Governor Juan de Oñate was returning from an exploration to the Gulf of California, he stopped to camp by a pool of fresh water at the base of a sheer cliff in the upper Zuñi River valley. Here, he, or more likely a subordinate, carved a now famous inscription on the cliff face:

> *Pasó por aquí el adelantado Don Juan de Oñate del descubrimiento de la mar del sur a 16 de Abril de 1605.* Here passed by the Governor-General Don Juan de Oñate, from the discovery of the South Sea, the 16th of April, 1605.

Antonio de Espejo had already noted this appealing campsite twenty-two years before, and members of Coronado's expedition had probably refreshed themselves here even before then. Situated, as it was, along an old Indian trail between the Zuñi villages (see p. 103), to the west, and Acoma Pueblo (p. 9), to the east, the site had long been a well-known travelers' landmark. When Oñate etched his memorandum on the wall, little did he realize a long inscriptive tradition would follow.

Juan de Oñate was someone who made a lasting mark on New Mexico history. Born in 1552 in Zacatecas, he enlisted in the military at a young age to join the war against the Chichimecas, a fiercely independent tribe in northern Mexico. At forty-three, with a distinguished soldiering career already established, he began planning his famous colonizing expedition to New Mexico. It took four years of frustrating delays before he set out on the six-month trek that would lead him

Ramon García Jurado inscription, 1709. (Photo by David Grant Noble.)

across the desert wastelands of Chihuahua and up the Rio Grande Valley to the Pueblo village of Ok'he, which he renamed San Juan de los Caballeros. Oñate remained in charge of the colony for twelve years, when his successor, Pedro de Peralta, moved it to Santa Fe.

Not to be outdone by Oñate, Governor Juan de Eulate contributed one of Inscription Rock's lengthiest Spanish contributions in 1620, while returning to Santa Fe from a trip to the Zuñi pueblos. His comments were followed by a few memorable words placed here by Governor Diego de Vargas, who is remembered for his reconquest of New Mexico in 1692. Vargas wrote,

> *Aquí estubo el General Don Diego de Vargas, quien conquisto a nuestra Santa Fe y a la Real Corona todo el Nuebo México a su costa, Año de 1692.* Here was the General Don Diego de Vargas, who conquered for our Holy Faith and for the Royal Crown all of New Mexico at his own expense, year of 1692.

In 1846, during the Mexican War, U.S. expeditionary forces from Missouri claimed New Mexico for the United States. In their wake came

Simpson and Kern inscription, 1849. (Photo by David Grant Noble.)

an array of newcomers: soldiers, traders, businessmen, ranchers, miners, and even tourists. The first Anglo-American inscription at El Morro was by the army surveyor Lieutenant James H. Simpson and his artist, Richard H. Kern. Their contribution reflects an interest in the inscriptions themselves: "Lt. J. H. Simpson USA & R. H. Kern Artist, visited and copied these inscriptions, September 17th 18th, 1849." They were followed ten years later by Lieutenant Edward Fitzgerald Beale, leader of an expedition through the Southwest, one of whose purposes was to test the use of camels for desert transport.

Surveyors from the United Pacific Railroad added their names to Inscription Rock in 1868; fortunately, they selected a more northerly route to lay their tracks. The Rock's most flamboyant signature was etched by one E. Pen Long, an individual about whom nothing is known except that he hailed from Baltimore.

Oñate's message of 1605 was by no means the first inscription to be etched here; the Anasazi Indians had already been using the pool for many centuries and had left their own figures on the cliff wall. The Pueblo Indians at El Morro were ancestors of the Zuñis who moved here in the 1200s, apparently seeking more favorable agricultural areas in a time of drought. At the top of El Morro they built a five-hundred-room pueblo, known as Atsinna, whose tiered apartment blocks surrounded a square plaza.

Mountain sheep petroglyphs incised by the Anasazi. (Photo by David Grant Noble.)

Archaeologists believe that in the early 1200s, Anasazi society in the region around El Morro was disrupted, possibly by internecine warfare, causing the people to abandon their many small communities and build large, massive, and highly defensive pueblos like Atsinna. Perched on top of the great rock with a view over the valley, this high-walled village was a virtual fortress. Its peak occupation occurred between A.D. 1275 and 1300, but tree-ring specimens retrieved from the ruins indicate that some people still lived here as late as A.D. 1340.

On a visit to El Morro National Monument, you will certainly want to follow the short trail from the visitor center to the inscriptions, and see the pool which drew so many explorers and travelers over the centuries. Allow about forty-five minutes for the walk. If you are more ambitious, the trail to the top of the rock and across the mesa is well worth the effort, for it will lead you to the ruins of Atsinna and stunning views of the valley. Indeed, this national monument offers not only a fascinating cultural experience, but a chance to become immersed in a place of unforgettable scenic beauty.

TIPS FOR THE TRAVELER:
While in the area, plan a visit to nearby Zuñi Pueblo (p. 103), whose old section and mission church are of special historical interest. The new El Malpais National Monument in Grants features an extensive lava

flow that is traversed by the same ancient trail that passes by El Morro. Inquire at the visitor center for directions to the trail head.

El Morro National Monument has a small campground. Motels, restaurants, and service stations can be found in Grants and Gallup.

SUGGESTED READING:

The Story of Inscription Rock, by Bertha S. Dodge (Canaan: Phoenix Publishing, 1975).

The Last Conquistador: Juan de Oñate and the Settling of the Far Southwest by Marc Simmons (Norman: University of Oklahoma Press, 1991).

EL RANCHO DE LAS GOLONDRINAS

El Rancho de las Golondrinas (The Ranch of the Swallows) is a Spanish colonial living-history museum located in La Cienega, fifteen miles south of Santa Fe and fifty miles north of Albuquerque. From Interstate 25 take the La Cienega exit and follow signs to the museum, which is open from April 1 to October 31.

During the Spanish colonial periods in New Mexico (1598–1680 and 1692–1821), *ranchos* and *haciendas* were scattered up and down the valley of the Rio Grande, from Taos to Tomé. Their landlords, or dons, with their peons cultivated grains and vegetables in the valley's fertile alluvial soils; raised sheep, pigs, horses, goats, and other livestock; and tended fruit orchards. Although supply caravans rumbled laboriously up the Camino Real from Mexico City every few years, they brought few of the necessities of daily life, and each ranch had to be a self-sustaining economic unit as well as a self-defending community.

Today, you can drive from Santa Fe (see p. 189) to El Rancho de las Golondrinas in less than half an hour, but in the eighteenth century it was nearly a day's ride along the rough *camino* from the capital city. Haciendas often served as *parajes,* or way stations, for travelers along the royal road, and supply caravans or military expeditions heading south from Santa Fe often spent their first night at Las Golondrinas. The ranch's proprietors prided themselves, no doubt, on the hospitality they offered not just to the caravans but to other travelers, including governors, generals, bishops, and ordinary folk. Here, before embarking on the long trail to Mexico City, they could savor, for a final time, the civilized atmosphere of Santa Fe.

Rancho de las Golondrinas. (Photo by David Grant Noble.)

Spanish farmers established *ranchos* down the Santa Fe River from Santa Fe in the seventeenth century, but these were destroyed in the Pueblo revolt of 1680. Those who were fortunate enough to survive the Indians' first strike took temporary refuge in Santa Fe's *casas reales,* then retreated to El Paso del Norte, where they remained in exile for twelve years. The *reconquistador,* Don Diego de Vargas, brought them back to New Mexico along with other hardy pioneers in 1693, and El Rancho de las Golondrinas was established about fourteen years later. The land was purchased from the Spanish crown by Miguel Vega y Coca, who built a family dwelling and several outbuildings on the property, probably including a defensive tower, or *torreón.* The farm and property subsequently passed to his daughter, María, who was married to Diego Manuel Baca, and it stayed in the Baca family for another two hundred years.

While we know few specifics about life at Las Golondrinas, we can make a few assumptions. With its fertile bottomland and lush pastures, the Bacas must have produced occasional surpluses. These they would have bartered with their neighbors, including nearby Pueblo Indians, for items they needed—cloth, furniture, pottery, footwear, and farm produce that they did not raise at home. In addition, they likely made a trip every couple of years to Chihuahua city to sell sheep, wool, or hides, and to purchase (at exorbitant prices) imported goods unavailable in Santa Fe.

In the eighteenth century, relations between the Spanish colonists and the Pueblos much improved as these formerly adversarial groups came together to defend against attacks by nomadic tribes. For Spaniards, to serve in the militia was a civic duty, and young men of Las Golondrinas probably joined numerous military expeditions.

The ranch was purchased from the Baca-Pino family in 1932 by the Curtin family, and some years thereafter, Leonora Curtin married Y. A. Paloheimo, a Finnish diplomat. At their own expense, the Paloheimos quietly spent many years in restoring the old ranch structures. They also acquired historic buildings and equipment from rural New Mexico communities, which they transported to their estate. After they had completed the job in 1972, the Paloheimos leased the property to the Colonial New Mexico Historical Foundation, to be opened to the public. Now operated by the El Rancho de las Golondrinas Charitable Trust, the buildings and grounds are open to the public as a cultural and educational museum, supported by private donations, admittance fees, and grants. On the first weekends of June and October, the museum holds festivals in which many historic activities from milling wheat to sheep shearing are demonstrated. At these times, you can observe *acequias* bringing water to turn mill wheels and irrigate fields, watch reenactors make soap and rope and weave blankets, and attend traditional music and dance performances. You can see how New Mexico's early colonists performed a myriad of other tasks. Additional festivals and special events are sometimes held on other summer weekends.

Las Golondrinas museum contains original or reconstructed elements of the old Baca hacienda, nineteenth-century additions to the ranch complex, and other historic Spanish colonial–style buildings that were imported intact from regional Hispanic communities. When you arrive here, you should first see the ranch house, whose living room, bedrooms, kitchen, storerooms, weaving room, servants' quarters, chapel, and defensive tower surround a central *placita,* or courtyard. Next to the main house are sheep sheds and corrals, food storage rooms, the later Baca residence, and an herb garden—for medicines were home grown, too. The basic building materials were adobe, stone, and wood. Originally, the earthen bricks, or *terrones,* were cut out of sod rather than formed of mud and straw and baked in the sun.

Using the trail guide, you can explore the entire two-hundred-acre museum. There is a blacksmith shop, wheelwright shop, molasses mill, and winery, as well as three water mills for grinding grain, two of which operate during the fall festivals. There is also a secondary farm complex, with its own family chapel, and a reproduction of a *morada,* or *penitente* meeting house.

Corn-grinding demonstration in Las Golondrinas farm house. (Photo by David Grant Noble.)

You will find that a visit to El Rancho de las Golondrinas offers a unique opportunity to see how eighteenth-century New Mexicans lived and to better understand New Mexico's four-hundred-year-old Hispanic heritage. Be sure to make advance arrangements if you are with a group and wish to be accompanied by a knowledgeable docent. For information on scheduled spring and fall festivals or to arrange for a guided tour, write to the El Rancho de las Golondrinas, Route 14, Box 214, Santa Fe, New Mexico 87505, or call (505) 471-2261.

TIPS FOR THE TRAVELER:
A visit to Las Golondrinas would be well complemented by visits to two other nearby historical museums: the Palace of the Governors in Santa Fe, and Pecos National Historical Park (p. 42) in Pecos. You may also enjoy visiting such regional Hispanic villages as Abiquiu (p. 137), Truchas (p. 218), and Las Trampas (p. 157). The Sangre de Cristo Mountains, just to the north of Santa Fe, offer many hiking trails in summer, and downhill and cross-country skiing areas in winter. Santa Fe has a wide variety of travel and tourist services.

SUGGESTED READING:
Coronado's Land: Essays on Daily Life in Colonial New Mexico, by Marc Simmons (Albuquerque: University of New Mexico Press, 1991).

THE SALMON HOMESTEAD

The Salmon Homestead is part of Salmon Ruins and Heritage Park, located on the south side of U.S. 64, just west of Bloomfield.

Unlike so many pioneer dwellings, the old Salmon homestead survived over many decades to find eventually new life as a historic monument. It consists of a restored farmhouse, bunkhouse, corrals, and root cellar. The site lies adjacent to the Salmon ruins, a partially excavated prehistoric Anasazi town.

In 1877, when Peter Milton Salmon brought his family to the banks of the San Juan River just west of the present-day town of Bloomfield, this region had only recently been opened for settlement. Fourteen years earlier, U.S. Army troops under the command of Kit Carson had defeated the Navajos in the region and removed most of the tribe to Bosque Redondo (see p. 258), on New Mexico's eastern plains. The Navajos' Long Walk to their internment at the Bosque had ended more than three centuries of their rule in this part of the Southwest.

Salmon was the son of German immigrants in Indiana. When the Civil War broke out, he headed west, only seventeen years old, settled in southern Colorado, and eventually married Mary Archuleta. Then, with their two young children, the Salmons moved to New Mexico to homestead a fertile parcel of bottomland near a river crossing that had long been used by travelers. Only a dozen Hispanic and several Anglo-American families preceded them. Although the Navajos had returned from their internment only a decade earlier and were a major presence in the region, they now lived peaceably with the white man.

Peter and Mary Salmon built a home and worked hard to get established in a still very remote and undeveloped region of the country. They planted a vegetable garden, fields of corn, and a fruit orchard; raised chickens, hogs, Angora goats, and other livestock; tended beehives; and made their own tools, clothing, and household implements. Peter even had his own still behind the corncrib. He also bought into a community irrigation system to provide water for the crops. In time, nine Salmon children helped carry out the farm's many chores.

The eldest Salmon son, George, eventually homesteaded his own plot next to that of his parents. George's land included the ancient Indian mound that was later named for him. It is his home and farm, built next to the ruins in 1901, that today make up a major attraction in the park. George Salmon constructed his family's house in the *jacal* style, in which juniper logs were set upright in the ground, then heavily plastered

Peter and Mary Salmon with their family, c. 1904. (Courtesy San Juan County Museum Association.)

with mud to form the walls. The roof was supported by massive hand-adzed beams, over which cottonwood poles and strips of juniper bark were laid. Dirt was layered on top to provide insulation in the cold winters and hot summers, and also to keep out most of the rain.

When you visit the homestead, you will see the family kitchen with its iron wood stove (probably the most popular room in cold weather), the living room with its cozy fireplace, and the bedroom. In recent years, the house has been refurnished with period furniture, household implements, and pictures of the family. From the house, you will be interested in touring the old *jacal* bunkhouse, corrals, and root cellar. Then continue on to the Indian ruins and finally the heritage park, which focuses on the Navajo, Apache, and Ute cultures in the region.

George Salmon was instrumental in developing Bloomfield as a settlement, and he eventually sold his place and moved into town, where

Salmon farm bunkhouse. (Photo by David Grant Noble.)

he opened a store. A series of subsequent owners of the old homestead maintained the buildings and guarded the Indian pueblo against vandalism and pot hunting. By 1968, when San Juan County purchased the property, the farm buildings represented the last extant homestead from early pioneer days. The county's objective in acquiring the site was to sponsor professional research at the Salmon Ruins and incorporate the pueblo and homestead in a public historical park. Today, the San Juan County Museum Association operates the park's museum, which has exhibits and a research library, bookstore, and gift shop.

In the 1970s, archaeologists from Eastern New Mexico University excavated about 30 percent of Salmon Ruins, which is composed of 150 ground-floor and 100 second-story rooms. The researchers determined that the site had initially been settled around A.D. 1088 by Chaco Anasazi people, who lived here for only about forty years while farming the bottomlands, as did the Salmons eight centuries later. After the Chacoans left, the town was nearly vacant for about a century, then reoccupied by Mesa Verde Anasazi, who stayed here until the late 1200s. At this time, the Anasazi Indians abandoned the entire Four Corners region. The two occupations, which parallel those of nearby Aztec Ruins, are reflected in the pueblo's masonry styles as well as in the designs of ceramics found at the site.

On your visit to Salmon Ruins and Heritage Park, stop first at the museum for information and a trail guide. It is open daily from 9 A.M. to 5 P.M.; the farmhouse, however, may only be entered by prior arrangement and in the company of a tour guide. You will need from one to two hours to tour the ruins, homestead, and museum. To arrange for guided group tours, call (505) 632-2013.

TIPS FOR THE TRAVELER:

You may wish to visit the nearby Farmington Museum, at 302 North Orchard Street, to view exhibits on the area's pioneer history. For an introduction to the region's Anasazi past, visit Aztec Ruins National Monument, in nearby Aztec, and Chaco Culture National Historical Park, located along New Mexico 57 to the south. In addition, Canyon de Chelly National Monument, in northeastern Arizona, offers a view into both Anasazi and Navajo culture. If the idea of hiking in a scenic desert landscape appeals to you, a trip to the Bisti badlands is recommended. They are located about thirty miles south of Farmington, along New Mexico 371. In Farmington, you will find a good selection of restaurants, motels, and other travel services.

SUGGESTED READING:

Ancient Ruins of the Southwest, by David Grant Noble (Flagstaff: Northland Publishing, 1991).

Aztec Ruins on the Animas: Excavated, Preserved, and Interpreted, by Robert H. Lister and Florence C. Lister (Albuquerque: University of New Mexico Press, 1987).

INDEX

A. M. Bergere House, 248
Abert, James William, 12, 179
Abiquiu, N. M., 137–41, 213; Apachean farms near, 118; sidetrips to, 76, 217, 328; mentioned, 135, 181, 211
Abiquiu Reservoir, sidetrip to, 302
Abo pueblo, 55–58; mentioned, 203, 293
Acolocu pueblo, 57
Acoma Pueblo, 9–15; sidetrips to, 38, 271; mentioned, 3, 5, 32, 35, 36, 57, 67, 80, 86, 87, 101, 136, 225, 321
Acoma: Pueblo in the Sky, Minge, 15
Acoma to Zuni historic trail, sidetrip to the, 15, 271
Agua Caliente, N. M., 234
Alameda, N. M., 144
Alameda pueblo, 20, 60, 61, 62
Alamogordo, N. M., military site near, 279; sidetrip to, 124
Albuquerque, N. M., 142–47; living museum near, 325; pueblos near, 8, 9, 15, 24, 25, 30, 35, 36, 55, 59, 64, 85; sidetrips to or near, 30, 38, 63, 67, 80, 89, 299; villages near, 189, 203; mentioned, 36, 38, 63, 67, 80, 85, 88, 164, 173, 192, 226, 272, 293, 299
Alcanfor pueblo, 20, 23, 39, 59
Aleman Station, 251
Algodones, N. M., 299
Alianza Federal de Mercedes, 215
All Pueblo Council, 76
Alvarado, Hernando de, 9, 20, 44, 59–60
American Indian Arts Institute, sidetrip to the, 248
Anasazi, the, 3–6, 8, 16, 25, 36, 323–24, 331; sidetrip to view culture of, 38
Anthony, N. M., 289
Antonito, Colorado, historic railroad

at, 300; sidetrips to, 119, 217, 302
Anza, Juan Bautista de, 116, 175, 180, 220, 225
Apache Canyon, 273
Apacheans, 113–15. *See also* Apaches; Jicarilla Apaches; Mescalero Apaches; Navajos
Apaches, 228, 330; Army policy and the, 227, 228, 239, 242, 244, 253, 259–60, 265, 266; Pueblos and the, 7, 26, 27, 36, 49, 50, 63, 106, 113, 116, 120, 225; Spanish settlers and the, 142, 144, 151, 157, 166, 171, 175, 182, 198–201, 204, 205, 230, 249, 254–56, 295; mentioned, 290–91, 303
Apaches de Nabajo, 113
Archaeological Conservancy, 240
architecture, colonial period, 217; homestead, 329–30; fort, 239, 247
Arenal pueblo, 60
Arizona, 3, 5, 113, 125, 129, 172, 228, 259, 332. *See also* Hopis
Armand Hammer United World College, sidetrip to the, 165
Armijo, Manuel, 144, 183, 187, 194, 246, 273
Arroyo Hondo, N. M., 211
Arroyo Hondo Pueblo, 189
art, mission, 188. *See also* retablos; santero; puebloan art, 23, 24, 34. *See also* crafts (arts and crafts); Taos art colony, 211–13
Artesia, N. M., 308
Ashiwi, the, 103
Astialakwa pueblo, 31, 79
Atchison, Topeka and Santa Fe Railroad, 145, 249, 297. *See also* railroads
Athapascans, the, 113. *See also* Apacheans
Atomic City (Las Alamos, N. M.), 8
Atsinna pueblo, 104, 225, 323–24
Axtell, Samuel B., 167, 169

Casas Grandes, Mexico, sidetrip to, 279

casas reales, 96, 190–92, 326

Catiti, Alonso, 66, 86, 87

Catron, Thomas B., 167, 169, 243

cattledrives, 303–309

ceremonies, 32, 42, 74–76; Apachean, 123. *See also* dances, public; feast days; festivals; fiestas

Chaco Canyon, 5, 90, 94, 104; sidetrip to, 15. *See* also Chaco Culture National Historical Park

Chaco Culture National Historical Park, sidetrips to, 38, 109, 332. *See also* Chaco Canyon

Chama, N. M., Apacheans near, 115; historic railroad at, 300; sidetrips to, 119, 217, 302

Chama Valley, sidetrips to the, 141, 302; village in the, 213; mentioned, 118, 134, 138, 149, 192, 302

Chamisal, N. M., 158

Cheyennes, 152

Chihuahua, Mexico, historic trail to, 293; mentioned, 142, 173, 197, 276, 277, 293–99, 311, 312

Chimayo, N. M., 147–51, 133; sidetrips at or near, 42, 55, 98, 160, 189, 198, 221; mentioned, 135, 186

Chimayo rebellion, 187

Chinle, Arizona, sidetrip to, 129

Chiricahua Apache, 113, 123

Chisum, John S., 168, 261, 307

Chivington, John M., 273

Chloride Flat, 200

Cibola, the land of, 105

ciboleros, 162, 258

Cieneguilla battle, 234

Cimarron, N. M., 151–56; fort near, 118; sidetrips to, 213, 267, 314, 321; mentioned, 116, 261, 314

Cimarron Cutoff, historic trail of the, 309; mentioned, 312, 313

Cimarron Indian Agency, 152

Cimarron River, 152

City of Rocks State Park, sidetrip to the, 292

Civil War, 47, 50, 54, 114, 121, 126, 144–45, 173, 200, 212, 226–27, 235–37, 241, 251, 255, 267–68, 271, 290, 292, 303, 317, 329

Clayton, N. M., 313

Cleveland, N. M., 177, 179

Cloudcroft, N. M., Apache headquarters near, 120

Cochiti Pueblo, 15–19; sidetrips to, 67, 89; mentioned, 27, 36, 64, 66, 87

Cochiti Dam and Reservoir, 15, 18, 67; Cochiti Lake, 19

Cochiti Lake, 19; Dam and Reservoir, 15, 18, 67

Code Talkers, 129

Colfax County War, 154

Colonial New Mexico Historical Foundation, 327

colonial period, 133, 325; missions of the, 55–59; sidetrips to villages of the, 30, 52, 119

Colorado, historical trail through, 309; mentioned, 31, 54, 68, 116, 175, 217, 235, 246, 271, 273, 300, 305, 307, 314, 319, 329. *See also* Antonito, Colorado

Colorado Plateau, 4

Colorado River, 125

Colorado Volunteers, 273

Columbus, N. M., 227, 275

Columbus Historical Museum, 278

comancheros, 162, 182, 258

Comanches, Apaches and 113, 116, 121; Pueblos and, 7, 39, 46, 50, 71, 91, 98, 225; Spanish settlers and, 138, 142, 152, 157, 175, 176, 180, 182, 208, 218–20; mentioned, 264, 266, 303, 312

Conchas, N. M., 308

Cook Spring, 229

Cooke, Philip St. George, 234, 242, 289

Cooke's Canyon, 241–42, 291

Cooke's Peak, 244; sidetrip near, 292

Cooke's Spring, 242, 244, 289

Cordova, N. M., 135; sidetrips to, 160, 189, 221

Corn Mountain, 106

Coronado, Francisco Vasquez de, 6, 9, 20, 23, 39, 44, 48, 57, 59–60, 73, 77, 85, 95, 105, 113, 115, 208, 225, 293

Farley, N. M., 313
Farmington, N. M., 125; sidetrips near, 109, 332
Farmington Museum, sidetrip to the, 332
feast days, 9, 15, 19, 30, 38, 51, 63, 67, 71, 74, 77, 85, 88, 98, 103. *See also* ceremonies; dances, public; festivals; fiestas
Fermi, Enrico, 281, 283
festivals, Apachean, 119; colonial, 327. *See also* ceremonies; dances, public; feast days; fiestas
fiestas, Santa Fe annual, 192; Taos Fair, 209–10. *See also* feast days
fishing, 85, 119, 124, 189, 202, 213, 302
Florida, N. M., fort near, 241; mentioned, 289, 290
Forked Lightning Pueblo, 42
Forked Lightning Ranch, 47
Fort Bayard, 228–32; sidetrips to, 202, 244; mentioned, 201; Fort Bayard Medical Center, 228, 231
Fort Bayard Medical Center, 228, 231
Fort Bliss, 235, 253
Fort Burgwin (Research Center), 232–35; Apaches and, 118
Fort Canby, 126
Fort Conrad, 235
Fort Craig (National Historic Site), 235–41; sidetrips to, 207, 244, 253, 284, 299; mentioned, 145, 205, 226, 229, 272, 293, 299
Fort Cummings, 241–44; sidetrips to, 174, 253, 279, 292; mentioned, 229, 289
Fort Defiance, 106, 126
Fort Fauntleroy, 267
Fort Fillmore, historic trail to, 289; sidetrip to, 174; mentioned, 172, 173, 226, 255, 272
Fort Lowell, 215
Fort Lyon, 267, 269
Fort Marcy, 245–48; mentioned, 194
Fort Selden (State Monument), 249–53; sidetrips to, 174, 207, 241, 244, 279, 299; mentioned, 172, 173, 229, 235, 249, 292, 299

Fort Stanton, 254–58; Apache agency at, 122; sidetrip to, 170; mentioned, 167, 168, 173, 226, 229
Fort Stanton Cave, sidetrip to, 258
Fort Stanton Hospital and Training School, 254, 257
Fort Stanton Marine Hospital, 256
Fort Sumner (State Monument), 258–63; historic trail near, 303; sidetrip to, 309; mentioned, 106, 122, 144, 153, 170, 256, 268, 269, 305, 308
Fort Union (National Monument), 264–67; historic trail near, 309, and photograph of wagon ruts, 313; sidetrips to, 47, 156, 165, 184, 275, 314, 320–21; mentioned, 118, 152, 162, 164, 177, 236, 237, 247, 251, 271, 272, 312, 314
Fort Webster, 200
Fort Wingate, 267–71; sidetrip to, 129; mentioned, 106, 126, 251, 259
Four Corners region, 4, 5, 16, 52, 72, 99, 331
Franciscans. *See* missionaries to the Indians
Frémont, John C., 151
Frijoles Canyon, 16, 64; sidetrip to, 85. *See also* Bandelier National Monument
From Hacienda to Bungalow: Northern New Mexico Houses, 1850–1912, Reeve, 166
fur trading, 210

Gadsden Purchase, 200
Galisteo, N. M., 273
Galisteo Basin, 69, 77, 185
Galisteo Pueblo, 87
Gallinas River, 161
Gallup, N. M., fort near, 267; pueblo near, 103; sidetrips near, 109, 271, 325
Ganado, Arizona, sidetrip to, 129
García Opera House, 207
Garrett, Pat (Patrick F.), 164, 169, 170, 173, 263
genizaros, 138–40, 181, 210
Gerónimo, 227, 230, 244

Manzano Mountains, 29, 56
Manzano State Park, sidetrip to, 59
Martinez, Antonio Severino, La Hacienda de Don, 212
Martinez Hacienda, sidetrips to, 94, 221
Matsaki pueblo, 103
Maxwell, Lucien Bonaparte, 151–53, 261
Maxwell, Pete, 261, 263
Maxwell Land Grant, 116, 151–55
Maxwell Museum of Anthropology, 146; sidetrips to, 30, 67
Mesa Verde area, 5, 68, 331
Mesa Verde National Park, photograph of Cliff Palace, 4
Mescalero Apaches, 120–24; sidetrip to visit the, 258, 284; mentioned, 113, 118, 167, 259, 269
Mescalero Indian reservation, sidetrip to the, 258. *See also* Mescalero Apaches
Mesilla, N. M., 170–74; historic trail to, 287, 289; sidetrips at or near, 244, 253, 279, 292, 299; mentioned, 168, 226, 235, 251, 255, 297
Mesilla Valley, 170, 249
Mesita, N. M., 36, 38
Mesquite, N. M., 289
Mexican War, the, 144, 171–72, 239, 245, 254, 289, 297, 322
Mexico, 3, 7, 57, 79, 120, 121, 139, 140, 161, 194, 200, 205, 251, 275–78, 296, 297, 311. *See also* Chihuahua, Mexico
Mexico City, historical trail to, 293; mentioned, 17, 142, 197
Middle Rio Grande Valley, 55, 61, 62, 120, 192
military operations, 229–30, 269; daily orders, 239; general duties, 242; posted routine, 250; the new era in, 278
Millicent Rogers Museum, 94, 213; sidetrip to the, 221
Mimbres Valley, 173, 291
mining towns. *See* Silver City, N. M.; Socorro, N. M.
missionaries, 136; colonial church description, 159; mission chapel at Abiquiu, 137–38; mission church at Isleta, 27, at Laguna, 38, at Pecos, 43, at Zuni, 109; Spanish village missions, 171, 181, 186, 191, 203. *See also* missionaries to the pueblos
missionaries to the pueblos, 12, 17, 28, 29, 30, 31, 32, 36, 40, 41, 45, 46, 48, 53, 56, 57, 60–61, 67, 74, 81, 83, 86, 87, 91, 96, 100, 101. *See also* missionaries
Missouri, historic trail from, 309; mentioned, 142, 194, 296, 297, 311
Mogollon culture, (Mogollon Indians), 25, 133, 198
moiety system, 70–71
Mojo pueblo (Moho pueblo), 60
Montezuma Valley, 5, 68
Monument Valley, sidetrip to, 129
Mora, N. M., 175–79; sidetrips to, 221, 267; mentioned, 211, 226, 247
Mora Valley, 175; sidetrips to the, 165, 179
moradas, 141, 327
Mormon Battalion, 246, 289
Mount Robledo, 253; Robledo Mountain, 171
Mount Taylor, 125
mountain men at Taos, listed, 210
Mountain Spring Ranch, 318, 319, 320
Mountain Villages, Bullock, 221
Mountainair, N. M., sidetrip to or near, 58, 59, 146, 207, 299; Spanish missions near, 55
Museum of Fine Arts, Santa Fe, 248
Museum of Indian Arts and Culture, Santa Fe, 89; sidetrip to the, 248
Museum of International Folk Art, Santa Fe, sidetrip to the, 221
Museum of New Mexico, Santa Fe, 166, 248, 253, 263

Nambe Falls, 41, 42
Nambe Pueblo, 39–42; mentioned, 81, 94, 147
National Park Service, 267, 274, 284
Navajo Nation, the, 260
Navajo Tribal Museum, 129

Plaza del Cerro, 133, 147–49
plazas, 133; at Albuquerque, 144, 146; at Chimayo, 147; at Santa Fe, 195
Poeh Center, 52, 54; sidetrip to, 98
Pohwoge pueblo, 69
Pojoaque Pueblo, 52–55; sidetrip to, 98; mentioned, 41, 68, 81, 94, 147
Pojoaque River, 69
Pope, 6, 17, 49, 66, 70, 73, 86, 191
Poshu pueblo, 96
Poshuouinge pueblo, 72; sidetrips to, 76, 141
Posiouinge pueblo, 72
Post of Santa Fe, the, 248
Pot Creek Pueblo, 48, 90, 234
Puaray Pueblo, 20, 61–62
Pueblo Indians, 3–9, 98, 133, 143, 323. *See also* separately by pueblo name and *see* government, puebloan
Pueblo Lands Act, 7, 33, 76
Pueblo Revolt, 6, 12, 17, 25, 26, 32, 40, 45, 49, 61, 66, 70, 73–74, 77, 81, 86, 91, 94, 96, 101, 105, 191–92, 203, 208, 225, 326
pueblo ruins, prehistoric, 20, 42, 119, 202, 329, 331; sidetrips to visit, 19, 38, 71, 85, 103, 119, 141
pueblos, 3; descriptions of, 12, 23, 26, 39, 79, 87, 100. *See also* Pueblo Indians
Punames, 100
Punta de Agua, N. M., 55
Puye Cliffs, 42, 81; sidetrips to, 55, 71, 76, 85
Puye Pueblo, 81; photograph of, 82. *See also* Puye Cliffs

Quarai pueblo ruins, 55, 57, 58, 203, 225; sidetrip to, 59
Quemado, N. M., (Cordova, N. M.), 186
Quivira, the land of, 44

Radium Springs, N. M., 299
railroads, and lifestyles, 7, 36, 106, 145, 146, 163, 194, 205, 211, 253, 266, 297, 314, 317; narrow gauge, 300. *See also* separately by name
Ramah, N. M., 106

Rancho de las Golondrinas, 325–28; sidetrip to, 221; mentioned, 133, 274, 299
Ranchos de Atrisco, 144
Ranchos de Taos, N. M., 90, 213; fort near, 232; sidetrip to 234
Raton, N. M., village near, 151, 161; sidetrip near, 156
Raton Pass, historic trail over, 309; mentioned, 305, 307, 314
Rayado Creek, 151
Rayado Valley, 118
rebellion, 226, 233. *See also* Pueblo Revolt; Taos rebellion
religion. *See* ceremonies; feast days
retablo, 159
Rio Abajo, 143
Rio Arriba County, 216, 217
Rio Bonito, fort near the, 254. *See also* Bonito River
Rio Bonito Valley, 166
Rio Chama, villages along the, 137; sidetrips to the, 302; mentioned, 6, 72, 94, 135, 189, 294
Rio Grande, forts along the, 229, 249; historic trails along the, 287; peoples along the, 6, 12, 15, 25, 48, 52, 56, 59, 64, 68, 72, 77, 79, 81, 85, 91, 94, 95, 99, 133, 203, 225, 325; villages along the, 137, 142; sidetrip along the, 213; mentioned, 83, 88, 120, 146, 186, 189, 236, 258, 293
Rio Grande Valley, villages in the, 157, 170; mentioned, 3, 5, 16, 20, 26, 36, 39, 44, 50, 52, 55, 64, 72, 77, 105, 125, 180, 181, 197, 226, 271, 289
Rio Hondo, 254
Rio Pecos, 120, 135. *See also* Pecos River
Rio Pueblo, 90
Rio Quemado, 148
Rito de la Olla, 232
River of Traps: A Village Life, deBuys and Harris, 160
Robledo, Pedro, 171, 293
Robledo campground, 249
Robledo Mountain, 171; Mount Robledo, 253